WOOD

SLAD

BULL'S
CROSS

CHELTENHAM →

THE
VATCH

SWIFT'S
HILL

LEY (2)

SLAD
FARM

BISLEY →

TOADSMOOR

OLD CHAPEL GARDEN

OAKRIDGE

R FROME

OLD
CHAPEL

CHALFORD
VALE

SICKERIDGE
WOODS →

COWCOMBE HILL

GOLDEN VALLEY

BAKER'S
MILL

A419

LONDON →

WILD ENCHANTMENTS

Honouring our indigenous plants

Walking the path of healing

Published by Quintessence Press

This book is a distillation of hundreds of experiences within the School of Intuitive Herbalism and those who work one-to-one with me, students and graduates of the school. I feel immense gratitude for every person who has been part of the school – thank you for being part of this beautiful process of (re-)discovery. In particular I want to thank the first waves of students who were very much part of growing the school: Hettie Peplow, Anja van der Geert, Sam Rogers, Jack Young, Fiona Owen, Emily Taylor, Šárka Forsyth, Cathy Williams, Marianne Saxton and Sara Ghanchi. I want to thank you all for sticking with me through the many twists and turns of creating a new (and ancient) way of working with plants. Sue Smee and Emily Taylor have been the most wonderful and constant allies as key editor and lead researcher for this book, alongside author Michael Malay who offered rich literary reflections, Phia Gourd who helped with research and Graham Frankland our proofreader. Thank you to the many others have have given useful reflections on specific chapters, all of which has been woven into the final draft. Finally thank you to Sarah and Paul Jackson, whose farm has been home to many of these experiences, Ruskin Mill, where it all started, and my partner Alena Štandová and daughter Líska for the steady love and support throughout. My gratitude to the plants is vast, and I hope it shines through every word.

These illuminations are the culmination of my life-long love and close relationship with plants, woven together with my herbal and Druidic studies of the past 15 years. It has been a rich and fascinating journey. I offer my deep gratitude to my loving and endlessly supportive and inspiring family; John, Laurie and Meri and also to their partners, Eden and Felix. I also thank the plants themselves for their wisdom and guidance.

CAUTIONARY NOTES - Please also see 'Working with plants safely' (page 236)

This book is not intended in any way as medical advice. It outlines suggested first steps of forming intimate relationships with plants and allowing them to teach us. Without a personal student–mentor or client relationship, we take no responsibility for the consequences of use or misuse of the techniques described in this book.

If you feel drawn to work with a herb internally (e.g. as a tea), research thoroughly with regard to safety, appropriateness and dosage, particularly with regard to suitability alongside any health conditions you have or prescription medication you are taking. Only some of the plants in this book are suitable to work with in this way. If in any doubt, seek advice from a experienced herbalist.

100% 100% 100% 100%

waterless   alcohol and   carbon   renewable
  LED   substitute free   neutral   energy

100%   100%   0%

recycled   VOC free   waste
FSC® stock   inks   to landfill

Printed in the UK by Seacourt Ltd (www.seacourt.net) in Oxford, currently the top rated B-Corp environmental printers in the world.

ISBN: 978-0-9929218-5-9

Preface

We invite you into a liminal space, a space where your dreams and your experience of the physical world might dance together, infusing each other with wisdom, insight and purpose.

My and Fiona's aim is to distil some of the insights gained from decades of experience of plant meetings, initiation and healing, into doorways that invite you to step deeper into relationship with plants.

Boundaried by the medium of book publishing, my doorways are of story, phrase and word. Fiona's are of visual beauty. Through these we hope to inspire you to find the living plants and allow all your senses to be touched, to smell, to touch, to feel, to hear; to seek out their presence and discover your own relationships.

We honour the other-than-human, the consciousness, wisdom and intelligence that we are surrounded by. We invite them to inspire and teach us. We honour all of you who do everything you can to nurture and protect the plants, trees, land and ecosystems of this earth. This is a time to step up, speak for voices unheard, act where action is needed and inspire others. The plants can help us dream into a future where we live in healthy symbiotic relationship with this planet and each other.

We already know all of this. We already know how to listen to the plants, the land, how to heal ourselves and how to live well. This knowledge is our birthright, embedded deep in the ancestral wisdom we carry in every cell.

The plants simply remind us, if we are ready to listen.

Also by Nathaniel Hughes and Fiona Owen
Intuitive Herbalism (3rd edition: 2019)
Weeds in the Heart (2nd edition: 2018)

Contents

Wormwood

Page 229

The plants will stretch you

If *you* allow them to, if *you* invite them in, the plants will stretch you.

Wormwood will awaken your warrior, Clary can help enliven your sensual joy. Mugwort might rekindle ancient knowing, and St. John's Wort your inner vision.

Every plant in this book will stretch you if you allow them to. I have never felt as stretched as I do in trying to honour them in these pages. Each chapter asked me to immerse myself fully in the plant's invitation, not as an academic, objective observer, from a safe distance of discernment, but as a lover attempting, in my limited way, to sing to the one I love.

Take a moment, right now. Close your eyes and bring to heart a place in nature, a plant or a tree that you love. How does it feel to bring this presence in? This book is about letting these beings in, letting ourselves feel them, letting ourselves be changed by them.

The writing is *entirely* experiential; everything is drawn from either my own experience, the experiences of my students and the ritual spaces we share, or those of my clients.

These experiences are shaped by my life and the lives of those drawn to this work. I am a cisgender, hetero, white male, and recognise the many privileges that come with this. At the same time, I am highly sensitive and prone to disabling sensory overwhelm – a facet of neurodivergence I only came to understand as a gift in my forties. This overwhelm previously meant I spent an immense amount of time learning how to regulate myself and how to differentiate trauma from neurotype. In these times I had to step out of the human-world, finding refuge in the holding of fire, woods and herbs. Fiona, likewise, found peace amongst her sensory overwhelm with the plants.

Perhaps this experience is why my heart opens easily to those who live at the margins of society, whose voices have been silenced and who carry the weight of our culture's shadow. It is often these individuals and communities who hear the plants calling most strongly and step towards them.

Our hope is that this book inspires you to deepen your own relationships with plants and explore further down this beautiful and challenging path.

This path is rich, but also difficult, since the plants reflect back to us the truth of ourselves. It is not only our brightness, but also our hidden and disallowed inner voices which are drawn into our awareness by the plants.

These parts of ourselves are both the most vulnerable and the most sensitive, and when we open into relationship from this place of vulnerability, we discover the depths of connection possible.

Re-awakening this sensitivity can take years, and the plants are the most incredible allies on this journey – a journey in which we inevitably find out why this sensitivity has been numbed, and how we might reclaim it.

I'm yet to work with someone who, in time, cannot awaken their forgotten, innate ability to listen to the plants, to let themselves be affected by the plants, to respond to them in their own unique way.

I train herbalists, and celebrate the many ways there are to be a herbalist. All are needed as more and more people awaken to the potency of our connection with nature.

Fiona, the artist I work with here, trained with me for seven years so that she might bring the herbs through more fully in her artwork. Claire, a movement artist, guides people into conscious dialogue with landscape and plants through movement. Glenn weaves spontaneous magical storytelling sessions for children centred around the plants, whilst Emily advocates for a remembering of our innate birthing wisdom and works with the plants to awaken this.

Hettie, one of the school's graduates, likened being a herbalist to being a mountain guide. Every plant opens up a new terrain, and as guides we use our knowledge and love of that landscape to support others to navigate it. Each journey is unique and every explorer has a personal experience, discovering and developing their relationship with this plant landscape, finding medicine, healing and learning.

The teachings in this book have emerged from hundreds of people's experiences over many years. Where possible I have attributed quotations, but I'm aware that many of the ideas, kennings and insights have emerged collectively through our work at the School of Intuitive Herbalism. I want to thank every single person who has been part of this journey, a journey I've had the privilege to witness.

Herbs can be medicine, in the conventional sense of the word medicine. They can also be teachers. Often they are both. You might meet Chamomile as a tea to treat eczema, just as Rose may teach you to tend to and live from your heart, and Lemon Balm release your creativity and vision. All is medicine for our soul; plants are not alternative or complementary, they are living beings that pre-date us evolutionarily, living beings that we are in relationship with.

3

In meeting plants in this way, we imbibe the medicine of the land. I suspect that the deepest medicine is in the dance and discovery of our living relationships, relationships with this ancient family who are always there for us. Many of today's struggles emerge from a sense of separation, from the land, from ourselves and from each other. I've come to see that our primary attachment wound is not from our mothers, but from the earth. Tending to our relationships to the plants and the land offers a way that we can start to heal this wound.

In a fast paced world, the plants offer us a chance to reconnect with something far older and deeper. As teachers they whisper truths, rekindling forgotten memories, and invite us to walk a path of profound connection and healing. As friends and allies, they companion us on the paths of our lives. As beings of light (quite literally), they give us vision and inspiration. As mirrors, they reflect back what we are and what we have blinkered ourselves from seeing.

We cannot live off light, but plants can. We need them to transform light into the substance we call food, which momentarily becomes us, before returning to the earth. In each plant's transformation of this light, they imprint their own unique being-ness, ancestry and wisdom, from which we might learn, should we choose to.

Let this book be a doorway into deepening your journey of relationship with the living world that surrounds and sustains us. Embrace the subjectivity of your own relationship and let the plants teach you to grow through your layers of projection into a deeper seeing. Let illusions of knowing dissolve, clearing space for ever deeper realisations to arise.

Radical plant wisdom

We are at a pivotal moment. Global capitalism continues to expand, despite the severe harm caused to both the planet and its inhabitants. At the same time, more people are becoming aware of the deep wounds left by colonial practices, which persist to this day. These harmful practices are closely linked to structures of oppression that target people based on perceptions of otherness – whether related to skin colour, class, gender, ability, or sexual orientation – forces that have long silenced and marginalised diverse voices, not only in the field of herbalism but throughout society.

Plants are resilient. Despite efforts to control them through monoculture, urban sprawl and herbicides, plants refuse to be constrained. Within herbalism, many powerful medicinal systems infused with human wisdom have been devised; however, plants will always grow beyond these constructs. Herbalism has been, and is, the people's medicine, rewoven in every generation in response to current-day needs. This constant grassroots evolution is its strength.

I encourage you to treat each encounter with plants as a mystery, to dive deeper, ask better questions, keep on learning, and embrace not knowing. Your relationship with the plants matters.

Plants can break through concrete. Similarly, they can challenge the ways we've tried to tame and domesticate ourselves, offering us radical doorways to new ways of being and inviting us to question everything we hold to be true.

The way we approach plants matters; if we approach them as commodities to be used by us, that is all we will see reflected back.

But when we approach them as living beings – our elders in evolutionary terms, bearers of the wisdom of hundreds of millions of years – a doorway opens.

My life, and Fiona's, is deeply rooted in animism, the belief that all things possess consciousness and are connected. This interconnected web, sometimes referred to as the web of Wyrd, is a symbiotic, eternal dance of life. This ancient spirituality, among the earliest in these lands and many others, shapes the narrative of this text.

Historically, animistic herbal practices have been subjugated, even erased, through violence and fear. The cultural wounds left behind by the wave of witch persecutions still reverberate today. I feel it's important to name this here, as meeting this wound is crucial to reclaiming our indigenous relationships with plants. It also touches a broader theme in healing.

In my clinical practice, I encounter daily the importance of coming into relationship with the trauma we carry. Healing requires tending to the ways we, our ancestors, and our loved ones have endured impossible situations and systemic violence. This process is a foundation for building true health, one that honours both our bodies and the lives of those who came before us.

As you open yourself to the wisdom of the plants and the land, you will face many thresholds – of trust, of faith, of letting go. The truths reflected by the plants often challenge our unexamined beliefs, asking us to make a choice: Do we cling to the known and familiar, or do we step forward into the new paths the plants reveal?

When I see people courageously cross these thresholds, I remember why I've committed my life to this work. It is by moving toward and through our own projections that we begin to see the world beyond the illusions of the mind. Each threshold crossed allows the wisdom of the plants to shine even brighter.

Value your own meetings with the plants – celebrate how these connections are shaped by the cultures you have grown up in and the lineage of your ancestors. Be gentle as you meet the wounds you carry, and embrace the gifts that the plants bring.

Together, let us cultivate a creative aliveness within herbalism, rooted in our own relationships. The strength of herbalism lies in its diversity, and your voice is a crucial part of this.

And perhaps, most importantly, if you find yourself disagreeing with something I write about a plant, great! This is a path where the plants themselves – and your own embodied wisdom – are the teachers. Dive deeper into your relationship with the plants, and use the grist of disagreement to strengthen your own journey.

A note on language: I have chosen to use the pronoun 'they' when referring to plants. This choice avoids the problematic gendering of plants and the objectification implied by the use of 'it'. As a term that can be both singular and plural, 'they' acknowledges the diversity within a single species, such as Lady's Mantle, where, despite variations across different climates and ecosystems, common traits persist.

This is not a book of cures.
It is a book of doorways

Each plant will touch some part of you, often multiple parts. Some of these are quickly obvious – Rose might touch your heart, Oak your longing for steadiness and rootedness. However, we are often only aware of a small proportion of those inner parts touched. As we deepen our relationship with a plant, more layers are revealed. In one moment, a certain mystery within ourselves reveals itself, in the next a realisation or new seeing of the plant. While some aspects hidden from our consciousness take time to surface, gnosis and revelation sometimes come suddenly.

This dance of meeting is like the lemniscate above, a journey deeper into ourselves alternating with a journey deeper into the plants. In the centre of this dance lies a sweet spot of intimacy, where we meet the plant in a space of shared magic.

As we awaken to hidden aspects of ourselves, some feel familiar and easy to recognise. Others, however, may appear shameful, dark, or unwanted – parts we instinctively avoid. The questions included in each chapter are designed to guide your inner reflection, allowing the essence of the plant to influence and direct your inquiry.

Some aspects of ourselves are buried deep in the shadows, emerging only in dreams, during vulnerable moments, or through intimate relationships. These parts can feel powerful, or they may terrify us. Yet nothing remains hidden unless it has, in some way, been exiled by ourselves, our culture, our sense of safety, our family or our beliefs.

Even the voices within us that speak of unclaimed power have a difficult journey before they can live consciously in our daily lives. Self-destructive habits and addictions might need to be met with honesty to make space for these hidden parts to find their home. Shame might ask to be named and embraced, old fears befriended, layers of rage discovered and depths of grief swum into.

Sometimes our inner authority, our sovereign self, struggles to know how to call and welcome home parts of ourselves. Sometimes we need to invoke something of our inner warrior (Wormwood, Horsetail), to make decisions ('decision' – to cut away) and enforce boundaries. Sometimes we need to open in compassion and patience (Rose, Mallow, Hawthorn). Sometimes we need more light to see by (Marigold, Mullein, St. John's Wort) and sometimes we need deep rest (Valerian, Chamomile, Vervain). Sometimes we need to be pushed through an initiatory threshold and sometimes all we need is a gentle reminder. Plants can be all of this to us and more.

In my practice, I see how essential it is to broaden our perspective on ourselves when exploring the deeper threads of health and illness. I hesitate to claim that our exiled parts directly cause illness – such a view risks being overly simplistic. The dance is far more complex. However, I believe that when we reclaim these parts, we unlock vitality and health that had previously been hidden.

Choose a card or open this book to any herb chapter and let the plant be a teacher you've chosen to pilgrimage toward. This might be just a brief encounter, but every meeting holds the potential to open a doorway into a profound inner journey. My hope is that my lyrical writing and Fiona's rich symbolism offer clues to help you find those doorways within yourself.

Whilst you can use this book for quick questions by jumping straight to the box at the end of each chapter, I would like to suggest that the richest experiences come from giving each plant some of your time, your love and your commitment. Take a moon cycle if you can, but even a few days can take you places yet untravelled. If possible, find the living plant. Read the chapter and notice what touches you. Importantly, not what *interests you* – this risks being too cerebral – but what touches you.

The touch may be sweet or raw. It could feel like an invitation, or it might remind you of something you've neglected to tend within yourself. It could come as a tickle, a strong emotion, or even revulsion. Sometimes, the touch manifests as indifference or disassociation – a numbing out, a sudden loss of focus. These reactions can be subtle and hard to spot, which is why friends, herbalists, or healers can be valuable guides.

Each touch is a doorway, and it's up to you whether you choose to explore it. In every plant's presence, many doorways can open, so don't feel pressure to focus on just one experience. However, treat all experiences with respect, as they are sacred gifts in the meeting between you and the plant.

Discover your own doorways, and ask yourself if your soul feels called to any of them. This is where your journey begins. The plants are there, waiting for us to pay attention. The challenge is not in asking them to communicate, but in learning how to listen.

Your path is unique to you

No matter your beliefs or life experiences, the plants will always touch you. However, your experience of, understanding of and framing of your plant meetings will be unique to you, unique to your cultural, biological and spiritual heritage. The extraordinary breadth of worlds touched is one of the things I love most about my work.

Some of you may approach plants from a scientific background. Science was my own first path, and I very much see the true pursuit of science as a spiritual pursuit of ever-deeper understanding. The exact biomolecular mechanism by which Rose interacts with our pheromones is as fascinating to me as the experience of what happens *when* Rose activates our own pheromones. For now, however, I invite you to approach plants from a place of vulnerability and intimacy, with deep emotional honesty and embodied connection.

When we meet a plant, we never simply meet a plant. We enter into a meeting that is itself embedded within a complex ecology, an ecology of land and human, of conditioned perceptions and semi-conscious intention. In psychedelic research this is sometimes referred to as 'set and setting'.

The more prepared a plant is, or the more it is wrapped in ritual, the more the plant meeting will also be carrying the implicit and explicit human intentions embedded within this particular set and setting.

My writing and Fiona's paintings are ritual preparations – they are one step removed from the living plant. Our hope is that they resonate with you such that you seek out and form *your own relationships* with the living plants. We love to share our experiences and inspire, but we invite you to nurture your own, inner-authority in your meetings with plants. Be cautious about deferring to anyone else's wisdom. Trust your experiences, be humble with your blind spots, and be willing to be challenged. Follow *your* unique path.

Remembering & Rekindling

In this chapter, I'll introduce a selection of approaches to walking this path. Given the scope of this book, these can only serve as introductions, but each approach holds unlimited potential. Be inspired by them, but also call upon any creative techniques that resonate with you. Draw from your own spiritual practices, seek reflections from friends, and learn widely from healers, therapists, and herbalists. The more sources of support and wisdom you engage with, the richer your journey will be.

The approaches we work with have evolved slowly and pragmatically over decades, often inspired by insights and skills shared by students. These practices have stood the test of time for one simple reason: they work. When we started the school, it was intentionally with a minimal framework, guided only by the desire to deepen our relationships with the plants. The reasons for this 'blank canvas' approach was due to the scattered and broken nature of our own indigenous heritage regarding plant ritual work.

In my early twenties, while studying herbalism, I spent years searching for authentic threads of indigenous plant rituals, only to find scattered fragments. These remnants offered little in terms of helping me understand the role of plants in healing. Over time, I came to realise that such animistic beliefs and rituals struggled to survive centuries of Christianity, though traces can still be found. My three years of reading every herbal I could find in the Edinburgh Botanic Gardens library both inspired me and painfully highlighted how much of our oral and ritual traditions have faded or been lost.

However, there are many gems in our heritage, though they often need to be kindled back into life and rediscovered, alongside the plants, such that

they become useful in these times. Many of them challenge the unexamined mythologies of modern life and the rampant commodification of capitalism, inviting us to choose new mythologies rooted in relationship to ourselves, each other and the land.

The wisdom of the Triskele, the lemniscate and the Three Cauldrons is invaluable in the school for helping open up our inner sensitivity to the plants. You'll find the Celtic Wheel of the Year, animal symbolism, rune and Ogham wisdom, sacred geometries and the wisdom of the elements woven deeply throughout this book. Our bodies and beings know the plants innately, but we need new (and perhaps ancient) language to know what they know.

The fabric of native healing plant rituals is ready to be reawakened. If this excites you, then you are reading the right book. There is much work (and play) to do to heal the wounds within this heritage.

Whilst some may look to other cultures to fill this gap in our heritage, my choice was to look to the plants of this land, the innate wisdom we carry within us and a wealth of scattered clues from our history. I believe that everything we need to know is there in the plants and our bodies, that we carry our ancestral wisdom within us, waiting to be activated, that if we pay attention, the clues are there in abundance.

Working with plants can be as simple as visiting the same plant over a series of days, sketching, journaling and dreaming. If you can, I recommend committing to a whole moon cycle, and hope that you find, amongst the techniques and frameworks I share in the next pages, ones that help to open doorways for you.

Think of each plant as a lover that you are slowly getting to know; how, given this, can you best turn up to, bring yourself, learn and grow from this new relationship?

Deepening into relationships with plants, the path takes many turns, and we might need to draw on different skills to find our way. The approaches described over the following pages are some of the key foundations of our work in the school. Each of these approaches is unlimited in how deeply it can be developed, and each will help the path unfold in different ways. I could devote an entire book to these approaches and more, but for now I hope these brief introductions and the web resources linked to this book will open some new doors for you.

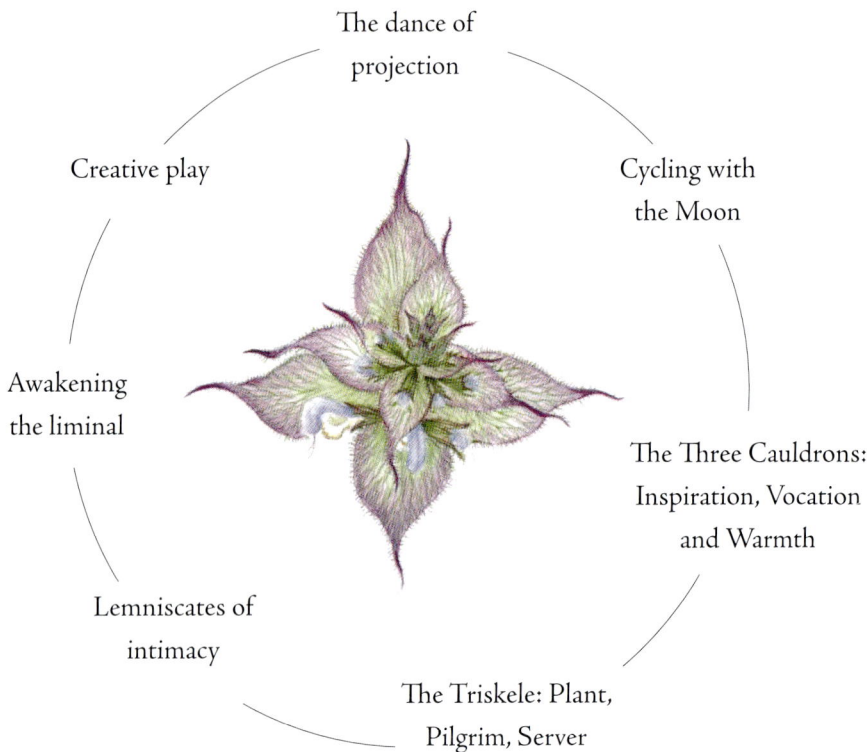

The dance of projection

Creative play

Cycling with the Moon

Awakening the liminal

The Three Cauldrons: Inspiration, Vocation and Warmth

Lemniscates of intimacy

The Triskele: Plant, Pilgrim, Server

Some approaches may be familiar, some may be new; all are powerful when used skilfully. Notice where your skills already lie and consider how you might deepen these. Don't attempt to do everything ... simply notice what speaks to you most right now and take this as a doorway.

The Dance of Projection: a Herbal Hall of Mirrors

We rarely perceive the world directly, instead relying on neurological short-cuts (heuristics), constantly projecting our preconceived model of the world. Understanding this is key to this work. I often suggest to my students that initially, more than 90% of everything that happens with a plant is a reflection of ourselves. Only by acknowledging this and stepping through the mirrors of projection do we begin to truly see the plant itself.

When twelve people explore their relationship with a plant, they will have twelve distinct experiences. This diversity should be celebrated. From the privileged position of witnessing many such journeys, I have observed that each of these varied experiences carries an invisible thread – a melody, a felt sense, a state of consciousness – that is the plant itself. The plants reveal themselves as the subtle currents beneath the projected drama of our personal journeys.

Common experiences from people meeting Rose, all summarised from two group ritual meetings with Rose in 2024:

"Tender. Opens my heart, touching all the grief that I'm holding."

"Supportive, mothering, safe. My body relaxes into a softness like falling into a huge duvet. Soft and enveloping."

"Sensual, soft, seductive, awakening the sensual in me."

"The scent is overwhelming, suffocating. I feel I can't breath. I want to push it away."

"It's trying to make me soften but I don't want to, I'm not ready. It shows up where I'm holding and defending myself."

"I'm drawn to the thorns, the toughness needed to survive in this world."

This snapshot of meetings with Rose illustrates a wide range of responses. A person whose encounter with Rose touches on grief might uncover deeper themes of longing and loss, ultimately inviting them into an experience of the love they seek. Similarly, someone who feels overwhelmed or suffocated in Rose's presence might be reliving the emotional suffocation they experienced as a child.

If this latter example were the case, and they formed a narrative that Rose itself is oppressive, that projection might close the door to both understanding themselves *and* a deeper understanding of Rose. However, if they recognise this as an inner experience triggered by Rose, a door to healing opens.

The key is to learn how to discern your own journey with a plant, and the wisdom to be gained from this, from the mystery of the plants themselves.

Both are valuable, but they are different.

I doubt that we can ever really 'know' a plant, and suspect that the appearance of knowledge serves as a plateau for the ego on a deeper journey of discovery. Many aspects of our experience will be coloured by, informed by and point to the plant, but the plant itself remains a mystery, impossible to 'capture' with our limited human consciousness.

Rather than viewing subjectivity and projection as problems, I encourage you to see them as gateways. By recognising and owning what is ours, and by being willing to confront what we cannot yet see, we take the next step – and a little more of the plant reveals itself to us.

One last thought and observation from my work: the more we are triggered, the more we tend to project, not just with plants but with the humans around us as well. These projections can be 'positive', for instance in romantic love, or 'negative', for instance in judging someone who is different from us or who triggers us. There is profound medicine in recognising and owning these projections as our own. Through this process, we open ourselves to the possibility of seeing a deeper truth in others.

Cycling with the moon

City life can lead us into city rhythms. Spend time away from the lights and noise, under the stars and subject to the shifting weather, and deeper rhythms become far more apparent – the sun's cycle through the year and seasons, the moon's (29.5 day) cycle and the daily rhythm of dusk, night, dawn and day. There is a lot to be learnt by starting to align our lives to the moon's rhythm, the quiet of the dark moon and the intensity of the full moon. Where possible, it is powerful to start a commitment to a plant on the dark moon and receive this plant for a full moon cycle. If new to working this way, I recommend reading up on the many ways to work intentionally with the moon.

• Shorter immersions can be just as valuable; if you find your journeys tend towards a few days rather than a whole moon cycle, that's fine.

• I'll often revisit a plant the same moon each year. For instance, *Amanita* often calls me around the harvest moon (around autumn equinox). Many years of revisiting a plant like this helps deepen the relationship with each year that passes.

• Sometimes when a plant particularly touches a strong and present life process, people might stay close with a plant for three moon cycles. I'd recommend taking a moon cycle break after this though to enable you to reflect and regain perspective.

• In committing to this you might call on any of the techniques outlined here, combined as is appropriate with taking the plant as a tea, flower essence or other preparation. Details on how to prepare plants, and dosage, can be found in many other herbals and websites, so much so I decided not to go into that much depth here. For those with experience of dieting and fasting with plants, this is a wonderful thing to weave in for a few days within the moon cycle.

• Even if you only connect to the plant for a few minutes each day, this is valuable and will deepen your relationship.

Three Cauldrons

In exploring the rich tapestry of Celtic wisdom, I found myself drawn to 'The Cauldron of Poesy' – an ancient Irish poem that dives deep into the mystical and creative forces that shape the poet's soul. This text, steeped in the traditions of the filí (poet-seers) of Ireland, offers profound insights into the transformative power of creativity and the sacred nature of artistic inspiration.

I approach this subject with a deep respect for its cultural heritage and a keen awareness of the painful relationship that has existed between Britain and Ireland. My hope is that in our work in the school we strive to honour the depths of wisdom from which this tradition has emerged.

This 7th-century poem speaks of three inner cauldrons: Coire Goiriath (Cauldron of Warming), Coire Ernma (Cauldron of Vocation) and Coire Sois (Cauldron of Inspiration), and I've included links for a full translation in the bibliography. Relating these cauldrons to plant wisdom represents a contemporary, personal approach to understanding these ancient concepts.

Each plant touches us in each of these realms of experience, though for many, one realm is dominant. Some tend towards vision, gnosis, seership and insight (Cauldron of Inspiration), whilst others have primarily emotional (Cauldron of Vocation) or somatic (Cauldron of Warming) experiences. This is particularly important as we deepen into this work; it is not unusual that a blind spot in the somatic realm leads to an excess of projection, fantasy and spiritual bypassing within the realm of vision. By reflecting on each of the cauldrons we have more chance of spotting our own blind spots.

Some questions to help you explore: How do I feel this plant in my body? How does this plant touch me in the realms of rhythm and warmth? How do I experience this plant affecting my emotions and felt sense of the space around me? What does this plant touch in me when I bring questions about my own vocation to them? How is my dreaming, journeying, visioning coloured by the plant? How does this plant inspire my creativity?

The Cauldron of Inspiration

"distributes wisdom in every art" and is "born on its lips" (upside down). The clear indication that this cauldron is born upside down invites us to discover how to turn and fill it with knowledge, wisdom and insight such that it "magnifies every common artisan, which builds up a person through their gift." Through the herbs I see this cauldron awakened when vision, sudden insight and realisation appear, often through conscious dream work/journeying. This cauldron is turned by "divine joy and human joy".

The Cauldron of Vocation

"must be turned by sorrow or joy" and is full only in the highest "great stream" (highest poetic grades) of wisdom and poetry. Sometimes this is translated as the Cauldron of Movement; I see this awakened by the plants in the way they stretch our capacity to feel, to stretch our emotions and our ability to be fully present in and respond to the the world around us, led by the truth of our soul (vocation).

The Cauldron of Warming

"distributes wisdom to people in their youth". This is spoken of less in the poem, but I have come to understand it relating to embodied vitality and the warm healthy animal of our bodies. This is particularly relevant in the work of healing as so many are disassociated from their bodies. The plant, awakening visceral, felt sensations, can speak directly to the body, shed light on what we are holding there, and help orientate it back to vitality and health.

Translations from 'The Cauldron of Poesy' by Erynn Rowan Laurie

I've given some examples drawn from experiences in ritual below. Every plant meets every cauldron in a different way, and this also varies amongst different people. Yet the longer we work with the plants, the more the constant song of their presence becomes clear.

——————— *St. John's Wort and the Cauldron of Inspiration* ———————

"When I close my eyes I see an eternal beacon, a flame that never goes out."

Glenn Thorne (2024)

A remarkably common experience of St.John's Wort, where people often describe experiencing a pillar or sword of penetrating light.

——————— *Clary and the Cauldron of Vocation* ———————

"I wish to speak of the maiden in me. To acknowledge her stuck sexuality, the numbness of a wounded womb and the immense grief around all of it."

Nathalie Alcock (2024)

I might have linked this to any of the cauldrons as Nathalie was speaking of deep somatic memories of her womb (lower cauldron), whilst also connecting back to another time (seership - upper cauldron). I've included it in the middle cauldron as the strongest presence at the time was grief … this middle cauldron 'must be turned by sorrow or joy'.

——————— *Mallow and the Cauldron of Warming* ———————

"I find myself spontaneously touching my face, exactly where my jaw was broken and bones fractured in a car accident 56 years ago."

Ann White (2024)

This is a good example of the ways the work with the plants will often guide us to places in the body that may not have fully healed from past injuries.

Lemniscates of intimacy

In every relationship between two, a third comes into being. This unique 'we' is an expression of the meeting of two, in this case, of human and plant. As we deepen into connection with plants, some time is spent exploring *what the plant touches in us*, whilst some is spent *discovering the beauty, colour, scent, geometries and ecology* of the plant.

This back and forth movement, feeling ourselves, feeling the plant, is no different from the dance of human intimacy. At one moment, one person's rhythms and needs guide the dance, in the next, the focus shifts to the other. Somewhere, delicately hidden in the middle of this dance, are moments of ungraspable intimacy, where two become one for a moment. Though this moment can't be grasped, it can be cultivated, and the cultivation is done through love, vulnerability, spacious listening, empathy and self-awareness.

A simple exercise to explore this is described in the Marigold chapter – simply rest a Marigold on your palm. Let yourself feel into a lemniscate – flowing between your palm and the flower, and explore what needs to happen to let yourself feel this presence more deeply in your body.

We enter into meetings with plants many times; this cycle is illustrated below. With each cycle of meeting, our connection to the plant grows and the relationship deepens.

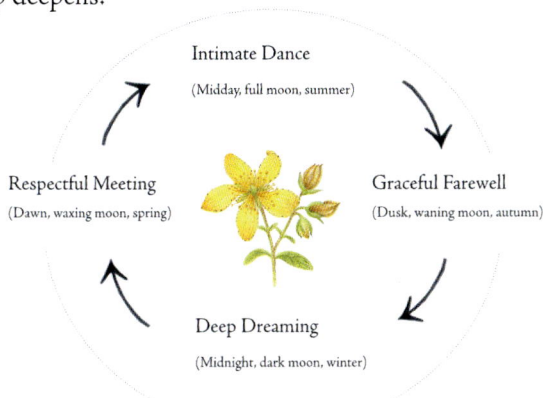

Intimate Dance
(Midday, full moon, summer)

Graceful Farewell
(Dusk, waning moon, autumn)

Deep Dreaming
(Midnight, dark moon, winter)

Respectful Meeting
(Dawn, waxing moon, spring)

Plant

How do I know you better? How do I
receive you? How do I thank you?

Pilgrim

Which part of me is pilgrim to this plant?
How do I commit to this pilgrimage?

Server

If I were in service at the grove/shrine
of this plant, what would my role entail?

The Triskele (illustrated here) is an ancient symbol that can be called on in many
ways. Within the school we've found a simple approach that invites rich inner
discoveries. Let one spiral represent the plant, one represent the part of you that is
pilgrim to the plant, and one the part of you that is serving both the plant and the
pilgrim. Imagine a place where this plant is venerated – a shrine, temple, clearing,
garden. Why would you choose to make a pilgrimage to this place? What parts of you
are pilgrim (for instance, it might be the part of you that feels lost, scared, or a younger
part of you)? If you were in service to the plant and part of your role was to welcome
and help the pilgrim receive the teachings, healing and blessings of the plant, what
might your role involve?

This simple approach allows an important distinction when working with plants
alone. There is often part of us, a part that might feel unknown or vulnerable, that
wishes to learn from the plant. Yet for this to happen there will always be another part
of us that facilitates this meeting. When working alongside a herbalist, the herbalist
becomes the server, allowing you to be fully in your pilgrim.

Depending on how familiar you are with the journey of healing – I'm sure many
readers here are already healers and practitioners themselves – you might choose to
explore each of the pilgrim and server roles differently. Both can offer just as profound

teachings; the pilgrim role will tend to meet us in our inner growing edge, whilst the server role can teach us not only how to care for ourselves better, but to do so in a way that is guided by the plant and that can also be extended to serve others.

When I train herbalists, the first couple of years are primarily in the role of pilgrim, but as they start to share their plant love more widely, they cultivate the server and meet the professional thresholds that unfold on this path.

─────────── *Part needing to let go – as pilgrim* ───────────

"In all the years of illness I just needed rest and to be cared for, but I was having to do the outward role of carer. Lemon Balm helps me put down these deeply habitual responsibilities and simply take the rest I have yearned for so long."

Emily Taylor (2023)

─────── *Contraction in response to overwhelm – as pilgrim* ───────

"Wormwood welcomes that part of me that contracts against something overwhelming. It ignites a fire in me and opens a door to standing tall."

Emma Sampson (2023)

─────────── *Serving at the shrine of Nettle* ───────────

"I'd make Nettle oil, Nettle soup, Nettle juice … my job would be to massage people and feed them, bring them back from states of deep depletion."

Notes from Insight Herbalism class (2023)

Creativity and play

We learn best when we play. Not only that, but play releases our creativity, invites us to let go of perfectionism and outcome and allows all manner of influences to be expressed. In the school, at least in the initial stages, there is often far more un-learning than there is learning!

I often invite students to write *bad* poems about the plant. It is surprising how this invitation feels so freeing and more often than not unlocks surprisingly profound poems. There are many creative ways to explore plants:

• **Sketching, painting and sensory art**: Creating 'felt sense' pictures of the plants. Be playful and experimental – start with a simple colour and stroke on blank paper and see how it does or doesn't feel resonant with the plant. Scrap it and do another. Keep going, each time refining your marking, guided by the plant.

• **Musical exploration:** Explore how music can capture the essence of a plant. Experiment with simple rhythms or melodies, noticing which musical styles or genres resonate with different plants. If you're comfortable with singing or improvisation, consider how you might let the plants sing through you. Many global traditions have songs tied to specific plants – how might you discover or create songs for native plants?

• **Movement and embodiment:** Movement can deepen your connection with plants in a physical and intuitive way. Try this simple exercise: imagine being in an Oak forest versus a Silver Birch forest – how does your body want to move in each environment? How might you echo the form, gesture and growth patterns of the plant, allowing your own body to be an instrument of sensing. If you are inhibited around movement and dance, start with a simple rocking rhythm and explore how different plants affect it. For me, for instance, Rose invites a flowing sensitivity in my movement, whilst Vervain invites an aligned stillness.

• **Touch** is fundamental to health, and many people don't receive nearly enough. In our school, we explore the different qualities of touch that each plant offers. Where Primrose might offer spacious tenderness, Wormwood offers purposeful focus and edge meeting; where Mallow invites flowing sensuality, Angelica invites an opening, stretching and extending quality of touch. Whilst you can explore this on your own, it is a wonderful thing to playfully explore with a friend, giving each other short exchanges and reflecting how each felt.

+ **Playful rituals:** I appreciate simple, authentic rituals – free of dogma and unnecessary complexity. Be playful in creating rituals: light candles to honour a plant at dusk, celebrate seasonal changes with fires or herbal washes, or incorporate herbs into initiation rituals to support friends in life transitions. One of my favourites is a cold wild-water dip followed by a warm herbal infusion poured over my head, offering cleansing and renewal. For those drawn to deeper experiences, consider spending solo time in nature, with only plants and water, to deepen your presence and connection.

+ **Create games** mapping human personalities, caricatures and archetypes to the plants. It can be surprising how revealing this is when letting yourself play here. How do you relate to these caricatures? What do they reflect about you?

+ **Sensory play**: Focus on one sense at a time and give yourself time to go beyond your initial impression by finding five descriptive words for each initial word. For instance 'soft' might be an initial word describing the touch of Mallow, but as we allow more of these experiences, qualities such as 'velvety, warm, graceful, light, inviting, flowing, tender' emerge in this space. Try this with all of your senses, including the sense of presence that defies categorising in any one of the 'classic' senses!

+ **Storytelling**: Create stories centred around a plant, drawing on both your experience of the plant and any folklore that feels resonant with you. Allow space for magical landscapes, gods, archetypes, magical characters and life's thresholds to flow into your stories. Children love this!

+ **Journal**: Keep a journal just for plants, or even better, a journal for each plant. Gradually add to this with your experiences, learned wisdoms, sketches, dreams, reflections and poems.

Liminal awakening

Cultures the world over have developed ways of working with alternated states of perception, though dreams, journeying, psychedelics and ritual. To develop skilfulness in this is to become an edge-walker, with one foot in the realms of the unseen, the ancestors and the energies that constantly surround us, and one foot firmly in human consensual reality.

We all do this spontaneously at times. Perhaps we are affected by an unusually potent dream or a momentary experience that takes us out of time for a moment. Most people I meet can relate to these places where a greater wisdom breaks through the shell of our consciousness.

Three approaches that we work with in the school are:

• Explore your **night-time dreaming** by keeping a notebook next to your bed and noting down themes emerging from your dreams. Invite the plants in, perhaps by having a leaf or flower next to your bed or drinking a cup of the herb's tea intentionally before sleeping. Notice the subtle shifts (and sometimes not so subtle!) that the plant brings.

• Develop a daytime practice of letting yourself rest, lie down and drop deeply into your body. Let your awareness **explore sensations in your body** and notice what happens when you invite the presence of a plant to affect this. There is a guided meditation in the online resources linked to this book to help introduce you to this.

• Explore working with either **drum journeys or guided journeys**, ideally supported by someone with whom you feel aligned, who has experience in this. I recommend having a specific and clear intention when doing this. Vague intentions tend to lead to vague journeys.

Not all approaches work for everyone; find what works for you and nurture this.

Oracle wisdom

This book and set of cards have been designed to serve multiple purposes, and one of these is as an oracle deck. Many have asked why we didn't include any keywords, names or numbers on the cards – this was intentional. We wanted the plant and your relationship with it to be central. Any interpretations that we added on the card risk inhibiting you in finding your own meaning. Of course, I trust that you will resonate with much of the meaning-making in the herb chapters of the book, but hope that there's a few plants at least where you strongly differ! By not adding text to the cards we offer these homages to the plants as invitations to your truth, not an assertion of ours.

Sometimes you will simply be called to work deeply with a plant that you know. Using the cards as an oracle opens up the possibility of discovering new doorways, new plants and new aspects of yourself, and as such is a wonderful way to start a deeper journey of relationship. With the web resources linked to this book I've included a recording where I suggest some simple interpretations of the Three Cauldron and Four Direction spreads illustrated opposite.

Single card

Whenever I've worked with cards I find myself mostly using this very simple approach. The key here is to be clear about your intention or your question. The painting – perhaps the plant, perhaps the symbolism or the animal – will touch something in you. How does this cause you to reflect back on your question? Each plant can be thought of as a different friend or mirror, each reflecting back a slightly different perspective. Notice particularly where you feel any charge – excitement, rejection or confusion – often this indicates that there is more to explore here.

Three Cauldrons

The model of the Three Cauldrons (*page 18*) is useful in challenging us to see beyond our habitual forms of perception, by inviting a reflection on what is alive in our body, in our soul (and sense of purpose/vocation) and in our seeing (inspiration). Possible questions you might explore:

+ How the different plants meet these different aspects
+ How these cauldrons are, or aren't, aligned
+ Which seem clearer and which more vague
+ How alive or dormant/hidden each feels

This initial spread can then serve as a starting point to dive deeper into whichever cauldron or herb is speaking most strongly to you in this moment.

If you were to draw this particular spread, you might consider (amongst many possible doorways):

Clary in the lower cauldron – Clary invites you to reflect on your relationship with the powerful animal of yourself and your raw sexuality. How do these relate to your experiences of vitality and empowerment in the world?

Bramble in the middle cauldron – Bramble is a tough pioneer plant. How do you relate to this with respect to your own sense of vocation and purpose? Bramble also creates an ecological haven for others – how does this resonate with your own life path?

Angelica in the upper cauldron – Angelica invites an expansiveness of vision and breath, clear sight and standing tall. What helps open this place in yourself right now and how much do you feel this in your life?

You might also consider how all three might relate to each other within your own life and body. Often there are significant clues to be found in the alignment (or lack of it) within your own being.

Four Directions

This spread works well when you have already formed your own inner relationships with the directions. If you haven't explored this, I very much recommend it, as it has proved a powerful way of orientating within our inner realms. Each person will have their own associations with each direction, though some simple themes may be:

- North/Earth – ancestors, dreaming, patience
- South/Fire – warmth, strength, courage
- East/Air – emergence, inspiration, clear sight
- West/Water – consolidation, intuition, wisdom

Explore how each card speaks to your relationship with each direction and then choose one to dive deeper with. This spread also suits working with the Four Elements.

Working with cards in this way is about trusting in your deeper knowing, beyond the surface of your mind.

- Honour this by making a ritual space, taking time first to be present with your own body and breath.

- Bring your question to heart. Keep it as simple as possible, and if your question is too wide, refine it down to whatever is most present and important.

- Choose a card, or a spread.

- For a quick reference go to the summary box at the end of the herb chapter and let whatever touches you be touched, and trust what emerges for you in response. There are many possible doorways with each card, follow whichever one feels most potent in this moment.

- Consider how you might see your questions through the lens of this plant.

Ancient Teachers
of this Land

Angelica

In marshy meadows and at the sides of canals, Angelica stands tall, striking in this watery setting with their umbrella of white-green flowers and strong hollow stems. Though occasionally mistaken for Hogweed, or even Hemlock, a brief familiarity with each plant makes Angelica easily identifiable. Reaching over six feet tall, they grow with formidable vigour. The name, *Angelica archangelica*, comes from a folk tradition, likely linked to their well-regarded medicinal qualities, that they were a gift from Archangel Michael, carrying within them a sword of clarifying light. Rising from and stabilising the muddy banks of the brooks which define the damp valleys of Stroud, this plant brings a bright, commanding presence.

> Architectures of light
> Demanding our vibrant uprightness
> Opening clear bright doorways
> To parts lost in darkness
> Reminding our spirit
> How to fly

When nibbling on a little Angelica root, I instantly feel the penetrating aromatic quality of this plant, a clarifying charge moving straight to my sinuses and lungs, activating, stimulating, clearing. Our nose and lungs are our meeting point with the air element, and air wants to move; to breathe and to be breathed, to dance and penetrate, to flow and merge in vast currents and tiny vortices. In these deep valleys of Stroud, moist air can sometimes slow and become stagnant, the perfect environment for mould and their spores,

conditions our lungs can find challenging. Angelica, with their clarifying embodiment of brightness and light, can be a balance and antidote to these dampening forces on the breath.

"The moment I took a few drops, my breathing easily dropped to my diaphragm, I felt like I was growing bigger and wider, a feeling of clarity, trust, power and bigness."

Kate Harris (2023)

Breath is life itself, and breathing well invites in vitality. Awareness around our breath features in many spiritual traditions around the world, and for me breath has the potential to open us further to Wyrd. An ancient Welsh concept, Wyrd represents the intricate interplay of life's unseen threads, a weaving together of events at levels of subtlety beyond our understanding. I associate feeling in flow with Wyrd as a place of inspiration and spontaneous insight, intricately tied to the breath, flowing into our being with each inhalation and finding expression through our words, songs and actions.

Right now, *in this moment*, how free and deep is your breath? Take a moment to allow this dialogue between you and your breath. Take a moment to feel gratitude for this lifelong companion.

Angelica tends to offer the following invitation to people: breathe a little more freely and slowly, relax your diaphragm, release your shoulders and straighten your spine. With the softening of the breath there is a subtle expansion of the being, a sense of uprightness and bigness, a momentary glimmer of the angel of ourselves. Several people have shared with me something similar after inviting Angelica in: "It feels dangerous to be this big", as the plant reveals, through the breath, habitual patterns of contraction.

Sadly, modern life leaves many heavily burdened, feeling the weight of the world on their shoulders, and in the contraction of their breathing. Mouth breathing, shallow breathing, overly fast breathing, nasal inflammation, chronic respiratory infections and sleep apnoea are common and can have a strong correlation with many health conditions, including hypertension, growth abnormalities and asthma. In my practice, I often see people with chronic respiratory problems, and see how grateful they are to feel Angelica's expansive aroma and penetrating brightness go so directly to lungs that have felt congested and stuck.

Angelica's traditional reputation across Europe is wider than just this potent action on the lungs, and it goes back centuries; Culpeper summarises Angelica well, "it resists poison, by defending and comforting the heart, blood, and spirits; it doth the like against the plague and all epidemical diseases … [The stalks and roots] … are good preservatives in time of infection: and at other times to warm and comfort a cold stomach."

Since the development of antibiotics in the mid-20th century, infectious disease has become less of a concern, though with ever-increasing warnings about antibiotic resistance, and little in the pharmaceutical repertoire for viral infections (Angelica proved a friend to many in Covid times), it seems wise to not forget our pre-penicillin remedies. Extracts of Angelica have proven themselves potently antiviral, antibacterial and antifungal. At this moment in history, herbalists often find themselves supporting fewer acute infections and more often supporting chronic health struggles, in which compromised breathing is often a significant factor.

As Culpeper alludes, Angelica's affinity isn't just to the lungs, but also as a warming, enlivening stimulant to the digestion and blood. The different preparations bring out different qualities. The decoction brings an aromatic bitterness perhaps more suited to the gut, whilst the hydrosol, essential oil and spagyric bring out the highly penetrating aromatics that speak to the breathing. My preference is to nibble on a little of the fresh root, which covers all of this and leaves you in no doubt of Angelica's potency.

To seek to know Angelica is to seek to know our own breath, to find a companion on a lifetime's journey of learning how to infuse our body with breath and life. Angelica can serve as a companion when we lose connection to our own power, when we get stuck in the mud of life, when we forget how to fly. The invitation is very physical, Angelica is deeply

Centred awakening

Rippling release

Green growth

Enveloping brightness

Earth dragon

Twinkling waters

Bringer of stars

Vibrant earth

Fizzing soil

Edge affirming

Flowing roots

Earth spirit

Dragon's breath

Sacral warming

Pathfinder

Marsh light

Inviting excitement

Unmasked potential

Sparkling upwards

anchored in the earth, but they are also very much in the realm of the spirit, light, possibility, vision and expansiveness. Gently but insistently, Angelica helps us discover ever-expanding architectures and possibilities within ourselves, reminding the breath of geometries of freedom and flight we may have long forgotten. As a swan rises up from marshes, Angelica can remind our spirit how to fly.

Light bringer · Dragon's breath · Awakening pulse · Angel's wings

How do I invite the fullness of my breath and my brightness?
How do I experience the connection between these?
Which situations cause my breath to become smaller and tighter and why?

Where do I find a sense of expansion, inspiration and vision?
Where might my visions be blocked or become lost in fantasy?

How do I experience Wyrd – the living web of interconnected life?
How might I have separated myself from my spiritual life and why?

Traditional: Angelica is traditionally considered a tonic and warming herb, with carminative, anti-spasmodic and expectorant properties. As such, the roots and leaves have been used medicinally for conditions of the lungs: coughs and colds; bronchitis and asthma; and for clearing catarrh. Their warming, stimulating and bitter nature also makes them useful for digestion, invigorating for the stomach, relieving spasms and indigestion. The stems, due to their aromatic, sweet smell, have traditionally been candied and used in desserts.

Botany: *Angelica archangelica*, family Apiaceae (formerly Umbelliferae), commonly known as the carrot, celery or parsley family, which includes the benign Cow Parsley and the highly toxic Water Dropworts. *Angelica archangelica* is a large plant growing eight to ten feet tall. They have an unmistakable aromatic fragrance, a pungent sweet smell and taste. They are biennial, and if not allowed to go to flower will grow for several years. The root is harvested in the autumn of its second year of growth, and the leaves in the summer.

Safety: Angelica is a strong herb and should only be used in pregnancy with professional supervision. Not to be confused with *Angelica sinensis* (also known as Dong Quai). In large quantities they can cause photosensitivity when used both internally and externally. Extreme caution should be taken if harvesting from the wild as several plants in the Apiaceae family are highly toxic, and in the case of Giant Hogweed, cause burning and blistering of the skin if juices from the broken stems come into contact with the skin.

Correspondences: ᚛ Fearn (Alder) – growth, protection, resilience, strength, endurance. ᛝ Fehu – abundance, fertility, spiritual protection, flowing energy. ☉ Sun – brightness, cosmos, heavenly realms, penetrating light.

Meeting Angelica: Seek out streams and canals where Angelica grows to spend time in their presence. Find high quality dried root, tincture or spagyric from a herbalist to work with Angelica internally.

Herbalists and ritual: I carefully dig up a one-year-old Angelica plant from the herb garden in autumn (at this point they are short and leafy) and encourage people to smell and handle the living root, which is so potent it has an immediate effect. I prune a little of this root for use in dreaming and infusion before returning the plant to the soil, ready for the second year of growth and flowering. Dried root and tincture can be used, but often lack the potency and clarity of the fresh plant. Spagyric preparations and hydrosols are my favourite preparations for Angelica. Groups are generally readily responsive and open to this plant, though they can be overpowering to some.

Bluebell

One dusky evening, I took a small group up to Randwick woods. We scattered ourselves in the fading light and the liquid floor of bluebells. Dusk, a liminal time, cast a glow on the swathes of bluebells, making them shimmer in the half-light. I caught glimpses of movement around me, a scatter of laughter, two people playfully chasing each other before disappearing amongst the trees. It took me a while to realise that the rich scent was starting to make me a little woozy. In these liminal woods my inner three-year-old was enchanted by a kaleidoscope of small fascinations.

Bluebell offers a playful, mischievous invitation – a call to dance, to play, to set aside adult responsibilities in the warm embrace of a May evening. The young Beech leaves, radiating their fluorescent greens, the flowering Wild Garlic and the occasional Wood Anemone scattered amongst the deep blues saturate the senses. And at the same time, there is something slightly intoxicating in the ever-changing shades of blue, evoking ancient cautionary tales; never fall asleep in the realm of the Fae, for you may never awaken.

How close is your sense of childlike wonder? Does it sparkle in your daily life, or has the flatness of routine dulled it? Where is your inner child – the one who sees the world with fresh eyes, finding fascination in everything?

During the years I suffered with depression, the world became two-dimensional, unsaturated. The cruellest trick of depression was to convince me that it spoke the truth. It was in this place, at the age of 20, that I started to hear plants whisper a deeper truth. All the plants call us back to the magic of life, the multi-dimensional, pulsing, thriving rhythm of life. But Bluebells have a particular place in my heart as enchanting custodians of spring's playfulness.

I wonder if it is, in part, the pursuit of wonder that can feed substance addiction and a life lived at a distance from worldly concerns. Our dance with wonder carries so many possibilities, but also dangers, if we were to ever forget, within the infinitely colourful dreams of the plants, that we are, indeed, human. The forest nymphs beckon, as do the sirens of Greek mythology, and their call is powerful, enchanting, seductive. They sing back to us our deepest desires and resisting them can take the strength of Odysseus. Yet, remember that Odysseus did not resist alone; he asked his sailors to tie him to the mast pole. We, too, need our friends to help us stay grounded in reality.

The blue of the flowers constantly shifts tone, as the light of the day and the weather change. Fiona found this the most difficult flower to paint, as if the blue refused to be captured. Sitting among these nodding flowers feels like being in a shifting sea where nothing remains still. Some find this enchanting, while others are unsettled, drawn into Bluebell's realm.

Bluebells spread slowly and, like Wood Anemone, often indicate an ancient woodland. They come into leaf and flower just before the woodland canopy closes over, reducing the light. In this way their growth pattern is like a woodland version of meadow Cowslips, which grow quickly on tall stems before the long grass can overtake them. Bluebell pollen hides deep within the flower, released only by 'buzz-pollination', a unique trick of bumble bees as they explore the woodlands in search of early spring food. The sweet scent of the flowers is mild on a cold day, but becomes strong and intoxicating in the early evening, after the woods have been warmed for the day in spring sunshine.

I grew up too fast, slipping into seriousness and false maturity. Bluebells and the magic of the spring woodland widen my eyes and wake the mischievous child in me. However, it's not just the child who awakens, there is also a hint of Pan in their invitation. And here is the sense of threat sometimes felt amongst them; like Elder they lead us on the road that winds about the fernie brae, the road to fair Elfland, from which it's unclear if we ever return, and if we do, we are perhaps changed in ways beyond our ken.

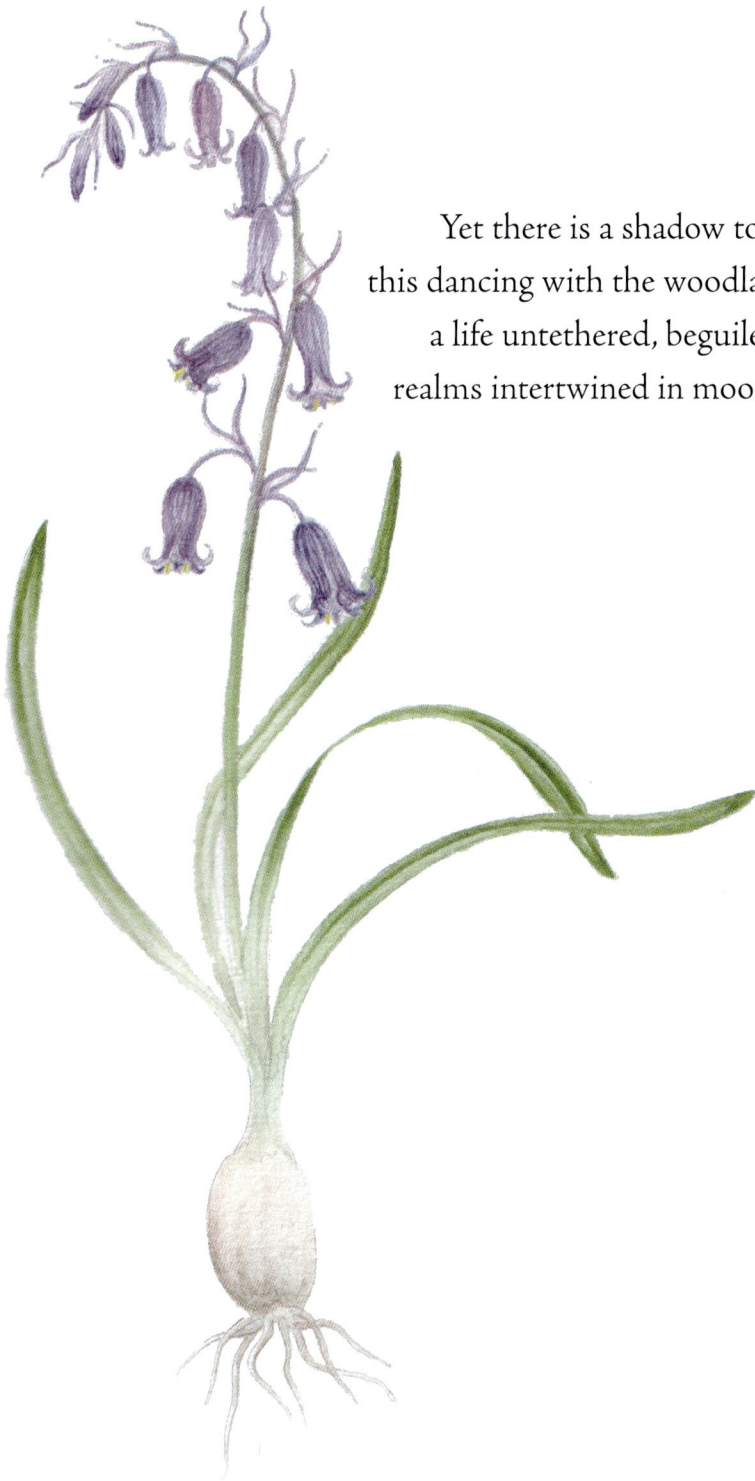

Yet there is a shadow to this play,
this dancing with the woodland Fae,
a life untethered, beguiled in dream,
realms intertwined in moonlight's gleam.

The journey into adulthood is delicate, fraught with dangers and missed rites of passage. Could Bluebell speak to the threads of unincorporated childhood dreams, waiting to be woven into the fabric of our lives? Healing often feels like re-parenting our younger selves, but what if the reverse is true?

> What if it is our younger selves who guide us, reminding us how to be held trustingly within the earth's embrace, within the ever-present web of love that has always surrounded us?

These child wisdoms, breathed into the adult self, bring with them the bardic skills of conscious enchantment. Folklore suggests that ringing a Bluebell summons the Fae, and perhaps they do, or, perhaps it is our remembering that is summoned.

As a writer, I'm a weaver of words, striving to help you rekindle your connections with the wild. As a parting thought on this journey, consider this: the sticky starch from the bulbs of Bluebells was once well known. It was traditionally used for binding books, quite literally the adhesive of linguistic enchantment.

Dream weaver · Liminal whispers · Childhood calling

How do I invite in my sense of wonder in nature? How do I listen to this voice and trust its importance in my life and decisions?
Whose enchantments am I really living by?

How do I make space for the inner children I've become distant from?
How are my inner children unconsciously guiding my decisions in ways that harm me or keep me stuck?

Traditional: All parts of the Bluebell are considered poisonous, even the sap can be irritating, so Bluebell doesn't feature much in traditional herbalism. However, Bluebell flower essence is called on for helping promote joy, feeling supported and opening the heart, particularly if feeling shut down by grief and heaviness. A thick pungent glue was traditionally made from the bulbs by grinding them into a pulp, and the sap from the stems was used by fletchers to glue feathered flights to their arrows.

Folk names: Auld Man's Bell, Bell Bottle, Blue Rocket, Blue Trumpet, Bluebottle, Bummack, Calver Keys, Cover Keys, Crake Feet, Crawfeet, Crawtraes, Cross Flower, Crow Bells, Crow Leek, Crow Picker, Crow-Flower, Crowfoot, Crow's Legs, Crowtoes, Cuckoo Flower, Cuckoo's Boots, Cuckoo's Stockings, Cuckooflower, Culver Keys, Dog Leek, Dog's Leek, Fairy Bells, Fairy Flower, Goosey Gander, Gowk's Hose, Granfer Gregors, Granfer Greygles, Granfer Griddlesticks, Grammar Greygles, Greygles, Pride of the Wood, Ring O'Bells, Rooks Flower, Snake's Flower, Snapgrass, Single Gussies, Squill, Wild Hyacinth, Wood Bells.

Botany: *Hyacinthoides non-scripta*, Asparagaceae – asparagus family. Bluebell is a perennial plant that grows from a bulb, producing three to six linear leaves, all growing from the base of the plant, An inflorescence of five to twelve flowers grow along the stem, which droops towards the tip. The flowers are arranged in a one-sided nodding raceme. Bluebell is native to much of western Europe with the most dense populations being found in Britain and Ireland and their infamous 'Bluebell woods'. Bluebell is a protected plant in the UK meaning it is illegal to uproot them.

Safety: All parts of the Bluebell can be toxic as well as cause dermatitis. I have personally experimented with making hydrosols which are extremely potent and with which I'd be very cautious. A flower essence (containing no material substance of the plant) is an ideal way to work with these.

Correspondences: ᚠ Luis (Rowan) – protection, inspiration, mysticism, divination, enchantment. ᚱ Lagaz – water, intuition, psychic ability, deep emotions, creativity, regeneration. ♆ Neptune – dreams, intuition, the deep unconscious.

Meeting Bluebell: There's a unique enchantment in encountering a swathe of Bluebells as dusk settles on a balmy spring evening. The warmth invites the heady scent and the dusk offers a doorway to the liminal. Though true of many plants, I particularly recommend spending time alone with the Bluebells in this dusk light.

Borage

Borage, dispeller of sadness, bringer of ease to a broken heart, friend to those exhausted in despair or adversity. Herbalists for over two millennia have praised these delicate plants for the capacity to 'expel pensiveness and melancholy', comforting the heart and bringing joy.

In the heat of summer, I steep Borage flowers in hot water and then chill this infusion with ice. This cooling drink has an earthy, satisfying flavour, and a remarkable ability to drain away the hot agitation of a humid, fly-ridden day. The plant's cooling effect mirrors that of a mountain stream, offering a refuge from the heat and gently easing the grief that burdens us. In ritual settings, it is a welcome antidote to the haze invoked by Valerian or Clary, reliably balancing and moderating some of the more delirious aspects that emerge when meeting these two plants.

Young pink flowers mature to a deep vibrant blue, which, once pollinated, droop in hairy clusters. The plant has moist, hollow, and delicate stems, all covered in fine hairs that shimmer like a white halo in the sunlight. The stems are juicy, tasty and easily snapped, but the irritating hairs protect the plant from potential herbivores. Whenever I've spent time with Borage I've felt a desire to become small and crawl under their canopy, feeling the invitation to deep restorative sleep within their protection.

Fiery passion, momentarily cradled

In ancient, cooling hands

A cascading refuge

Allowing grief, finding equilibrium

Borage imparts a moist coolness and resilient nourishment, providing the strength to endure life's intense moments and deep sorrows. This plant comes into their own when we are feeling overwhelmed, spun around and having lost our ground.

In my first ever experience of intentional dreaming with Borage, I had a spontaneous image of an army, waiting just before dawn for battle, in the midsts of a woodland edge. There was a sense of anticipation, fear, excitement, but all held within a cool determined focus. Courage, the 'moral strength to venture, preserve and withstand danger, fear or difficulty', is a quality long associated with Borage, something I see in people whenever we meet Borage; centring, balancing, holding and nourishing. Whatever struggles are unfolding in someone's life, Borage draws out a place of cool, calm resilience within them.

In fear or passion, the heart can *feel* inflamed, pounding, hot and beating fast. Adrenaline and the extra oxygen delivered through vasodilation prepare us for action as the body becomes suffused with oxygenated blood. Sometimes this can be overwhelming, inhibiting clear thought and purposeful action. At times, this fiery intensity is sustained through prolonged challenges or excitement, driving one to the brink of exhaustion.

In this breathless, hot state, Borage is a cool rock in a stream, draining away the remnants of the excessive fire within us and returning us to equilibrium.

When I first trained as a herbalist, I was taught about Borage as a tonic for

the adrenals – of particular value in helping people coming off steroids. In general, steroids are given in acute or chronic inflammatory states, of the gut, lungs, skin or even the blood: the pharmaceutical go-to for inflammation and 'excess-fire'. Calling on Borage, a plant rich in the anti-inflammatory gamma-linolenic acid *, when coming off steroids (which can be difficult) is useful.

It is not unusual when working with people suffering from chronic inflammation for themes of deeply embodied, unexpressed anger to emerge *. Borage can hold a door open here, to meet and integrate this in a way that touches us at both a physiological and a soul level.

Friend in grief and untapped rage

Daring to dream of sisters bright

Standing strong in ritual tight

One of the tricky aspects to working with anger is that if it has been long suppressed, when we do come into contact with it, it can feel overwhelmingly powerful, even unmanageable. For many, their response to this can be to shut it back down as quickly as possible, potentially losing the opportunity to really see what lies behind it. A good therapist might hold a safe space for this enquiry; likewise, Borage can prove a powerful ally here. A plant that moderates, cools and holds this process, used skilfully, can help integration unfold slowly, minimising the risk of the sorts of therapeutic setbacks that can happen if someone becomes scared of their own unexpressed emotions.

Cool shade on hot day   Starlit cave

Cascading cosmos   Rhythm of the night

Delicate grief   Softening tightness

Hackles soothed   Restorative rest

Restorative rest · Cooling passion · Tending grief

How does it feel to have hand at my back, supported in my
day-to to-day courage? How do I ask for this?
*Where might I be attempting to solve problems from a place
of will, passion or fight? Might I be missing support that is available?
Have I normalised any lack of support I experienced in childhood?*

Thresholds of grief or anger have power – where might I be able
to travel deeper into myself, into these thresholds?
Where do I feel I have to contain my anger and manage my grief?

How do I receive the sort of cooling, rest and nourishment
that Borage can offer?
Where do I override my need for rest or where does it feel impossible?

Traditional: Borage has been typically been used to soothe respiratory conditions due
to their demulcent properties, and as an emollient for inflamed and sore skin. They
have also been traditionally been used as a tonic for the heart, particularly for weak
heart conditions and palpitations, and to support the system due to exhaustion and in
times of convalescence. Borage seed oil (sometimes known as 'Starflower oil'), high in
gamma-linolenic-acid (GLA) is commonly used for menstrual problems, eczema, and
allergies. The fresh, cooling and moistening juice of leaves can be applied to burns and
insect bites. I often call on Borage to support people after an intense or overwhelming
experience, as a way to come back to themselves and out of a short-term sympathetic
stress response.

Botany: *Borago officinalis*, Boraginaceae, is a familiar plant in many people's gardens.
Native to the Mediterranean region, Borage is a hardy annual that thrives in various
climates, known for its vibrant blue, star-shaped flowers and fuzzy, grey-green leaves.
Borage produces an abundance of nectar, making it a very attractive pollinator plant.
The covering of fine irritating hairs are known as trichomes, and protect this moist
(and rather tasty) plant from herbivores. Borage is easy to grow from seed, often
germinating in a couple of weeks.

Safety: There are some concerns about Borage (along with others in this family) containing toxic pyrrolizidine alkaloids (PAs), though the concentration of these and actual risk is disputed and controversial. Commercially it is possible to buy PA-free extracts, whilst if working with the actual plant, it is advisable to keep both dosage low, and the length of time it is taken for short. Plants that potentially contain PAs should be avoided in those with any form of liver disease, on medications that affect the liver and in pregnancy. The hairs on Borage can sometimes cause irritation when handled.

Correspondences: ᛖ Fearn (Alder) – protection, strength, resilience, inner resilience. ᚠ Feh – true wealth, prosperity, abundance, exchange, generosity, stewardship, growth. ♃ Jupiter – expansion and the path forward – Borage here offering the support that allows this.

Meeting Borage: If you have access to any plants, I recommend lying down on the ground, encountering Borage at 'insect level'. The extracted seed oil (commonly available as Starflower oil) is a gentle way to meet the plant over a moon cycle. If you have liver disease or are pregnant do check the safety section.

Herbalists & ritual: Borage flowers through the summer and is a beautiful plant to meet on a hot day, helping balance this heat and thus revealing their qualities. In the school we've often enjoyed preparing ice cold infusions and experiencing these through a plant sprayer on otherwise unbearably hot days. The effect is immediate and prolonged.

Bramble

The most tenacious of all the Rose family, tough and fast growing, Bramble is a force of reclamation of the wild. Bramble is often an early coloniser of land disturbed by humans; there are few places in the UK where they cannot be found. They will be one of the first plants to appear in abandoned building sites, along pathways and at the edge of fields. They thrive in the edge-realms of human cultivation, be that of agricultural monoculture or of concrete.

Bramble is nature's push back to humans' push forward.

Until Hiroshima in early August 1945, nothing short of a large asteroid had the power we now have to destroy all other life according to our impulse to dominate. A team with trucks and chainsaws can raze hundreds of years of forest ecosystem in a matter of hours. We have immense power and with that power comes immense responsibility. To understand Bramble is to understand how we might choose to walk in the path of a different power.

Brambles find their home in the edges and the gaps, and what they do there is a gift to life. With their tangled knot of thorns, impenetrable to humans (unless we carry sharpened steel), they weave a zone of safety.

Surrounded by this protective web of thorns, Bramble's nectar provides food for many insects, the chaotic weave of stems provides safe habitat for birds, small mammals and grass snakes, and the berries food for birds, foxes and badgers. In a handful of Bramble tangles near where I live, I've seen Robins, Wrens, Thrushes and even Blackbirds take refuge in their protection. What might look messy to us is actually an ecological paradise.

"Bramble is sometimes considered an undesirable plant or a 'thug' that outcompetes other wild flowers; however, these findings confirm that it is highly valuable for flower-visiting insects. Wherever conflicts of interest and management strategies allow, bramble should be maintained and promoted for wildlife and insect conservation."

Insect Conservation and Diversity 2020
Royal Entomological Society [*]

Not only are Brambles an ally to all this animal life, they provide protection in which saplings can grow, helping regeneration of Oak, Willow and Birch forest, protecting tender young growth from grazing deer. [*]

There is an ancient and widespread understanding that iron is detrimental to the Fae. [*] Iron (and thus steel) is a potent symbol of humans' utilisation and manipulation of nature according to our will, with an impulse that is in equal parts constructive and destructive. To put it simply and bluntly, chainsaws couldn't exist without iron. Is it any wonder then that the Fae, the spirits of place, the beings of the living ecosystems of nature, fear iron?

The loss of the Fae is not the loss of some childish whimsy; it is a harbinger of utter environmental destruction and a warning bell to our own unchecked colonising impulses. Personally I've always been drawn to the unkempt Bramble in the corners of people's gardens, bordering the overflowing hedgerows and the wrapping of solitary copses of trees in the centre of meadows. These are the places where nature regenerates itself; these are the places where I have always felt renewed.

The grass snakes that take refuge in Bramble are a rare sight now in Britain, and when, in the carefully tended Horsley valley, I crossed paths with one for the first time, some deep memory and a quiet respect was touched in me.

The legend of St. George slaying the dragon is renowned, with deep mythological origins. It speaks to the conflict between the earth powers of the dragon (snake) and the powers of the Sun-god, in this case represented by the Christian militant St. George. This archetypal conflict plays out in our inner lives and in our relationship to our body, challenging and inviting us to find the place of trust betwixt the wild wisdom of our body and the expressions of our thought and will.

This archetypal conflict becomes critically important in various medical contexts, especially during childbirth, where the inherent wisdom of the body often needs to be carefully balanced against the call for medical intervention. Bramble is a reminder that the wild has its own wisdom, older and deeper than ours.

Bramble fruits abundantly, and the tightening qualities of the young leaves are so astringent that they have been used to secure loose teeth. Their roots are just as fast-growing and tenacious as the strong stems, covered in the thorns that inspired the defensive barricade invoked in Sleeping Beauty:

> "But there went a report through all the land of the beautiful sleeping Briar Rose (for so the king's daughter was called), so that, from time to time, several kings' sons came and tried to break through the thicket into the palace. This, however, none of them could ever do, for the thorns and bushes laid hold of them, as it were with hands, and there they stuck fast and died wretchedly."

> *Collected and published by Jacob and Wilhelm Grimm 1812*

If nature exacted her revenge so directly on us, as she did with the princes, perhaps we would be more reticent to pick up the chainsaw. The sort of reticence that is still found today in Iceland when a building project threatens to disturb a Hawthorn or the Fae.

Where do we listen and wake up to the rapidly collapsing ecosystems, and where do we close our ears?

Where do we choose to feel more, *even though it hurts*, and where do we withdraw and numb ourselves?

Numbing is a natural response to a situation that feels beyond our control. In the case of environmental destruction, self-numbing offers no path forward. It is time we awaken from our numbed state and begin to truly listen – to the plants, the land, to the creatures that inhabit it, and to the deep, ancient rhythms of the wild.

Where might others – people or the land – need more of my thorns, tenacity, and protection in a way that truly serves them?
Where might I be being overly defensive, overly protective, or even overly caring?

How does it feel to step into my wild, unkempt and unknown parts?
Where have I allowed myself to be led by others' dreams and needs, or become suffocated within someone else's protection?

How do I step towards my wild, creative fruitfulness?
Where has my inner and outer world become barren through disconnection?

How might I be a better guardian of the land?
What does it mean to live in relationship with land and place?

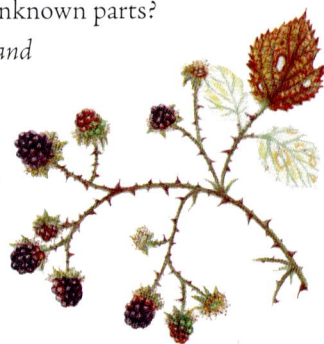

Traditional: The well-known fruit of Bramble, blackberries, have been used since neolithic times. The ripe berries made into a decoction have been recommended as a gargle for sore throats, and like other deep purple and red fruits they are full of antioxidants and rich in vitamin C, proving useful for seasonal colds. The leaves have a strong astringent action, used to staunch bleeding wounds, for inflamed gums and mouth ulcers, and to treat diarrhoea and haemorrhoids. With their thorny, winding, impenetrable branches, hedges made of Bramble were used as defensive and protective barriers around settlements.

Botany: *Rubus fruticosus*, is a member of the Rose family (Rosaceae) native to Britain and Europe that has naturalised in Australia and America. There are thought to be around 400 micro-species of Bramble in Britain alone. A sprawling prickly shrub with small white-pink flowers and the unmissable dark purple 'black' berries. Leaves are harvested in summer and the berries in late summer into autumn.

Safety: The only real risk with Bramble is cuts and scrapes when harvesting blackberries, and, of course, eating too many berries can cause a sore belly.

Correspondences: ᚋ Muin (Vine) – growth, transformation, fertility, abundance, fruitfulness, joy, pleasure, resilience, regeneration, soul protection. ᛗ Manaz – community, consciousness, social connections, cooperation, collaboration, humanity, rationality. ♂ Mars – courage, leadership, passion, initiative.

Herbalists and ritual: Harvesting berries (especially with children!) is always a joy, the challenge and the abundance making for a very satisfying excursion – do always think about how to reciprocate and thank the Bramble for this abundance. Celebrating Bramble around Lamas (1st August) feels perfect, as the British summer subtly shifts into a time of fruiting. Celebrations can take many forms, but simple offerings and lighting candles to the Bramble with space and time to feel their teachings always feel deeply reconnecting and life affirming to me. As with all of the Rose family, there is something here that gently lifts and opens the heart if we can let it in.

Chamomile

Harvesting Chamomile is a slow but satisfying process. With each flower plucked, a soft musty scent is released and the pollen leaves a fragrant dust on the fingertips. Commercially, of course, this has all been mechanised, or at least hastened with a 'chamomile rake', otherwise we'd be paying a fortune for this, most familiar of British herbal teas. Even the profoundly non-herbal have heard of Chamomile and, musing on this, it seems appropriate, given British culture's rather complex relationship with anger.

English language is abundant in idioms relating to anger: 'seeing red, blow a fuse, up in arms, spitting fire, on the warpath, boiling, steamed up, hot-headed, hot-blooded, hot under the collar'. There's a consistency in these idioms and the folk understanding of anger as an emotion of fire, a fire which heats an inner fluid in a sealed container, venting sporadically as the pressure becomes too much to contain. Sometimes controlled so well (in appearance at least), that anger simmers away quietly under the surface, only to show itself in frustration, resentment, defensiveness and passive aggression. These more subtle forms of anger, in my experience, are the more common ways of expressing this fire amongst many.

> Spacious breeze,
>
> To the knotted fire,
>
> Of our confused passion.

The flowers infuse quickly in boiled water, releasing their musty scent in the steam and golden glow to the water. The taste is full, bitter, sweet and aromatic and yet at the same time light and spacious like the plant itself. I've often seen them thriving on the cracked and sun-hardened soil at the edge of meadows in Devon, along with their close relatives Pineapple Weed and May Weed with which they can be easily confused.

Whenever I've brought Chamomile into a ritual space the effect is immediate; the room suddenly opens out, the space between individuals seemingly bigger. There is a sense of a deep collective out-breath, of unacknowledged bodily tensions released; people become more pensive, quiet, and time slows. This is an unhurried space, the opposite of intensity. Chamomile's presence in the room is like the cooling mist a little distance from the hard rocks and fast water of a powerful waterfall. There is a lightness and a letting go, a quiet joyfulness that makes long-held resentments fade away into unimportance.

I wonder if what I'm seeing in the human ecology around me mirrors how these plants inhabit their own ecology. Chamomile is a plant that can hold its own, it has a characteristic called 'allelopathy'; as it grows it releases chemicals that inhibit the growth of plants around it, making more space for itself, reducing the pressure to fight for the light, water and nutrients it needs.

> "I feel like I can breathe fuller, like more air can enter my nose, throat, chest, lungs. My heart space feels like it is getting more air. I feel softness, a sense of grief … like a grief for the softness that I haven't been feeling before connecting to this. I want to lie down with the sweetness of the plant and the smell of the soil."

> *Melissa Rose Spencer (2024)*

Distilling Chamomile is a beautiful experience – floating on the surface of the fragrant hydrosol are tiny dark blue dots of chamomile oil, coloured by the molecule chamazulene, a potent anti-inflammatory and analgesic. Once after distilling, I was about to clean out the distillation pot and, noticing there was still quite a bit of extremely well decocted water in with the flowers, I decanted and drank a little. The brew was so strong that the effect was immediate and potently psychoactive. It gave me a new-found respect for Chamomile; for the next hour I could hardly walk straight or form a sentence without losing my thread of thought.

Chamomile has a long history for those experiencing constrained, tense heat – just as much when this heat is felt as inflammation in the gut or the skin, as when it is felt in the heart and the emotions. This is a plant of light, air and balance, a cooling breeze to the simmering confusion of anger and resentment.

Our fire sometimes serves to defend us, our soldiers invoked to protect us. Sometimes, if we struggle to find support and other strategies, these soldiers risk becoming embedded, habitual, seeing danger where there is none, even keeping those who come towards us in love at a distance. Like Hiroo Onoda *, the Japanese soldier who didn't realise the Second World War was over until he formally surrendered in 1974, our inner soldiers are reluctant to leave us unguarded.

Chamomile's magic isn't to quickly resolve such deep patterns, rather they offer a space where we might more clearly see what we are holding on to and if – and how, with deep gratitude for all it has done to protect us – we might find a way to let it go. Within the holding of Chamomile is an invitation to soften our defences, hyper-vigilance and reactivity, finding space simply to be present in the moment.

Spacious expansion
Gentle touch
Freedom and flight
Airy flow
Innocent play
Delicate gold
Soft sunlight
Spacious breath
A feeling of hollowness
Summer gateway
Space to dream

Invitation: To find space within ourselves, a freshening breeze to the fullness of our lives.

Where might my life flow with more ease by letting go a little more and giving an issue or relationship more space? *Where might I be getting overly engaged, perhaps motivated by anxiety or a need to feel in control?*

How is my relationship with my internal fire? How might Chamomile guide me into a deeper understanding of this?
How might I be judging my own fire, passion and anger in ways that inhibit me finding creative, healthy expression?

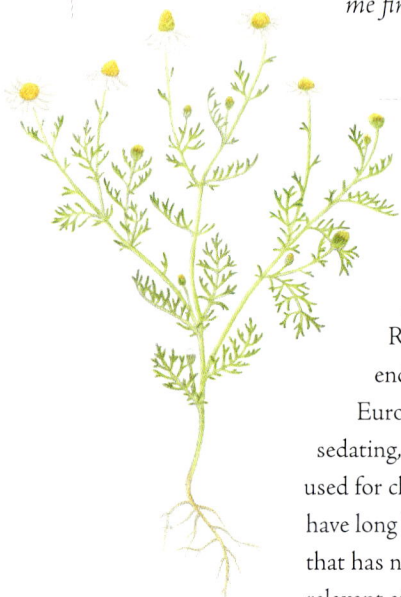

German Chamomile (the Chamomile shown on the card) Matricaria chamomilla, is an annual, growing taller and with more spacious leaves than Roman Chamomile. They offer a comforting, sweet, end-of-summer warm infusion and have featured in European herbalism for millennia. They are soothing and sedating, with anti-inflammatory properties which can be used for children, the elderly and everyone in between. They have long been a staple in Europe for menstrual cramps, a use that has now been well researched.[*] The carminative and relaxant effects make them useful for digestive disorders, including indigestion, Crohn's disease and IBS. Topically these qualities are useful for sore and irritated skin conditions such as eczema, psoriasis, nappy rash in babies and sore nipples in breastfeeding mothers, and healing wounds. They are also supportive for asthma and seasonal allergies. The flowers have a sweet, potent, rich and evocative scent that is best experienced from the living plant as inevitably some of this is lost in drying. Chamomile has been researched extensively for many conditions; I've given an overview of this in the endnotes.[*]

Roman Chamomile, Chamomile nobile, also known as 'Lawn Chamomile' is a perennial and tends to grow closer to the ground, thus their traditional use as a lawn. Though often used interchangeably with German Chamomile, these are a lot more bitter and more stimulating to the liver and digestion. Otherwise, the uses, relaxant and anti-inflammatory effects are similar to German Chamomile.

Botany: *Matricaria chamomilla*, Asteraceae (daisy) family. Grows throughout Europe and in other temperate regions. German Chamomile is an annual, growing from seed in spring and flowering from early summer.

Safety: Some people are allergic to plants in the daisy family, if so the fresh plant can cause contact dermatitis. Do not use the essential oil internally and avoid topical use in pregnancy. There is mixed research about Chamomile's safety in pregnancy – I've included an open access research paper ⚹ in the endnotes to read more on this, but in brief there is little evidence that moderate doses in the later stages of pregnancy present significant risks, and potentially have many benefits. Work alongside an experienced herbalist, midwife or doula here. If taking any prescription medications do check online for possible drug interactions.

Correspondences: ᛡ Ur (Heather) – heaven–earth connection, adaptability, independence. ᚢ Uruz – inner strength, health and vitality, endurance, protection, sovereignty. ☉ Sun – strength, vitality, self-expression, summer solstice.

Meeting Chamomile: A slow, spacious tea meditation with a good quality Chamomile tea is a very simple and effective way of meeting Chamomile. It is remarkable, when a tea is drunk consciously, over half an hour, with focused intention and without distraction, how deep it is possible to go into connection with a plant. For a plant that can be found in every supermarket, Chamomile can be surprisingly strong. These are easy and satisfying plants to grow from seed.

Herbalists and ritual: I particularly enjoy introducing Chamomile alongside distillation. The aroma escaping from the still is beautiful to journey with, the hydrosol can be added to a spray bottle and the tiny drops of black-blue essential oil carefully separated off the hydrosol. Chamomile invites spaciousness; be sure to allow plenty of time and space to dive in.

Clary

I have heard from several midwives an observation: that there is often a stage in labour where the mother, in pain and exhaustion, repeats, "I can't do this, I can't do this" – and that this seeming impossibility often marks a threshold to the final stages of labour. Birth can take us right to the edge of what feels possible, and beyond, asking for a deep surrender to the pulsing of the womb and trust in the body.

Every year I freeze a large batch of Clary in full flower – working with the whole plant is so much more potent than an oil or hydrosol. I remember supporting a friend in her birthing; I went to fetch the Clary just at the point she was needing to find some extra strength in the labour. They were sealed in a plastic bag and I still remember the visceral response to opening this bag, three metres away from the birthing pool. The smell of the plant alone unlocked a sudden power and strength to her contractions. This can be such a strong effect, care is needed with timing and bringing it into the birthing space.

Compared to the essential oil, the living plant is significantly more potent, containing deep, thick and resinous aromatics that don't seem to make it through the distillation process; it feels to me that these heavier pheromone-like compounds are key to Clary's power.

> Wild feminine, liquid life
>
> Womb's pulse – invoking life
>
> Calling in, pushing out
>
> Birthing yell, first breath

The scent is pungent and feral, some liken it to a more-ish body odour of a lover, awakening something deep within us, speaking to the wild animal of us. The words that emerge from ritual spaces are enthusiastic, immediate and evocative, as people taken by surprise by the forceful immediacy of this plant.

And yet this birthing ally is far more than this; the invocation to embodied wild aliveness can touch everyone, awakening the sensuality and power of the lower cauldron whilst simultaneously relaxing long-held tension – a perfect combination for dance, lovemaking and birthing.

This embodied enlivening doesn't just express itself through the physical; many people have shared an activating of their imagination, discovering a direct 'power line' between the lower cauldron (womb, pelvis, testes) and their creativity.

I've noticed this whilst writing this book, the richest, most flowing creativity comes when I can channel the aliveness of the lower cauldron into words.

Divine lover

BIRTHING YELL

No compromise

Deep permissiveness

LIVING FULLY

Life orgasm

Fertile aliveness

Musty growl

DRAGON'S TONGUE

JOYFUL EROS

Pure delight

Ecstatic muse

Clary is found in the wild in southern Europe, though grows well in Britain when carefully tended. The young shoots seem favoured by slugs, so we let them grow stronger in the greenhouse before potting them out, though after a while have found that they happily self-seed in the herb garden. Whilst the painting might appear exaggerated, it is not – the plant is a glorious, bold and potently scented presence in the garden.

"This feels pheromonal, dangerous even. Whatever I was feeling ten minutes ago is utterly gone and I feel awake and like I want to prowl. I feel like a cat around catmint – a bit delirious, wanting nothing more than to surrender to the pulses and desires of my body."

The potency of Clary means I'm cautious when bringing them into ritual; just as they can lead people into connection with their animal self, they can also touch any trauma held around this, layers of sexual trauma that are ubiquitous and ancestral: trauma and conditioning that I've come to see we all hold within us in different ways and to different degrees. Clary, along with Wild Garlic, Hawthorn, Elder, Meadowsweet or Mugwort, can touch our fear of our own wildness, of our own desires. These plants challenge our attempts to suppress or confine such aspects of ourselves.

Plants disregard our societal norms and expectations; instead, they beckon to our primordial selves, parts that precede the constructs of social convention and etiquette. Clary, in particular, serves as a potent reminder of this primal essence. I suspect this is precisely why herbalism has and will always exist at the fringes of the mainstream – plants resist assimilation into our constructed reality, continually pushing its boundaries. Plants speak to our indigenous selves, and though many romanticise this, the reality is that when we meet the sensitivity, needs and desires of these parts, the confrontation can leave us feeling challenged and even threatened by implications it presents.

If we truly invite the plants in, this is not a casual hobby, an interest or even an enquiry – it is a fundamental challenge to who we think we are and who we choose to be.

"Clary is a plant that helps us give birth to our true selves.
It's not tidy – it's messy, smelly, wild and free."
Emily Taylor (2022)

Sensual aliveness · Awakening roar · Ecstatic surrender

*What within me is ready to be birthed? Where can
I find and meet the thresholds of this birthing?*
Where am I resisting surrendering to the flow of my animal self?

How do I invite and allow my desires, visions and dreaming?
Where is my capacity for powerful, creative visioning blocked and why?

*What does it feel like to be in vibrant relationship with
my sexuality and the vital animal of me?*
*Where do I hold shame, guilt or fear around my sexuality? Do I carry
trauma (my own and systemic/ancestral) in these realms and how might I
find ways to meet this with compassion?*

Traditional: Clary has anti-spasmodic, nervine, antidepressant, anti-inflammatory and emmenagogue actions. They are well known for their use in the final stage of labour when mental and physical exhaustion may have become overwhelming to the birthing process. The relaxant effect means Clary has been used for headaches, asthma, insomnia, indigestion and pain from muscle tension, such as with menstrual bleeding. The plant is generally considered euphoric (lifting mood) and research indicates that they can invoke an increase in oxytocin.

The seeds have traditionally been soaked in water to create a mucilage used to help clean the eyes and reduce inflammation, alluded to in the name clary sage or 'clear eye'. Before brewing of beer became regulated, it was commonly used in the place of hops, making a highly intoxicating beer. Modern research is primarily into the uses of the essential oil, which has been included in various human trials looking at massage and aromatherapy in managing anxiety, labour pain, high blood pressure and stress.

Botany: *Salvia sclarea*, member of the mint (Lamiaceae) family, is a biennial native to southern Europe and the Middle East. The large, hairy leaves carry a strong, musky fragrance when crushed, and in their second year, tall flower spikes of white, pink and lavender tubular blossoms appear. The flowers have an even stronger scent than the leaves, particularly around the calyx where a sticky, scented resin can be found. Clary likes heat, sun and a dry soil, and is known to be drought resistant.

70

Safety: If using Clary Sage essential oil, always dilute it in a carrier oil before applying it to the skin and perform a patch test on a small area to check for sensitivities. Do not use the essential oil internally. Avoid using Clary Sage during pregnancy due to the risk of miscarriage. The oil can amplify the intoxicating effects of alcohol and interact with sedative medications, so avoid combining it with alcohol or sedatives. Although rare, there have been reports of Clary Sage triggering seizures in individuals with epilepsy. More commonly, excessive exposure to Clary Sage can cause headaches. Due to their strong hormonal effects, it is advisable to consult a professional herbalist if you are taking any medications, including contraceptive pills. Clary Sage has potent effects during labor, so unless you have significant experience and confidence with herbal remedies, it is wise to work with a doula, midwife or herbalist who has expertise with this herb.

Correspondences: ᚋ Muin (Vine) – growth and vitality, living in harmony with natural cycles, fertility and creativity, resilience. ᛗ Mannaz – the human experience, community, interdependence, harmony, communication, relationship, social bonds. ☉ Sun – warmth, aliveness, strong sense of self, purpose, enlivening.

Meeting Clary: If you have access to a living plant, the presence is so potent that little guidance is needed here! I find the essential oil far less potent and often variable in quality, so whilst this can sometimes be a good initial meeting, it falls far short of the actual plant.

Herbalists and ritual: Clary Sage supports people in transcending their ordinary human experience, connecting them to their more primal, animalistic nature while simultaneously enhancing inner vision and intuition. It reveals an abundance of possibilities and encourages explorations of personal sovereignty within community and relationships. Clary Sage invites a sense of potency and skill in holding space, often evoking a radically honest and authentic environment that demands clear communication and awareness of projection and transference dynamics.

Cleavers

As I write, rain pounds down on the roof, much as it has throughout December. Under this ceaseless downpour, the ground has become marsh-like and mud is everywhere. It is early January and the young Cleavers stand cheerful and sprightly amongst the mud, their vitality a stark contrast to my dwindling patience with the constant presence of water. Yet their lively demeanour nudges me toward embracing the very element I find myself growing weary of.

This is a plant that grows as if they were water flowing slowly upwards. Their growth is a winding journey, not choreographed by erosion forces like a river, but by the dance of light and the intricate patterns woven by neighbouring plants.

Collecting a little Cleavers, they rest on my hand; they feel animated and vibrantly alive. There's no trace of the heaviness that's been weighing on me recently. It's a constant source of wonder to me how much I forget in the realm of plants; in this very moment, it feels like precisely the medicine I've been seeking.

Cleavers can only sustain their own height up to a certain point. Once they extend beyond the span of a hand, they lean on, gracefully wrap themselves around and intertwine with any neighbouring plant in a fluid weave. My hand glides along their tender bright green leaves and nimble stalks and I can't help but smile. For a moment I'm lifted out oppressive eternal dampness, feeling an urge to move my body with the fluidity of a water snake.

The Cleavers' growing stem puts out whirls of tidy laminate leaves, and from each node a captivating micro-Cleaver, an axillary stem, emerges, mirroring the elegant pattern with six or seven leaves in each whirl. There is a rough, slightly sticky feel to the leaves and stems; the result of thousands of tiny hooked bristles, the bristles that allow Cleavers to latch on to and climb over surrounding vegetation.

At this point in the year, the Cleavers stand at ten centimetres, far from flowering and seeding. Before long they will put out minuscule white flowers, succeeded by hairy seeds that cluster in pairs, reminiscent of miniature testicles. Cleavers, a member of the Rubiaceae family, share their botanical lineage with the renowned coffee plant. Unexpectedly, the seeds emit a distinctly coffee-like aroma when fried.

I've stumbled upon a distinctive method of preparing Cleavers, and its appeal has resonated with many who've learned about it. Place the fresh plant in a sizeable, transparent glass flower vase and immerse it in cold spring water, creating what I call a 'living water'. With daily water refreshments, Cleavers thrives in this submerged environment, entering into a living osmosis with the surrounding water. The result is a water imbued with the essence of the living plant, offering a truly unique herbal infusion. I recommend allowing this watery dance to unfold for approximately eight hours, ideally basking in sunlight, before sipping the water and replenishing it with a fresh batch.

This lively water is deeply satisfying, hydrating and pulsing with aliveness. It invites movement and dance, dispelling any stagnation within us. Our body's hibernatory reflex in winter can leave us feeling weighed down and lacking motivation. Cleavers offers a delightful means to usher in an early awakening come spring, encouraging movement and rejuvenation.

Clear harmony

Fluid freshness

Crystal waters

Outreaching arms

Sweet stream

Tangle sparkles

Water snake

Subtly spiralling

Bristling beauty

Water snake · Subtle spiral · Fluid self

What encourages flow and fluidity in my body?
Where am I allowing myself to become too still and stagnant?

How do my emotions flow and what helps them move with more ease?
Where and why do I feel emotionally stuck?

What does healthy interdependency with others feel like?
*Where am I overly dependent or avoidant in a way that might smother
other people or keep others at a distance?*

Traditional: Cleavers is valued in herbalism as an excellent spring tonic, lymphatic
remedy, diuretic and immunomodulatory herb. They are traditionally considered
useful in eczema, psoriasis, urinary tract infections and for reinvigorating the body
when convalescing from illness. In my clinic I find many people seem chronically
dehydrated and don't enjoy drinking water – Cleavers' living water is helpful here, not
just in helping people drink more, but in re-enlivening their relationship with water,
both that which they drink and the waters of their own body.

Botany: *Galium aparine,* family Rubiaceae is easily recognisable with whirls of
lanceolate leaves and the whole plant covered in sticky 'velcro-like' hairs. Cleavers
possesses a quiet resilience, thriving in diverse environments and playing an essential role
in the ecosystem as a pioneer species, often marking the first green in disturbed soils.

Safety: Cleavers is generally considered safe, though I have heard of people having very uncomfortable choking if eating the fresh plant. May rarely cause contact dermatitis. Theoretically, as Cleavers is considered a diuretic they should be used with caution on people already taking diuretics.

Correspondences: ᚄ Saille (Willow) water, spiritual growth, forgiveness. ᚺ Sigel – vitality, brilliance, sun. ☽ Moon – water tides, rhythm, change, intuition.

Herbalists and ritual: Cleavers is a wonderful and generally straightforward herb to bring into ritual, always use fresh and preferably along with spring water in some form. The space Cleavers tends to invoke is often playful, light and flowing – suited to dance or authentic movement practices. I highly recommend hydrating well with Cleavers' water before and during any ritual with them!

Dandelion

Many people have never looked closely at a Dandelion flower. They are one of those plants that is so ubiquitous that we hardly even notice them, made invisible, or worse, into the quintessential 'weed' by their very success. But look closer and the beauty to be found here is exquisite.

The flower we see is composed of hundreds of ray florets radiating from a central 'involucre,' and deeper in the centre of the flower, there are hundreds more central hollow disk florets. Each disk floret contains five stamens rich in pollen that attracts and nourishes bees, butterflies, hoverflies and beetles. The scent is subtle and sweet; you often have to bring your nose right up to a flower to savour it. The flower heads are edible and surprisingly sweet due to the nectar that rests in the disk florets.

Once pollinated each of these central disk florets transforms into one flying seed, and it is hundreds of these together that form the iconic seed heads much loved by children. These seeds are just part of Dandelion's success, not only do they travel great distances on the wind, but they stay viable for years, dormant in the soil. Once a new plant starts to grow, the powerful taproot draws up nutrients from the deeper soil, making the young plant strong and resilient in multiple soil and drought conditions.

Far from taking these plants for granted or perceiving them as weeds, I see Dandelion as the most adapted survivor of a plant. In this tenacity they don't just serve themselves, but feed countless insects whilst the tap roots either stabilise weak soil or break up compacted soil, aerating it and drawing nutrients from the depths, which then become available to neighbouring plants once the Dandelion decomposes. Perhaps you can tell from my enthusiasm in writing about them that I'm rather in awe of their success, resilience, adaptability and ecological reciprocity.

So given all of this, why do many think of them as undesirable weeds?

I suspect the answer lies in a the desire for a certain controlled aesthetic in garden design. If, as seems essential in these days of looming environmental collapse, our gardens need to become ecological havens, Dandelions have an essential place in this. If they were rare, they would be considered a wonder.

Every gesture of a plant is a fractal of their entire being, with Dandelion's living movements beautifully reflected in their medicinal qualities. For centuries Dandelion has been valued for enlivening and cleansing qualities, being particularly activating of the blood cleansing and detoxification roles of the kidneys and liver. In the 17th century Culpeper wrote of their "opening and cleansing quality", a quality that made them "very effectual for the obstructions of the liver, gall and spleen". Little has changed in herbalists' perception of Dandelion, but unfortunately, Dandelion has never been a particularly fashionable plant to draw research funding, meaning research is limited.

Acedia's foe, spirit stirrer

There is an old word that Fiona introduced me to I'd like to revive here: 'acedia', a state of 'listlessness or torpor'. In the 13th century, Thomas Aquinas described acedia as a lethargic grief rooted in loss of spiritual direction "on account of the flesh utterly prevailing over the spirit." I wonder if this might be akin to the disempowered state of freeze that many find themselves in faced with the realisation of both environmental destruction and our complicit entanglement with it. Given the challenge to keep on turning up to this truth with integrity, rather than succumbing to the gravity of even more materialistic comfort seeking, Dandelion strikes me as a fine remedy on many levels.

To invite Dandelion is to call in vitality and dynamism, to be challenged to move any stagnancy in your body and will that is keeping you stuck. It is here, and maybe appropriately within the Dandelion chapter, I feel I need to burst a bubble of potential magical thinking. Simply inviting Dandelion consciousness in will itself not promote change. Dandelion will not 'make' you exercise more, drink more water or eat better. What they can do though, is put a spotlight on your own denial around areas of stagnancy in your life.

Under this gaze, habits of inertia gradually lose their grip. Imagine cohabiting with a vibrant, dynamic athlete; their very presence illuminates our own less-than-ideal lifestyle choices, be it a poor diet or excessive screen time, gradually nudging us towards healthier, more life-affirming habits.

This insight aligns with a key tenet of this book. The plants alone will not heal us. However, they can be our close companions when we choose to embrace the journey, step through our inner resistance and walk the path of our own healing.

Where are the places of stagnancy within me? How do I encourage them into movement? *How do I lose connection to my life force through habitual stagnancy?*

What life-affirming changes do I need to make right now? *Where am I holding on too tightly?*

How do I nurture my physical dynamism? *Which habits of diet, behaviour and exercise are weighing me down?*

Traditional: Dandelion leaf is well regarded as a diuretic, * whilst the root is favoured for skin problems, liver and gallbladder support, * and as a hypoglycaemic in type 2 diabetes.* The latex sap has been traditionally used to heal warts. Research also points towards an anti-tumour effect, suppressing gastric and colon cancer cell proliferation *in vitro.* Traditionally Dandelion is often used by herbalists as a nutrient-rich spring tonic and to help clear stagnant heat from the body.

Botany: *Taraxacum officinale*, family Asteraceae, grows wild in most parts of the world, having followed settlers as they have moved, thriving in human 'anthropogenic' environments. The genus of *Taraxacum* is extensive, with over 2500 known species. This perennial plant is characterised by its distinct, jagged, 'tooth-like' basal leaves and a deep, robust taproot typically harvested in the autumn of its second year. The stalks of the flowers are hollow excreting a latex-like sap when snapped, and has bright golden yellow flowers, which when they turn to seed create the classic white puffball-like Dandelion clock.

Safety: Possible allergic response to Asteraceae (Compositae/Daisy) family. Possible drug interactions due to diuretic effect. Large doses can cause diarrhoea and gastric irritation.

Correspondences: ᛖ Tinne (Holly) – strength, protection, vigour, courage, warrior, summer solstice. ᛏ Tir (Tiwaz) – justice and victory in conflict. ☉ Sun – core identity, brightness and bigness, vitality, authority, life direction.

Personal meetings: Dandelion suits a committed moon-cycle plant diet in spring or early summer, taking a little of the root, leaf or flower every day for a moon cycle. This works particularly well combined with a weekly fasting day.

Herbalists and ritual: Dandelion tends to provoke dynamic encounters that benefit from having a lot of outdoor space to expand into and play in. I've encouraged people to graze on Dandelion flowers, drink juiced leaves and nibble on fresh root, all of which can invite an intense physicality, sometimes with release of long-held anger and frustration. Though a very common and much used herb, I would advise a fair degree of experience before inviting a group into Dandelion ritual, as the effects can be quite provocative and cathartic. For sure, anyone working in this space should have explored their own relationship with their physical dynamism lest their own unconscious habits become mirrored within the group dynamic. This encapsulates the challenge of working as a herbalist and ritualist in this way; we always need to have done the work ourselves.

Control
Responsibility

Surrender
Trust

Elder

The liminal zone between our dream world and our waking world is a potent, creative, generative place. Elderflower, in the lead up to summer solstice, releases a sweet, narcotic scent that instantly blurs the line between wakefulness and dream, between the Wyrd and the manifest, between our human selves and our mythic selves. Elder can open us to the realms of omens and portents, sensitising us to the subtle nudges we can easily miss.

The presence of the Fae is rarely so visceral as when inviting Elderflower into the space. The smell invokes a hazy, dreamlike space, an inner quieting and drifting off into reverie. Elder opens the door to the liminal with ease. For some this dreaming space is blissful and ecstatic, an awakening to the aliveness in Nature. For others, it leads to places of old wounds, darkness, fear and even terror. As with Mugwort, it is entirely unpredictable where each person will travel in a journey with Elder. But some things are constant. Elder promotes a softening of the edges, a blurring of dream and manifest reality, a potentising of emotions (or a numbing if the emotions touched are too powerful) and a gentle narcotic spell-weaving.

In the ancient ballad 'Thomas the Rhymer' no-one knows for sure what the 'Eildon Tree' was, but Elder is a likely candidate and, from my experience, is a very likely portal for Thomas to be taken into Fae for seven years.

"Light down, light down, now, True Thomas,
And lean your head upon my knee;
Abide and rest a little space,
And I will shew you ferlies three.

O see ye not that narrow road,
So thick beset with thorns and briers?
That is the path of righteousness,
Tho after it but few enquires.

And see not ye that braid braid road,
That lies across that lily leven?
That is the path to wickedness,
Tho some call it the road to heaven.

And see not ye that bonny road,
That winds about the fernie brae?
That is the road to fair Elfland,
Where thou and I this night maun gae.

But, Thomas, ye maun hold your tongue,
Whatever ye may hear or see,
For, if you speak word in Elflyn land,
Ye'll neer get back to your ain countrie."

Selection from the ancient ballad
'Thomas the Rhymer"
The Underworld Initiation,
R.J. Stewart, 1998

The moment I bring Elderflower to my face, the scent is almost overwhelming, yet at the same time more-ish. I'm torn between pushing it away and drawing it closer. Letting myself drop into this space I have a distinct feeling of a vine wrapping itself slowly around my wrist and up my arm. It's slow, perhaps like a snake, but not threatening. Around the circle, the sounds of others are distant and mixed; crying somewhere, giggling somewhere else, a sense of everyone travelling in their own reality, carried by Elder.

I find the somewhat saccharine notions of Faerie often seem unhelpful and very out of alignment with people's experiences of the Fae, not least their darker, trickster tendencies. The word 'faerie' is likely made up of

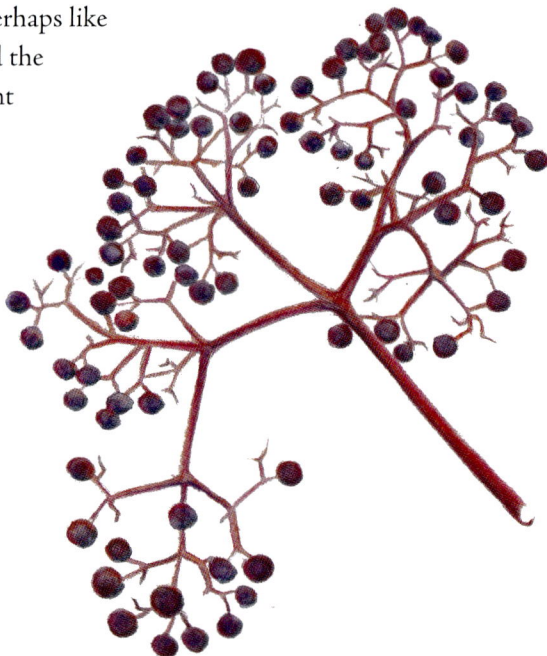

two etymological roots, the French verb 'faer', meaning 'to enchant' and 'rie' being the Old English for 'place of'. I encourage this interpretation; to experience Faerie is to experience a place of enchantment. When understood this way, there are few people who would claim to have not had an experience of Fae.

To experience Fae is to visit a place in nature where the veil between worlds becomes thinner, to enter a liminal space in which our habitual projections on the world are momentarily challenged. Just for a moment, we might glimpse a deeper ecology, beyond our understanding and perhaps even our capacity to understand. Within this humble experience of wonder and liminality is a remembering of our fragile place in the world and with that, perhaps, the desire to live in greater balance and reciprocity with the invisible weavings of life. If we see a woodland purely as timber, we will treat it as such. If we see the same woodland as a thousand-year-old living being, an ecology that we can only grasp the edges of, we will listen more carefully before felling a tree.

Dissolving slumber

Heady seduction

Sweet enchantment

Bewildering mustiness

Enveloping enticement

Whispering dream

Alluring stupefaction

Light density

Time expanding

Invitation to Fae

Distant bells

Irresponsible adventure

Doorway opening

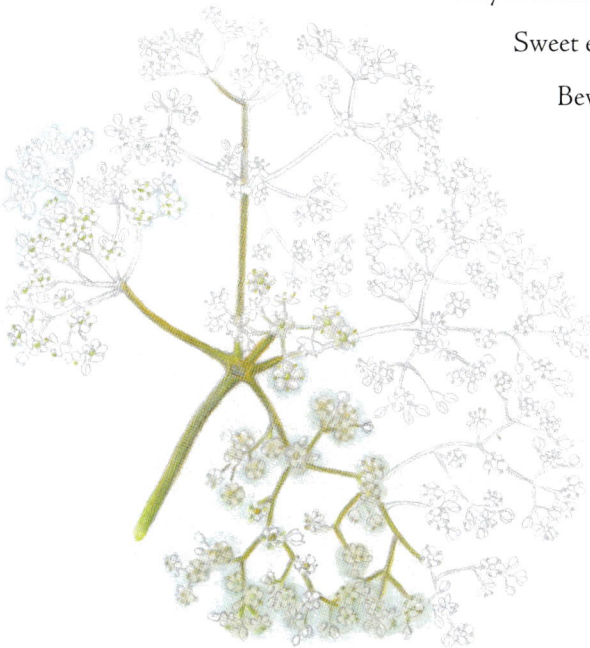

The land whispers messages that are both devastating and deeply counter-cultural. Messages that are fundamentally at odds with global capitalism and mythologies of never-ending growth. It asks us to feel the grief of ecosystem destruction and calls us to wake up to our drive to do things differently. Grief avoided gradually suffocates our will to action. By feeling it, allowing of it, a greater clarity and purpose emerge within us. I believe this is part of the liminal delirium invited by Elder, to feel and be moved, to sob and rage, to sweat and purge the weight of the disallowed and unexpressed within us.

Elder's offerings, both flower and berry, are renowned as reliable companions in fever. They don't suppress the fever; they draw it out further, opening up the sweat and pushing us through a threshold of delirium. In biomedicine today, fever is seen purely as physiological response to infection; however in many traditions, the delirium and dreams of fever are significant and offer insight into the root cause of the illness. Elder accompanies us in these realms, helping purge the inner demons that have clustered too closely around our light.

Beyond control · Fever's invitation · Whispered dream

How can I allow my dream world and liminal experiences
to bring creativity and healing to my manifest world?
How do I pay attention to subtle nudges and omens?
Where might I be leaning too much, or too little into this?

How much do I allow illness, fever and times of confusion to be
doorways for deeper enquiry and initiation?
*Where am I overly suppressing or managing these in ways that deny myself
the possibility of learning from them?*

Traditional: Known as 'nature's medicine chest', Elder has a long history in Europe, particularly for fever and respiratory infection, where they help not by suppressing fever but by inducing sweating. Modern research has established potent immune-modulating *and* antiviral ability, and clinical trials support Elder's use in speeding recovery from influenza *. There is a rich folklore throughout Europe about Elder's ability to ward off evil spirits. 'Pan pipes', also associated with the Fae can easily be made from Elder due to the easy removal of the pith.

Botany: *Sambucus nigra*, family Adoxaceae. Elder is a fast-growing tree, often small and shrub like, commonly found in hedgerows. The wood is very light, with a large spongey pith – many cultures have warnings against cutting and burning Elder wood, in part in respect of the sanctity of the tree and also as it burns with an acrid, toxic smoke, due to the same cyanogenic glycosides that can make the unripe berries toxic. The dense white clusters of creamy white flowers have a potent scent in early summer and the juicy berries appear in abundance in early autumn.

Safety: The unripe berries of Black Elder can easily cause nausea and vomiting, but this is not so when simmered or tinctured, which breaks down the cyanogenic glycosides that cause the toxicity. The bark and leaves are considered poisonous, but the flowers and berry (when prepared properly) are generally regarded as safe in moderate doses across Europe. This is not the case for all species of Elder – the berries of Red Elder, sometimes found introduced in Britain and common in North America are considered far more poisonous. Due to its potent immune-modulating effects, individuals with autoimmune conditions should consult a herbalist before using elderberry products.

Correspondences: ᚏ Ruis (Elder) – cycles of life, death and rebirth, transitions, protection – guarding against negative energies, healing, ancestral knowledge, wisdom. ᚱ Raidho – direction, guidance, journeys (spiritual and physical), higher truth, protection, healing, beginnings and endings, cyclical growth, purpose and courage.
☽ – Moon, specifically dark moon – death and rebirth, transformation, crone, rest and renewal.

Meeting Elder: Dreaming under an Elder tree when in flower in early summer is an ideal way to meet Elder. In autumn, collecting, simmering and making a syrup with the berry (enough to support immunity through the winter) is deeply satisfying and gives a visceral encounter with the juicy berries.

Herbalists and ritual: I always approach working with Elder with a deep respect and humility, knowing well that, apart from a potent invitation into liminality, I couldn't guess at what Elder might ask or invite of us in ritual. Generally, I only suggest students work with Elder once they are more experienced, due to the range of inner terrains and forgotten memories that might be presented to navigate. Well-suited to dusk rituals.

Fennel

Take your time to savour a Fennel seed. So familiar, yet, if we pause to truly taste, smell, feel and listen, they unveil their many layers. A sweet potency, a gentle oiliness, the invitation of lively brightness. They exude immediacy, a clarity and vibrancy, being both permeating and protecting, gentle yet mischievously inviting, stimulating yet calming. The seeds, green and fresh off the plant in late summer, are at their most potent.

As I gently touch the bright green fronds of the Fennel plant, it seems remarkable that such a substantial presence is woven from something so fine, more air than substance. They stand tall in the centre of the herb garden, at once fragile and robust, confidently filling the space with their impressive six-foot stature. I like to think this particular plant is so tall because it is so loved, and lyricism aside, the carefully applied love of well-fermented cow manure undoubtedly contributes here.

> Clear bright bell,
> Of sweet sensual fullness,
> Permeating, penetrating,
> Protecting and proud

In ritual meetings, I often see Fennel bring a call to clarity in those who let this plant in, a call to vibrancy – a desire to shake off any lethargy and muddiness. It's unusual that Greek gods appear in my journeys, but on one of my first meetings with Fennel I had an acute sense of Apollo – confident, young, toned, athletic, gazing purposefully over the sea. In Greek mythology, when Prometheus stole fire from the gods, he hid it in a Fennel stalk. This association with fire is interesting. In India, Fennel seeds are often given after a meal, not only for their taste and carminative action, but also because they are understood to support *agni* ('digestive fire') whilst balancing the *Pitta dosha*, which, when out of balance, can present as 'fire out of balance' – excess heat, acid or inflammation. A picture emerges for me here of affirming our inner fire whilst also helping contain it.

There is a particular exercise that I often feel called to bring in when working with Fennel. It involves recognising that we extend beyond our physical bodies, and may come into deeper relationship with this non-physical self. This space around us is permeated with aspects of our being, as much as the space around is is subtly permeated with the pheromones and subtle scents we constantly release. How big is this space around you? How does it change in different situations? Can you recall a time when you felt expansive and bright in the 'sphere' of yourself, confident in the space you fill?

As we move in the world, we all extend beyond our physical bodies – we know this well when an energetic or especially charismatic person enters a room. In its most vibrant, this non-physical bubble of self gives us all the space we need to move and breathe freely; it also allows us to be responsive to our will and exert agency over our life, choosing what we let in close and what we keep distant. Micro-violations of this personal space might each, on their own, seem a small thing, but repeated experiences of this can have a profound effect on our identity, self-confidence and sense of safety.

Fennel offers an invitation to fill this space we inhabit, for it to be firm but fluid, responsive, alive and gently pulsing, responding to the moment and our agency, not the echoes of past violations.

In my clinic it sometimes seems to me that such vibrancy feels a distant dream as we try to find peace with internalised layers of personal, cultural and ancestral trauma that burden us.

Working with plants attracts wonderful, sensitive, empathic people, but with this sensitivity often comes the difficulty of knowing and caring for the boundaries of self. Some routinely let others in too close, getting confused when they struggle to determine which feelings are 'I' and which 'you'; some

manage this by armouring these edges, keeping others at a distance, which then denies them the closeness, trust and intimacy they so long for.

As we dive into these Fennel-inspired exercises with our non-physical selves, experiences can vary widely. Some may feel strong and clear around their heart and head, while the area around their pelvis may feel vague and uncertain. For others, as they delve deeper into this inner space, they might encounter tender, raw emotions. Many I work with describe their experience of this non-physical space around them as tight and constrictive. For some it feels full of holes and erratic – like long–abandoned fishing nets. For others it's like toughened leather, or so hardened it feels impenetrably metallic. Some lack definition, allowing too much in, in others the opacity blocks everything out. As with all the work I do with the school, what is most important is to allow *your* experience and find the ways to describe it that feel right to you.

In Fennel there's an invitation to know oneself simultaneously in the elements of earth *and* air. We can let ourselves be invited into grounded embodiment *and* spacious awareness, the fine airy sensitivity of the fronds balanced by the robustness of the plant and seeds.

As these fronds listen and respond constantly to every tiny gust of air, so might we welcome our awakened sensitivity without being thrown off-balance. So many of us have become numbed to this level of sensing, but if so, it is simply lying dormant, waiting for the right time and situation to awaken.

In the fullness of our awakened sensitivity, we become more able to receive the magic of the natural world, a magic of aliveness that can bring us to the fullness of *our* fruiting. I find it fascinating how these relational experiences map onto the well-established oestrogenic * effects of Fennel seed – the fullness and fertility that comes with oestrogen corresponding to the oily fullness of the seeds.

Fennel is such a gentle ally. Sitting with these beautiful, spacious, airy plants invites a deep clear breath and a rekindling of our sensory, sensitive selves, a stepping into clarity and brightness with exquisite gentleness.

Permeating power

Dormant potential

Still and solid

Gently pulsing

Strength without walls

Opening and expanding

Expanding warmth

Warm cliff breeze

Dispersing chatter

Soothing nerves

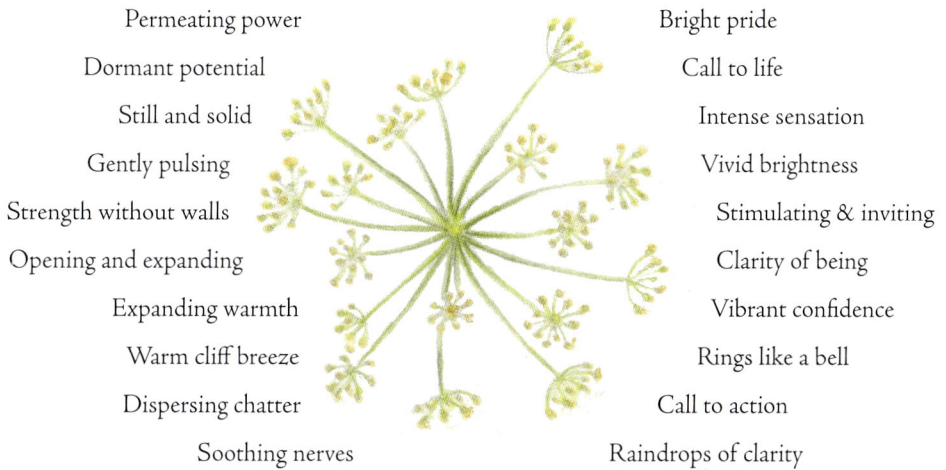

Bright pride

Call to life

Intense sensation

Vivid brightness

Stimulating & inviting

Clarity of being

Vibrant confidence

Rings like a bell

Call to action

Raindrops of clarity

Bright aliveness · Oestrogenic fullness · Subtle sensitivity

Invitation: Relaxation and fullness where there is tightness and contraction.

What does it feel like to live confidently with my sensitivity?
Where do I numb or override my sensitivity?

Where do I need soothing, brightening and uplifting?
Which foods weigh me down? Which make me feel lighter?

What helps me feel full and fertile, both literally, and fertile with creativity?
Where do I feel depleted?

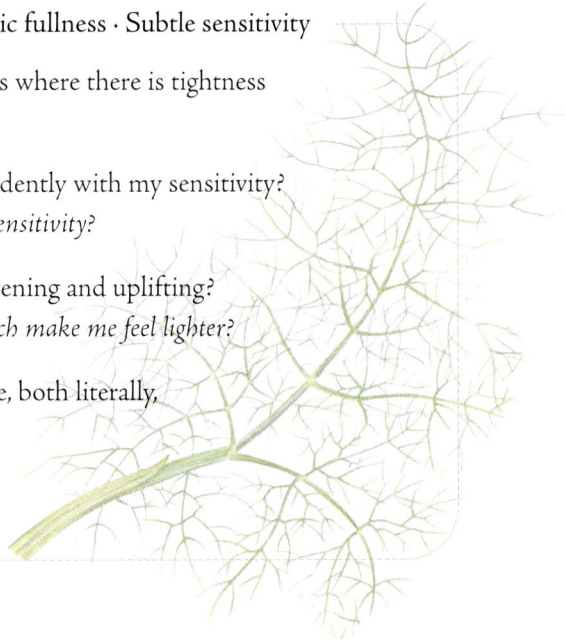

Traditional: Traditionally used for bloating and to ease indigestion and intestinal pain, Fennel is anti-inflammatory, diuretic and anti-spasmodic. Fennel has been long used by nursing mothers to ease colic in babies, both by drinking the infusion which then transfers into the breastmilk, and small doses that can be spoon-fed to the baby directly. Fennel seed also helps to increase breastmilk production and has oestrogenic effects which can be helpful with menopausal symptoms, polycystic ovary syndrome and a wide range of other conditions that respond to phytoestrogens (see research links ⁎ for more on this). The relaxant and anti-spasmodic effects are not only helpful for intestinal cramps, bloating and indigestion, but also in bronchitis and asthma. As an anti-inflammatory, Fennel is valued in arthritis.

Botany: *Foeniculum vulgare*, Apiaceae or Umbelliferae family, commonly known as the carrot family. Fennel is native to Mediterranean countries and now cultivated around the world in temperate regions. Seeds are harvested in autumn when they have turned brown, but younger green seeds are my personal favourite. Whilst the seeds are commonly used, the feather-like leaves can also made into teas and added to salads. The root is also edible.

Safety: Fennel seed is considered safe in culinary quantities, but it is good to be aware that they are oestrogenic and high doses can cause digestive discomfort. The oestrogenic effects mean that I'd recommend taking professional advice from a herbalist if you have any hormone-sensitive conditions, such as endometriosis or breast cancer. Avoid high doses in pregnancy.

Correspondences: ᛇ Eadha (Aspen, Poplar) – strength, protection, overcoming adversity, interconnectedness, adaptability, resilience, shielding, endurance. ᛖ Ehwaz – cooperation and teamwork, harmony in relationships, transition, adapting to change, unity, progression, achieving desired outcomes, bright future, loyalty. ☿ Mercury – communication, intellect, mental agility, communication, sensing and processing information.

Meeting Fennel: Fennel seed is readily available to explore with a slow tasting meditation (give yourself half an hour to slowly chew a seed, noticing everything you feel). However, if you have a chance to watch a Fennel grow and can eat the green seeds, I recommend this as the fresh seed is so much more potent than the dried.

Herbalists and ritual: I find that every time we work alongside Fennel we need a lot of space! For this reason, Fennel suits working outdoors and explorations of our non-physical space (sometime known as aura and etheric body), seeing what Fennel brings to this experience. Every plant can be explored in this way, but I've found that certain plants such as Fennel and Marigold are useful access points for those new to this. Fennel often brings a curious combination of being both dynamic and calming at the same time. More advanced work would involve working with Fennel to meet and journey into the wounding we carry in the non-physical.

Fern

In this valley woodland, wandering into its shadowy, moist embrace, I feel a sense of timelessness growing with each step, each step taking me further out of human time. The lush green of the Ferns – Lady Fern, Bracken, Polypody and Hart's Tongue – is welcoming, and being here feels like an ancient homecoming. These plants have been growing here for over 360 million years, long before the dinosaurs and flowering plants. This primordial world, shared with Horsetails, and even more ancient mosses and liverworts, speaks a different language from that of our more recent evolutionary flowering companions.

> Soft, moist, web of life,
> slowly becoming,
> patience, ancient wisdom, reciprocity
> Green blanket of love softly enfolding,
> gentle sound of water trickling.
>
> *Meltem Konkin (2024)*

Like rocks, these ancient plants carry the story of the world within them, leading us into deep pre-verbal memory, into the possibility of remembering the earliest days of our evolution into human form. In forest fires, Ferns are the first plant to renew, with a resilience to survive not only events cataclysmic enough to destroy the dinosaurs, but those far more frequent forest fires. To be amongst the Ferns is to be in a place where the drama and narratives of our present-day human experience fade away, and a quiet space can be found for another way of knowing – beyond story, beyond language.

> "The child in me
> feels safe and full of enchantment
> Connected to earth's magic and mystery
> There's tonic here for a world-weary soul."
>
> *Heather White (2024)*

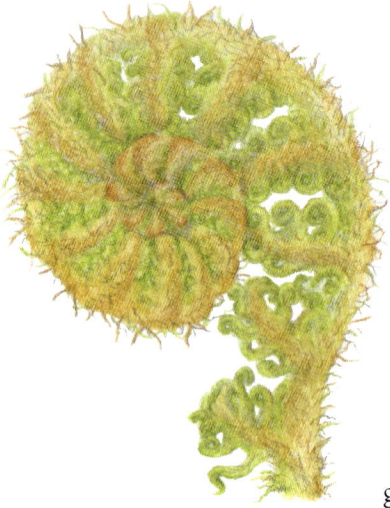

These plants have been one of the hardest to write about; to attempt to put into language something that mostly touches the pre-verbal in me is, I guess, bound to be tricky. I spoke with a friend to try and find words, and we both recognised the feeling of being something of an interloper when walking through the thick Ferns found near the Devon coast or in the woods of Stroud.

The feeling is not exactly that I am unwelcome, but more as if I'm a momentary guest in a different reality. Fiona spoke of her experience painting Ferns: "They feel like a cloak of invisibility, guardians of secrets, offering protection and the sense that I need to look deeper through the layers of myself. As I paint them I feel I'm being drawn downwards, quite the opposite of Bluebells, feeling like I'm being led somewhere earthy, rooty, damp."

I feel there is a similarity with Bramble here in their resilient colonisation of land, but in a different way; whilst Bramble protects a rich ecosystem of saplings, insects, birds and small mammals, Fern speak to me of an earlier stage: of soil made into plant; of enlivened earth; of a deep greening of the world. Curiously, Ferns are known to accumulate cyanide and a number of heavy metals in their roots, meaning they are used for bioremediation – drawing these contaminants out of the soil and so helping to restore human-abused land.

Unfurling ancient earth wisdom

Thriving in the moist half-light of the canopy

Oldest of plants, beyond the reach of human time

Ferns (along with Primroses) are the only plants in this book which will grow happily inside – a fact that led to a decades-long Victorian 'Fern-craze', the precursor to our current enthusiasm for houseplants. Most common house plants are not native to Britain, generally originating from tropical and sub-tropical regions. Ferns are one of the few that are indigenous to these lands.

There is rich folklore surrounding Ferns; they were believed to flower once a year at midnight on Midsummer's Eve. It was believed that if someone discovered this elusive Fern flower, they could gain the ability to enter the spirit world or the realm of the Fae, and perhaps even be granted the magical gift of invisibility. Young women would sometimes carry Fern spores, with the hope that the first male they saw afterwards would be their future husband.

I'm aware that whilst many people reading these words would love to spend more time deep in the wilds of nature, the reality is that most of our life is spent indoors; with this in mind I'd like to suggest a simple experiment. Buy several Polypody Ferns to have next to your bed and spend a week sleeping with them; then move them out of the room for a week. As the third week comes around, bring them back in and notice how the room feels different with their presence, how you feel about your room, perhaps even how your dreams might be subtly affected by them.

Ferns can invite us into a parallel reality; even a small Fern-filled wood metres from a busy road or urban area can offer a momentary refuge from a busy, human pace of life. They invite us to step into this space, make time to be timeless and trust in what might emerge from our connection to the woodland ecology and the deeper, quieter parts of our being that are awakened here.

Can I make space to step out of my usual pace of life into 'Fern time'?
What sort of resistance comes up when I try to do this?

How do I honour and meet my non-verbal, pre-verbal self?
What do they have to teach me?
How do I override, judge or deny these parts of myself?

What within me is slowly unfurling into being?
Where am I not giving enough space for the emergent and unknown?

Traditional: Hart's-Tongue Fern has been used as an ointment for piles and burns, as well as traditionally for diarrhoea and dysentery. Male Fern and Lady Fern have both been used historically to treat worms; however, doses large enough to paralyse the worms (which were then expelled using a laxative) also risk being toxic to humans. Bracken rhizomes have been ground into flour to make a type of bread, and broken fronds can be used to produce a yellow dye. Various Ferns have historically been mixed with fat to create wound salves, and fronds have been used as wraps to help preserve food. Bracken has been used traditionally for the lungs, rheumatism, and the womb, though reports of this are scattered, and I've not met anyone actively working with them in this way. Ferns appear rarely used in herbalism today, potentially due to concerns about their toxicity.

Botany: Peak growth for Ferns happens in spring and summer, during which new fronds, called fiddleheads, unfurl and mature. In autumn, they begin to die back; some species' fronds turn brown and wither. In winter, deciduous Ferns lose their fronds, while evergreen species, such as the Hart's-Tongue Fern, maintain their fronds throughout the year.

Ferns reproduce through a two-stage life cycle known as alternation of generations, which includes both asexual (sporophyte) and sexual (gametophyte) phases. The dominant, leafy diploid sporophyte produces haploid spores in structures called sori on the fronds' undersides. These spores germinate into small, heart-shaped haploid gametophytes (prothalli) that carry both antheridia (sperm-producing organs) and archegonia (egg-producing organs). Fertilisation occurs when sperm swim to an egg, forming a diploid zygote that grows into a new sporophyte, thus completing the cycle. This reproductive method allows Ferns to efficiently spread and colonise new areas.

Safety: Many Ferns are toxic and should not be consumed. In Japan, Korea and Indonesia, certain young shoots are used in cooking, but are always prepared carefully to reduce toxicity; even so, epidemiological studies suggest a link between Fern consumption and increased risk of oesophageal and stomach cancers in humans.

Correspondences: ᚠ Luis (Rowan) – spiritual vision, strength, seeing beyond the surface, protection, heightened awareness. ᛚ Lagaz – intuition, psychic ability, water, flow, trusting instincts and embracing change, emotional insight. ☿ Mercury – the messenger who travels between worlds, deeper communication, curiosity, adaptability.

Meeting Ferns: Spend time alone in woods abundant with Ferns. I recommend taking some warm things to lie on amongst them and take time to become absorbed in their realm.

Herbalists and ritual: Ferns always seem to invite quite solitary meetings – I enjoy inviting a group to quietly scatter themselves around a woodland for a while, before coming together to reflect on how our state of consciousness has shifted. Back inside, spacious drawing sessions with Fern tend to invite a deep quietness, invoking a space beyond the noise of thought, touching something slower and deeper in everyone.

Fly Agaric

To stumble upon a stand of Fly Agaric whilst walking in woods is to be instantly transported. *Amanita muscaria*, Ambrosia, Berserker mushroom, Son of Thunder – some of the many names given to this fungal wonder, each one a little clue to some of their rich reputation. I have come to affectionately know them as 'Birch brothers', due to the beautiful way their growth pattern follows the root-lines of Silver Birch trees and their symbiotic relationship with this tree.

> What you see are just the fruiting bodies of a massive being, a potentially ancient mycelium, extending extensively in an intricate web of life beneath you.

My approach to getting to know them over the past 20 years has been slow and simple: spending a moon cycle in their presence once a year when they are fruiting. Each encounter reveals a little more of their essence. Lying among the Ferns, Birches, and Amanitas on a warm autumn evening is profoundly transporting. While many traditions involve ritually imbibing them, my experience has shown that their presence and proximity alone possess unquestionably potent medicine.

The Evenki, Yakut and Koryak peoples of Siberia, the indigenous peoples of Latvia, Estonia and the Kola Peninsular in Russia and the Saami people of northern Scandinavia all have traditions of calling on Fly Agaric for spiritual, divination and healing rituals. Beyond Eurasia, traditions linked to Fly Agaric have garnered extensive interest (and controversy) since Wasson's book, *Soma: Divine Mushroom of Immortality* (1968), proposed it as the 'Soma' of the Vedas, the sacred drink of the gods *. If you enjoy rabbit holes, I highly recommend exploring this further!

For centuries, English literature has been awash with often-repeated myths and folklore about Fly Agaric, each perhaps containing grains of truth, but so coloured with creative fantasy and evocative writing it can be hard to navigate.

Andy Letcher's book, *Shroom*, casts a respectful and critical eye over this literary heritage, helping to separate fact from fiction and avoid the romanticised tales shaped more by British colonial fantasies than by indigenous truths. If you'd like to explore further I've included a selection of books in the endnotes, including Baba Masha's in-depth *Microdosing with Amanita Muscaria*, which systematically shares and reflects on hundreds of experiences.

In my work, we explore our relationship with Fly Agaric purely by being in their presence; spending time with them, dreaming with them close by, inviting ourselves to be wrapped in their consciousness.

Many years ago, when I first met them, I decided to invite them into my dreams by placing several dried mushrooms wrapped in cloth near my bed. Life became unexpectedly busy and I forgot about them, only to wake five nights later wondering why my dreams for the past five days had such a persistent intensity to them – a low pulsing drumbeat where each beat poured more life, more energy into my dreams. I suddenly remembered the dried mushrooms and moved them to another room, but I could still feel their influence. Finally, at three in the morning, I buried them in a clay pot at the far end of the herb garden. Only then did everything go quiet. Perhaps it was their potent scent, but it took a lot to feel free of their influence.

Plants, met skilfully and respectfully, can help us to escape the gravity of ourselves. Our familiar perceptions, our sense of self and ways of relating to the world are embedded in well-worn neurological and somatic pathways. Changing such embedded beliefs and behaviours is difficult, but it is exactly here that the plants (and mushrooms) can be our allies, guides and teachers.

Throughout this book I reflect on the ways different plants wake us up, break us out of our familiar ego bubble of perception. Wormwood calls out

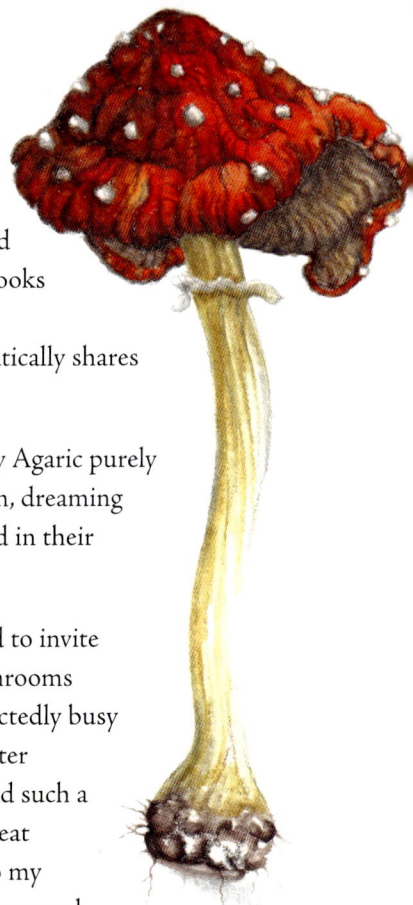

the warrior within, Mugwort stirs the deep unconscious, Lemon Balm opens the possibilities of our heart's dreaming. When met with intention, I've seen Fly Agarics act as rocket fuel, helping people overcome the gravity of themselves. We don't need to ingest them for this, but let ourselves deepen into relationship, letting them teach and guide us through noticing the subtle shifts in our dreaming as we let ourselves be affected by them.

Personally, I've had uncanny experiences where my dream state flows seamlessly into manifest reality when around these mushrooms. Synchronicities, a sense of flow, and the spontaneous unfolding of events align more fluidly with the previous night's dreams. Seemingly insurmountable blocks and tangles in my life show themselves with more clarity, such that life can better flow through to untangle them. Fly Agaric seems to weave my dreams into an unseen mycorrhizal web, a layer of becoming that precedes the manifestation of events. In these realms, the issue of free will becomes questionable; am I dreaming my reality into being, or am I being dreamt into existence?

I suspect it is more of the latter – the dream dreaming me, sometimes allowed to flow, sometimes held back by my choices. They guide my dreaming towards the web of Wyrd that was always there, helping align me with a deeper purpose beyond my understanding. I've seen similar themes echoed in others; Fly Agaric invites a bigness and a boldness to trust in themselves and the unseen paths their soul is travelling. The seemingly impossible becomes less impossible and more a surmountable challenge we can walk towards.

When meeting them for the first time, almost everyone is surprised at how welcoming and warm their presence feels, though someone occasionally has a different response. Claire, for example, found their presence overbearing and overwhelming. Such strong responses often indicate strong medicine.

Knowing this, she decided to face into her discomfort and meet what they had to teach her. She realised how she had been making herself small in response to overbearing life experiences. She moved from a strong rejection to a deep welcome in a few hours, later creating an amulet from Fly Agaric and she wore this as one of her closest plant allies.

I've come to deeply respect these beings, and only call on them when feeling stuck, when some unseen inner or outer blockade seems to be keeping me trapped (be that in my creativity, relationships or work) and I feel out of sync with my path and purpose. Somehow, often in unexpected, and often in challenging ways, they seem to guide me back home, to a place where my outer actions align with my inner dreaming and I feel I can walk more surely forward in the world.

The active ingredient *is* the relationship

When I first trained as a Medical Herbalist we were taught about the correct dosage of plants. In practice I quickly discovered that individuals' responses to herbs varied immensely, and not necessarily according to the classical understanding of dosage. Some people responded profoundly to tiny drop doses, whilst others were unmoved by 'heroic' doses of the same plant. This was one of the key observations that led me down an experiential and relational path in herbalism; a path that led me to found a entire herbalist training school centred around our relationships to the plants.

I slowly started to realise that people's responses to plants were *not* primarily affected by the dose, but by their readiness to receive the plant. This readiness is rarely conscious; whilst many might, on the surface, believe and say that they wanted to receive the medicine of the plant, other, more hidden parts of them were not so sure.

Wormwood, for example, can help release one's anger and transform it into living passionately. Who wouldn't want that? The truth is that many would resist this, as the process of learning to ride one's anger is not easy; the path is likely to ask that you revisit the roots (often traumatic, often deeply ancestral) of that anger. Parts of us say 'yes' and other parts resist. It is no wonder an individual's response is … so individual.

Few herbalists attempt to force the body to do anything, preferring instead to invite it into balance, change or growth. Most herbs in this book will not override an invisible 'no' within you (though there are plenty that will); their more subtle magic only appears once the inner doors are open. Once these doors are open, pharmacologically minuscule amounts can catalyse a profound transformation.

Though some of you might feel tempted, don't dive headlong into experimenting with Fly Agaric internally. Spend time with them, discover their invitations, discover *your* inner gates, discover how to let them in simply by virtue of their presence. This is slow work, but such a rich path for those willing to walk it – and this practice of opening these inner gates will serve you well, little by little, letting yourself receive the magic that is all around.

Wyrd pathfinder · Dream weaver
Mycelial power

Where do I feel stuck, as if an insurmountable barrier is blocking my growth? How might a wider perspective reveal a path through? *Where might I be choosing to be stuck out of fear of change?*

How do I deepen my relationships with the felt, yet unseen realms? How might I better let love, trust, faith, magic and creativity flow? *Where might fear or my need for control be limiting me?*

How might I better cultivate and trust my intuition? *Where do I doubt or second-guess my inner guidance?*

Traditional: While the hallucinogenic nature of *Amanita* has been the focus of much narrative and lore, Fly Agaric also has a long history of medicinal uses including for pain relief, neuralgia, inflammation, anxiety, as well as being a stimulant. There is an increasing body of scientific research supporting these traditional uses.[*]

Muscarine, muscimol, muscazone and ibotenic acid are four psychoactive constituents found in Fly Agaric mushrooms. Unlike other hallucinogenic plants which have an effect on serotonin receptors, studies on the active component muscimol show it to be potent $GABA_A$ agonist, which is likely to contribute to the traditional use for pain relief as a poultice or tincture applied externally. There is also growing research interest in how Fly Agaric might have a role in Alzheimer's disease and other neurodegenerative conditions.

Unlike most of the plants in this book, entire volumes have been devoted to Fly Agaric. Whether you are intrigued by Soma, folk medicine traditions, reindeer lore, shamanic practices, radical perspectives on Christianity, micro-dosing, Viking Berserkers, dubious Santa Claus theories, Lewis Carroll, psychoactive urine, Baba Yaga, Kami mountain deities, or the highly politicised modern history of psychedelic culture, you will find countless avenues to explore through the books I recommend in the endnotes.

Botany: *Amanita muscaria*, commonly known as Fly Agaric, is a basidiomycete fungus belonging to the genus *Amanita*, within the sub-kingdom Dikarya of the fungi kingdom. There are several variations and subspecies of *Amanita muscaria*. Fly Agaric is a mycorrhizal fungus, forming symbiotic relationships with various tree species such as birch, pine, oak, spruce, fir, and cedar.

Fly Agaric is easily recognisable by its bright red cap, which can sometimes appear scarlet or orange, adorned with white wart-like spots. The gills are white to cream-coloured, closely packed together, and attached to the stalk. The stipe (stalk) is white and typically bulges at the base. The spores are white and oval-shaped. Misidentification could occur with *Amanita rubescens*, commonly known as the blusher, which has a paler reddish-brown cap and cream spots and is similar in size.

Amanita muscaria is native to temperate and boreal regions of the Northern Hemisphere, including higher regions such as the Hindu Kush mountain range in Iran, as well as the Mediterranean. However, it does not naturally occur in Central America. Molecular studies suggest that its origins are in the Siberian region, where it is famously known for its use by shamans. From there, it spread across Europe, Asia, and North America.

Safety: The use of *Amanita muscaria* falls into a grey area of legality in some countries. People taking medications that affect GABA, choline, or glutamate should not consume *Amanita muscaria*. Additionally, individuals with severe mental health issues, such as bipolar disorder or schizophrenia, should avoid psychoactive plants such as this. Although it is considered toxic in most modern field guides, *Amanita muscaria* was historically consumed in parts of Europe, Asia, and North America after careful preparation. Traditional methods, such as drying or boiling the mushrooms, can reduce toxicity. Common symptoms of *Amanita muscaria* poisoning include nausea, vomiting, dizziness, hallucinations, and confusion. In case of suspected poisoning, it is important to seek immediate medical attention.

Correspondences: ᛇ Ioho (Yew tree) – complex interplay of life and death, strength and renewal, wisdom, spiritual protection. ᛉ Elhaz – embodying protection, spiritual connection, awareness, vitality, and inner strength, importance of vigilance, protective nature of higher forces. ♆ Neptune – dreams, intuition, depth of feeling, resilience, guardianship, the unconscious.

Hawthorn

There is something deeply inviting about Hawthorn trees, particularly those grazed by sheep, who, in nibbling the lower branches, carve out a wonderful sheep-human hollow around the trunk. Taking refuge in these hollows, leaning against the dense wood of the trunk, there is a feeling of being held, of protection, of being buffered from the world and the weather.

We spend a day attempting to identify all the plants growing within two metres of a Hawthorn on Swift's Hill. There are easily 50 different plants, many of which are core to the British herbal tradition – it is incredible to realise that within the protective ecosystem of this tree one could weave a fairly complete pharmacy. Protective Bramble and Nettle surrounded the trunk, radiating out to the richest diversity of plants around one metre away; as is so often the case, diversity was thriving at the edges.

The berries and the flower of Hawthorn are so mutually distinct in their actions I sometimes find it hard to think of them as the same being. The heady May scent of the flowers invokes a Bacchanalian fuzziness, a voluptuousness deeply fitting to their flowering at Beltane; Fanny's poem on the following page speaks to this wonderfully. And the berries, in autumn, offer something a lot steadier, stiller; they offer deep nourishment, resilience and holding.

Hawthorn, with their seasons of flower and berry, can touch within us the tender place of the lover we long for and the grandfather we never had. Hawthorn offers an invitation to magic and the steadiness of heart that keeps us walking our path towards it.

Our hearts want to grow. Something in our soul calls us out of the familiar. In love, in passion. These are forces of growth, and so often, the very growth our soul longs for can also be a path of pain and bruising. If though, in this bruising, we harden our hearts, we also calcify the very cradle of growth. Living and loving come with a risk.

Little secret closed buds
so full and ready to burst,
you sing a sweet spring melody,
the glorious chorus
of the luscious swirling of life,
of the shining cup of plenty.

That lilting tune
of unharnessed pleasure
of unpossessed joy
flighty, flirting, light-filled
lascivious lounging.

Yes, you are life
throbbing through veins
laughing,
twirling,
live a little!
Chiding, whirling.

In your full, fecund fervour
your amorous innocence,
you are the rapturous orchestra of delight
a lollipop lullaby,
a disobedient feast

Little buds,
full to the brim just about ready to burst
bring on the bloom I say,
bring it on!

*Bacchus' Heartsong
(a Hawthorn tree at Beltane)
Fanny Soirat (2023)*

If our foundations of love and attachment have been wounded, our resilience to withstand the inevitable heartbreaks of living is also challenged. In this, few plants are equal to Hawthorn in the strength and resilience offered to our heart.

This resilience is not just within the emotional and interpersonal realm. It is also very physical, with many research papers attesting Hawthorn's benefit in early heart failure and a wide range of other cardiotonic properties. Studies have found them to be positively inotropic and negatively chronotropic, literally strengthening and slowing the heartbeat.

114

Where the flowers bring a whimsical invitation, the berries offer a steady hand at our back. There's a unique quality of calm that descends in the space as Hawthorn berry, prepared as a gentle decoction, weaves its way through each person. A simultaneous settling and a softening. Everyone appears more clearly defined, more solid in themselves and at the same time deeply and steadily engaged in their explorations and journeys.

There's a stillness here, as if we are in the presence of something ancient and weighty that invites a gentle humility. A gravitas that people can lean into and be held. But this holding isn't the holding of the mother or lover – of Rose or Mallow or Viburnum, or Clary – it is a quiet solidity, a solid ground that can calm emotional and mental storms.

Many share their experience that an archetype of grandfather is here in the space. At a time in our history when there is such change and confusion, Hawthorn touches a memory we may not even have from this lifetime – a memory of complete trust in the holding of this steady presence.

"It feels like coming home"

I once had an unexpected experience with a Hawthorn. As I approached, I asked the now habitual question, "May I come close?" The answer was no.

I stopped and sat with the refusal, giving myself space to hear why that might be. The message came through clearly. "You are too full to fit within my embrace." This was humbling, and true. My heart and head were in overwhelm, my body in a fine tremor.

I realised that if I wanted to receive of Hawthorn I needed to have space to receive. I set off back down the valley to the small brook at the bottom – cold water has always held, for me, an ability to clear away the noise. It wasn't deep enough to immerse myself, but as I splashed my face and chest with the crystal clear water, a layer of fog cleared and the internal noise quietened. Returning to the Hawthorn was like returning to a warm kitchen. We can let the plants fill us, but only if we make space to be filled.

Hawthorn is a tree of many parts: the heady, floral exuberance of their May blossoms and the steady, nourishing depth of their autumn berries; the strength of their wood and the sharp protection of their thorns. Each part offers a different kind of medicine – touching the lover's longing and the quiet resilience of the grandfather we never had. Hawthorn invites us to explore both the magic of the unknown and rekindle the steadiness of heart needed to journey there.

Hedgerow guardian · Beltane's breath · Grandfather's embrace

How can I call on Hawthorn to help strengthen my emotional and physical heart?
Am I giving time to listen to the needs of my heart?

How might I rekindle the bright-eyed, wonder-filled Beltane wild youthfulness of myself? *Where have I lost connection with this?*

What does it feel like to feel held, safe and supported?
How might I be trying to 'hold it all together' myself when perhaps I might not need to?

Traditional: Hawthorn has long been used in traditional folk medicine and been extensively researched in clinical trials. Culpeper speaks of the berry powdered in wine as 'good for the dropsy', a symptom of heart failure. Hawthorn is valued support for congestive heart disease, angina, high blood pressure, and irregular heartbeat. Hawthorn is well-regarded as a valuable remedy not just for the physical heart, but also for the emotional heart – calming anxiety, bad dreams and insomnia, and in Chinese traditional medicine the berries have long been used to calm the Shen and aid food digestion. Hawthorn trees have a long tradition in these lands of being a gateway to the land of the Fae and are often venerated with clouties at sacred waters. Berries, young leaves and flowers are all used medicinally.

Botany: *Crataegus monogyna*, Rosaceae. These thorny shrubs or small trees are found throughout temperate Europe, blooming with white or pink flowers in the spring and producing dark red berries, known as 'haws', in late summer to early autumn. Commonly found in hedgerows, they make excellent hedging trees – their name literally translates to 'hedge thorn'. They thrive in poor soil and have shallow roots, yet stand up well to stormy weather, bitter winds and long winters. Hawthorns can take on a variety of distinctive dwarf forms when exposed to harsh weather, such as on coastlines or open moors. They feel very close to my heart, and their nature and proliferation are intricately woven into the landscape and creation of this land.

Safety: Due to the potent and useful cardiovascular effects, I recommend only combining Hawthorn with heart and blood pressure drugs with the support of an experienced herbalist. Otherwise, Hawthorn is generally regarded as safe and often used as a food as well as a medicine. The tree in blossom has a curious trickster quality, so be cautious what you wish for, Hawthorn may hold you to your word.

Correspondences: ⊣ Huathe (Hawthorn) – ritual protection, magic and spirituality, boundaries, spiritual growth and change. Ν Hagall – adaptability, ability to weather the storms of life, transformation, destruction and regeneration, change, cleansing. ♂ Mars – initiative, purpose, action, physical strength, survival.

Meeting Hawthorn: Find a friendly-looking Hawthorn to rest under and let yourself dream in their presence. Berry tincture in a little warm water or decoction of the berries are beautiful ways to receive Hawthorn.

Herbalists and ritual: rituals around Beltane with Hawthorn blossom can easily unlock a rather other-worldly, playful, sensual and dreamy Pan quality in people, well suited to a spacious warm spring day. The trickster quality can often come through and the blossom be quite provocative. I find that preparations of the berry in late autumn and winter are almost universally well received, the warming heart-affirming qualities quickly bringing grounding, harmony and connectedness to a group. Hawthorn is a potent witness and ally for intention setting, spell casting and rekindling the experience of wonder.

Horsetail

Horsetail carries memories from a time long before humanity, thriving in a verdant world of ferns, mosses, lichens and liverworts around 280 million years ago – well before the arrival of flowering plants. Pausing as I walk along the Horsley valley to sit and let my hand run over these rough, strange leaves, I'm transported to another time momentarily. The younger beings of the valley fade from my awareness, leaving me with a deep sense of something ancient and elemental.

Horsetail, rising from this marshy expanse, once grew up to 30-metres tall, bearing witness to both the evolution of dinosaurs and their eventual extinction 65 million years ago. Like Bamboo, a far younger plant, Horsetail is unusual in how they accumulate a very high proportion of silica dioxide. This silica, the same substance that gives strength to the concrete we use for the buildings we live in, is deposited in their cell walls, giving the plant its form and strength.

In their antiquity, Horsetail speaks to the ancient in us. In their rich silica structure they speak to the silica within us. When you peer through a window, you're looking through silica – a medium that is both bright and clear, characterised by crystalline, defined edges that permit the passage of light while keeping everything else at bay.

In ritual spaces with Horsetail, people are transported back to a more elemental time, walking ancient landscapes and watching the play of light on a pre-human world. Often journeys are very solitary, as if on a long solo retreat in a landscape where the earth energies dominate. Where some plants, like Mallow and Valerian, soften people's edges such that the group flows and dissolves together, Horsetail tends to individuate people within the group, happily together, but alone in their journeys.

The human body is its own community – a rich ecosystem where our cells coexist with fungi, bacteria and countless microorganisms, outnumbering our cells by roughly ten to one. Mostly, this ecosystem thrives in harmony, but disease often arises when it drifts out of balance. In the damp climate of Stroud, this imbalance manifests in people with prolonged coughs and bronchiectasis – conditions marked by a constant accumulation of easily infected fluid in the lungs. Chalford Valley, where Fiona lived for 35 years, is particularly damp and has earned the nickname "Snot Valley" due to its pervasive wetness. Fortunately, many local herbs, such as Elder, Thyme, Balm, Hyssop, Mint, and Wild Garlic, offer immune support and antimicrobial properties. Mallow and Mullein, with their soothing mucilaginous qualities, bring relief to troubled lungs. However, these herbs primarily address symptoms, soothing infections without repairing the structural damage.

Horsetail offers a different invitation. Their traditional use in restoring lung structure and integrity speaks of a capacity for rebuilding our inner architecture. This is the essence of silica: structure, crystalline boundaries, and well-defined edges. Horsetail's ability to protect and restore structure is mirrored in the effect on our bones and in horticulture; a spray made with Horsetail is a respected biodynamic approach to the mould that can thrive on plants in overly damp conditions.

In the human body, which contains only minute quantities of silica, silica dioxide serves as a structural catalyst rather than forming the substance of our bodies. Deficiencies can show up in weak nails, hair and skin and if prolonged, weak bones, cartilage and collagen. Horsetail has long been a folk remedy for all of these.

Seeing Horsetail emerge from the marshy ground is to see light, form and geometry emerging from a fertile primordial soup. Invoking Horsetail invites a clarification of our edges, a finding of ourselves in the structure of our bodies. Meeting Horsetail in ritual, a sense of vastness opens into the space:

> "It is like the full silence of an ancient stone circle or the infinite vastness of the stars felt from the surface of the moon.
> Elemental, raw, a frozen tundra with the horizon stretching far into the distance. Rock, wind and infinite space. Time stands still here."
>
> *Notes from blindfolded meeting with Horsetail. As is typical of blindfolded meetings like this, no one knew which plant was in the middle of the circle (2024).*

Like Wormwood, Horsetail has the power to strip away what no longer serves us, helping us rediscover our boundaries – but it does so in a different way. Where Wormwood awakens our will and stirs the liver, purging with fire and movement, Horsetail brightens our edges of self. They reveal the skeletal framework underlying the soft, fleshy aspects of our being, helping us sense the inner geometries of ourselves. In this way, Horsetail reveals where our boundaries have blurred, where we've lost sight of the edges that define us.

Horsetail sheds light on these entanglements and their potential to harm us. They serve as a reminder to our body and being of our inherent forms, archetypal structures capable of constant renewal. Their invitation extends beyond the restoration of health; they empowers us to construct resilience and strength, fostering a foundation that not only sustains us but helps us thrive in clarity and brightness.

Bright clarity · Geometric harmony · Crystal boundaries

What does it feel like to be clear in my choices, needs and boundaries?
Where and why am I stuck in unclear boundaries?
Where might unclear boundaries be affecting my health?

How do I stand tall and bright in my own being?
Where am I letting others' perceptions and needs hold me back?

Horsetail can shine a bright, revealing light; what am I now
ready to look at in myself that was previously in the shadows?
Where am I in avoidance?

Traditional: Horsetail has an ancient history as a styptic, staunching wounds when used topically. As a tea, herbalists value Horsetail for the high bio-available silicic acid content and thus the beneficial effects on bone resilience and the strengthening effect on hair, nails and skin. As an anti-inflammatory for arthritis and dermatitis, Horsetail has received some interesting preliminary research [*]. Horsetail also has a traditional reputation for supporting the health of kidneys and lungs.

Botany: *Equisetum arvense*, Field Horsetail, family Equisetaceae, is a perennial with deep rhizomes that are difficult to remove once established. Horsetail can be found all over the world, is one of the most ancient plants and loves to grow in damp, marshy conditions. The stems resemble tiny bamboo trunks with whirls of leaves. Other common Horsetails in Britain are Marsh Horsetail and Giant Horsetail.

Safety: Horsetail is generally considered safe in moderate doses, though care should be taken as Horsetail has thiaminase activity meaning they can break down vitamin B1, leading to deficiency. This has only been confirmed in cattle grazing on Horsetail, but does suggest caution in pregnancy, in alcoholism or with prolonged or high dosage. Easily mis-identified with Marsh Horsetail or Giant Horsetail, neither of which have as strong a reported lineage of safe traditional use as Field Horsetail.

Correspondences: ⸸ Ngetal (Reeds and Ferns) – wounding, perceiving our wounds, wound healing, clearing, letting go. ⵝ Ing – knowledge, perfection, harmony, peace, divine, successful conclusions, hope. ♄ Saturn – structure, discipline, tenacity.

Meeting Horsetail: I recommend experiencing Horsetail through touch, harvesting and drying a little to prepare your own tea for meditative exploration. Horsetail suits explorations related to boundaries, lungs, bones and the seership art of far-seeing.

Herbalists and ritual: Horsetail is a wonderful herb to work with around midsummer, as a counterbalance to ritual work with the more brightly coloured and scented plants that are abundant at this time of year. In my experience, Horsetail really suits spacious (both physically and temporally) outdoor work with plenty of opportunity to experience the plants through touch. Horsetail tends to take people into quiet individual and contemplative places; I often have the sense of individuals sitting on a cliff staring at the distant horizon on a solitary sea. This is a place for finding clarity of purpose. Sometimes Horsetail may feel somewhat unfriendly, or hard to relate to, like a harsh spotlight seeing beyond our performative selves, but with encouragement and support, this can be embraced as a powerful ally and teacher. Occasionally, while some find the space invoked by Horsetail deeply restful, others can experience fear at the sense of losing human-warmth and meaning. At the close of ritual work with Horsetail, I've often called on Rose or Hawthorn to help people return to a more 'human' mode of awareness.

Lady's Mantle

Many years ago, visiting the High Atlas mountains in Morocco, I was deeply struck by the acute contrast between the blazing red rocks and the narrow band of carefully curated green valleys. Water is precious here, and every stream is carefully channelled, bringing lushness, shady trees, coolness and life to a strip of land sometimes no more than 30 metres wide. The image of these cooling valleys amongst the heat resonates with what I see happen every time I invite Lady's Mantle to be received by a circle of people: an oasis of moist, refreshing, stilling coolness offering refuge from the intensity of the day.

There is a quietening, a spaciousness. Any chatty intensity or strong emotions fade into the space of a deep, deep breath. Time slows down. There is a delicacy to this plant that invites a delicacy in us when we touch them, cool, light and tender. As a group, it is as if we have been transported to an exquisite water garden, full of spring-fed pools and gentle clear streams.

In the womb, we are held within our own watery bubble, our amniotic sac, one of the many layers that hold us in safety as we grow. Healing is so often a reclaiming of the parts of ourselves that we have unconsciously exiled. This is where Lady's Mantle can offer their own gestational bubble and allyship.

When we discover these younger aspects of ourselves, they are often at exactly the same emotional and behavioural development stage as they were when they were exiled. This is such an important concept – we can't expect to meet the hidden four-year-old of ourselves and for them to instantly turn up to our expectations of adult life.

They need time and nurturing, we need to get to know them and allow them to find their dance; to be woven into the fabric of who we are. We can welcome them back into the family of ourselves, gently, tenderly, lovingly.

So many people have wounding around puberty and their emergence as an adult. For so many deep cultural reasons, not least centuries of patriarchal sexual repression and abuse, we have lost our initiations into adulthood. Those parts of ourselves not initiated often stay lost and stuck at the pre-initiation stage, deeply unconscious, showing themselves in our relationship to intimacy and sexuality.

Lady's Mantle is well regarded as an ally to the womb – and this is true, but I feel the reasons for this go far deeper than any physiological effect. This plant has the ability to hold the womb and all her history in a way that allows her to find her own balance, her own truth, her own expression.

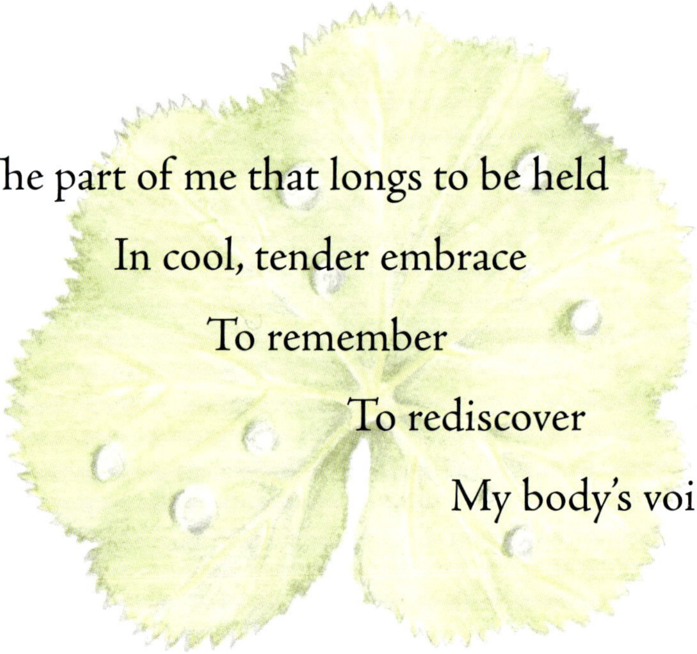

The part of me that longs to be held

In cool, tender embrace

To remember

To rediscover

My body's voice

Mothers embrace

How do I invite coolness and clarity into my life?
Where am I acting with too much heat, haste or passion?

Do parts of me need to be held and healed in the sacred womb?
Where am I overriding my need to give aspects of me time and space to 'gestate'?

How do I honour the energy of the womb – both symbolically and personally (my own womb/the womb I was gestated in)?
What does the phrase womb wisdom mean to me?
The womb can hold deep collective trauma – where might I turn away from this and how might there be wisdom and healing through turning towards it?

Traditional: Lady's Mantle has a long history in folk medicine, particularly as a wound healer and a women's remedy – balancing and regulating the menstrual cycle. They are recognised as an astringent, diuretic, anti-inflammatory, emmenagogue and vulnerary herb. Its astringency, due to the tannin content, staunches blood flow and promotes healing. The ariel parts are more commonly used and are also useful as an infusion or tincture for diarrhoea, and as a mouthwash for ulcers and sores. Research points to interesting topical anti-inflammatory and anti-tumour effects.

Botany: *Alchemilla vulgaris* is a herbaceous perennial in the Rose (Rosaceae) family with a unique way of holding droplets of water on their surface. Native to the British Isles, they are often found in woodlands, meadows and along roadsides. In gardens *Alchemilla mollis* is more commonly cultivated, used as a 'space filler' in herbaceous borders – spending time with Lady's Mantle in situ invites a sense of coming right down to ground level.

Safety: Generally considered a safe herb. Contains salicylates so caution in those with aspirin allergy. Seek professional guidance for use during pregnancy or if considering taking in combination with medications for blood sugar, high blood pressure or blood thinners.

Correspondences: ᚷ Eadha (Aspen) sensitivity, shielding in times of fear, endurance, adaptability, inner voice. ᛗ Ehwaz – harmony, unity, partnership, cooperation, journey, trust, loyalty and fertility ♀ Venus – earth, love, beauty, harmony.

Meeting Lady's Mantle: Spend time with this plant at dawn, when drops of water balance gracefully on their leaves. Let a leaf rest lightly in your hand, explore stroking your face or arm with them. A simple infusion of the fresh leaves (a leaf per cup) is a welcome way to meet this plant.

Herbalists and ritual: Lady's Mantle is a gentle plant to work with, tending to invoke a space of deep stillness, reflection, delicacy, tenderness and slowness. The ritual space invoked is ideal for quiet introspective work, and often gently touches themes around being held, grief, the womb and safety. They are a beautiful plant to combine with any somatic work exploring people's relationship with the womb. Work specifically with the womb often touches a place of deep ancestral grief, pain, tenderness and loss in people, so it is important as a practitioner that you've done your own healing work around this.

Tenderly delicate

Mother's tears

Still waters

Tender friend

Umbilical solace

Gentle womb

Timeless solace

Sadness portal

Cleansing stillness

Deep recognition

Womb waters

Tear catcher

Lemon Balm

To distil is to separate. With a plant, the light aromatics are lifted in the steam and the non-volatile compounds left in the distillation pot. Lemon Balm invites a distillation of self, creating breath and space within the knots of our heart's confusion.

'O troubled dust concealing

An undivided love

The heart beneath is teaching

To the broken heart above'

Leonard Cohen, 'Come Healing'

Even in our darkest days, the heart below knows love. Our hearts are layered, protected by a shield that absorbs the blows of life: a layer that, sometimes, we come to identify with as ourselves.

This shield takes the blows and, ideally, returns to its supple, transparent form, but not always. In the case of unintegrated trauma, particularly where a recent heart blow touches a deeper wound, this shield can, instead, harden and calcify. Rather than letting love heal this wound and returning to our innate trust, this ever-present shield holds on to it, keeping part of us in a state of hyper-alertness, valiantly attempting to protect us from future assaults. Sadly, this often causes us to close ourselves off from life and make choices that perpetuate our heart's caution, repeat our trauma patterns and hold love at a distance.

When out of alignment with ourselves, we can feel lost, unfulfilled, unsatisfied, searching. Yet as we find choices and actions that align with our hearts, a sense of purpose, clarity, vitality and aliveness emerges.

Lemon Balm breathes space into this confusion, helping us distil out the entangled knots. As this happens, we start to see them, untangled, as the multi-generational threads of trauma that they are.

Swirling high and clear

Friendly and majestic

Of bright mountain streams

Inviting space in our confusion

My training as a chemist taught me how to separate the component parts of a plant, yet in doing so I am no more likely to find the soul of the plant than I am the soul of a person by dissecting a cadaver. However, in the spiritual distillation offered by Lemon Balm we are offered the spaciousness and light to dream our dreams, embrace the threads of our wounds and imagine into the world we want to create together.

To invite Lemon Balm is to invite clarity, brightness and sense of possibility. People's imaginations are set free and their playfulness is allowed to breathe. Dreamful, childlike, unconstricted by doubts and fears. In the realm of Lemon Balm, anything seems possible.

Carl Jung evoked the mythological notion of *Puer aeturnus* and *Puella aeturna*, the eternal boy and eternal girl, to describe the adult child who never reaches true maturity. Like Peter Pan, the most well known *Puer aeturnus*, these individuals desire freedom and live in their imagination, whilst fearing the constraints of responsibility, repeatedly turning away from claiming their adulthood.

This is the shadow of the inner child, and I've met it often, dressed up in a myriad of forms. However, just as some become stuck in the playful naïveté of this inner child, others entirely lose their connection to this creative, playful part of themselves. Some sacrifice their inner child on the altar of responsibility, leading to a life devoid of joy, whilst others glorify them as the ground erodes under their feet, leading to an insecure life of fantasy.

The golden child needs our confident sovereignty – our inner King and our inner Queen – to bring their bright gifts to the world, to invite their play and their brightness. When the child is banished from the kingdom we prematurely age; yet if this child takes control, we infantilise ourselves, and potentially, if enough of us do this, our culture. If the inner sovereign appears to be missing, it's well worth considering who, or what, we have pledged allegiance to in their place.

This bright aliveness is mirrored in the nature of Lemon Balm itself. The genus name *Melissa*, derived from the Greek for honeybee, points to the plant's historical significance in attracting and calming bees. Ancient practices of rubbing Lemon Balm on beehives to attract and retain swarms, and the connection to the oracular Melissae priestesses who revered bees, reflect the profound relationship between nature and human spirituality. This theme is explored more deeply in the Lemon Balm chapter in our book, *Weeds in the Heart*, which I've included in the web portal for this book.

Somehow, and this is such a testament to the mystery of plants, the presence of Lemon Balm rekindles the golden child within us. Invigorated by this essence, doorways to forgotten possibilities open, and new paths beckon us forward, encouraging us to dream with the brightness of unbounded potential.

Golden child · Bright possibilities · Infinite love

How does it feel to allow the creative playfulness of my inner child?
How do I block my own creative playfulness?

When do I feel bright and clear in myself? What encourages this?
Where do I feel confused, stuck or heavy?

If anything was possible what would I dream into?
Where do I feel stuck and heavy; can I give these parts a voice?

What does sacred or divine love mean to me? Do I nurture this?
Where are the shields, scars and knots of confusion in my heart;
how might Lemon Balm help me tend to them?

Traditional: Lemon Balm is a well-known medicinal plant across Europe, respected for their calming effect on the mind and the digestion. Balm is often recommended for anxiety, depression, sleeping difficulties and overwhelm *, whilst research also suggests a useful role in dementia and Alzheimer's, being both calming and neuroprotective.* Balm's antiviral properties are often called on for treating cold sores.*

Botany: *Melissa officinalis*, family Lamiaceae, is a perennial plant found widely throughout Europe. They have a distinct bright lemon scent which is released when rubbing a leaf (Lemon Verbena is, as far as I'm aware, the only other common plant with such a citrus aroma, and is often confused for Lemon Balm). Lemon Balm's tiny white flowers are loved by bees, and the leaves can be harvested for tea from spring to late autumn.

Safety: Generally considered safe, but can influence thyroid hormone levels, decreasing thyroid hormone production. Patients taking thyroid medications, such as levothyroxine or methimazole, should avoid Lemon Balm unless working alongside a herbalist and their medication prescriber due to potential interactions that could alter the effectiveness of their prescribed drugs.

Correspondences: ᛂ Quert (Apple), bridge between worlds, wholeness, abundance, generosity, youth, beauty, wisdom. ᚾ Nied, the strength to face into challenges, rebirth through adversity, resilience. ♃ Jupiter, good fortune, expansion, abundance, prosperity, higher learning, optimism. Also correspondences with Quintessence, the element Air and the full moon.

Mountain stream

Bright aliveness

Space in overwhelm

Liquid light

Youthful joy

Infinite possibilities

Spiralling upwards

Penetrating brightness

Heart's companion

Expansive invitation

Meeting *Melissa*: Rubbing the leaves of the fresh plant, simple short infusion of the leaves. The hydrosol and essential oil are also beautiful ways to meet Lemon Balm if you have no access to fresh. Lemon Balm can easily lose a lot on drying; fresh is often far more potent.

Herbalists and ritual: Lemon Balm invites rituals that allow for space, lightness and play, whilst also giving the space for the shadow and wounded aspects of these that can equally easily appear. Distillation of Lemon Balm, movement, working outside and rituals inviting the inner child are all possible ways into deeper connection. Lemon Balm used skilfully can also shift the consciousness of a collective space that has become stuck or heavy, making Balm valuable in the closing and cleansing of a ritual space.

Marigold

With some plants we need to develop a discipline of attention if we want to let them in, filtering out the noise of the world to allow our ability to listen. Marigold is not like this. They broadcast loudly, permeating the airwaves, holding an easy pull on our attention and awakening our senses. They are one of the first plants I introduce people to in this work, often with the simple exercise of letting a Marigold rest in their hand.

I'm sitting beside a living Marigold installation I've taken to a festival. In the midst of the hubbub I witness repeatedly how these beings reach through, unlock people's smiles and touch a place of joy within them. Some speak of a warming felt in their heart, a kindling of their own inner warmth. Others speak of Marigold's brightness felt directly in their solar plexus, the penetrating brightness revealing any stuckness they carry here. Every evening a two-year-old boy returns to light the candles we set amongst the plants with a determination and joy that mirrors the Marigolds. As the festival closes I cradle a flower, with their waxy green sepals and bright orange florets; their presence in my palm feels warm, reminiscent of glowing embers.

Many describe a vibrating warmth slowly filling their palm, then softly radiating up their arm, releasing cold and numb strands within them and gently lifting their heart. One person describes an unfurling in this warmth, standing taller, bigger, brighter. I find it hard to maintain a serious or worried frown in the face of Marigold's optimistic smile, invited to sunbathe in their glow. It was Marigold who taught me that my ambivalence about exercise was rooted in my attachment to staying small. As my ligaments stretch and my muscles work, old habits of contraction are challenged to be released. Marigold invites the possibility of living with bright dignity, and in doing so reveals the ways in which we may have given up on this.

But what matters here are *your* experiences, *your* relationships, *your* sensations; these can't be found in any book. In every experience is a doorway; the key to letting plants in is recognising and walking through this doorway.

"I used to think that confidence meant being big and shining brightly. Now I realise it is letting myself shine so the cracks show."

Billie Rose (2023)

The word 'glamour' derives from the Old Scots 'gramarye', meaning an enchantment.* It might be thought that the word has lost its original meaning, but I'm not sure; perhaps it has just become normalised. To wear a glamour is to present a bright, enchanting version of yourself. Social media has refined this sport with devastating consequence to many people's mental health.* Sometimes we even become confused ourselves where the divide between our glamour and our true self lies.

Where is our brightness without wearing a glamour? What does that look like, feel like? Where do we feel safe enough to let this show? What if our brightness reveals itself through our vulnerability, not our performance of self? What is it like to feel our glow deep in our core, to rest peacefully in this and walk brightly and tenderly in the world?

Surely embracing this is the only way we stop being complicit in the game of appearances that leaves nobody, not even the apparent winners, fulfilled.

Many of the themes that I see emerge working with Marigold concern edges. The strengthening and healing of the lining of the gut, the ability Marigolds have to both help seal and heal wounds, and emotionally, the brightness that emerges in people when they become clearer in their sense of purpose.

Marigold may also literally 'brighten' our vision; the molecules lutein and zeaxanthin that give Marigolds their vibrant orange and yellow colours are also found in the macula of the retina, the part of the retina responsible for sharp, detailed vision. These molecules absorb and thus filter out ultraviolet light, protecting the retina.*

The capacity to bring brightness extends far beyond the human social-emotional sphere. Marigolds have long been respected as a companion plant, helping those plants around them thrive. This is possibly due to their effect on nematode populations *, helping contribute to a healthier garden ecosystem.

As I cradle the vibrant Marigold in my palm, feeling their warmth seep into my being, I feel deeply uplifted. They invite us to embrace our inner light, to let go of the fears and habits that keep us small, and to stand tall in our own brightness. Marigold teaches us to walk through life with both dignity and vulnerability, illuminating the world around us, not by wearing a glamour, but by allowing our inner light to be seen. In their presence, we are encouraged to reconnect with the deep, resilient spirit within us – a spirit that, like the Marigold, thrives not just by enduring, but by blooming boldly.

I take a deep breath of their complex fragrance and feel the sticky resins of their sepals. My smile broadens and my heart feels lighter in their presence, and a deep, latent optimism within me is gently rekindled.

How can I let the warmth and vibrancy of Marigold inspire me?
How do I overlook the beauty in and around me?

What does it feel like when I allow my boldness and brightness?
Why do I dim my brightness? How long have I been doing this? What triggers this? How might I let Marigold in?

How might I show my authentic self more?
Do I feel safe enough to unmask? What helps build this safety?

Traditional: Marigold is a staple in herbal medicine, primarily valued for its wound-healing and anti-infection properties. It is often found in skincare preparations and traditional remedies for gut healing. The antiparasitic effects of Marigold extend beyond soil nematodes, demonstrating anti-candida, antibacterial, antiparasitic and antiviral qualities. This potent ability to combat pathogens, combined with their role in activating lymphocytes and fibroblasts during wound healing, makes Marigold an impressive ally in treating surface wounds, whether on the skin, in the mouth, the vagina, or the gut. These healing properties are well researched, and *Calendula* extracts are commonly found in medicated dressings. The beneficial effects of lutein and zeaxanthin, compounds found in Marigolds, also help prevent glaucoma, diabetic retinopathy, macular degeneration, and cataracts.[*]

Spiritual heritage: Marigold has a rich spiritual heritage; in India they are widely used in festivals as symbols – auspiciousness, vitality and joy, bringing the light of the sun. In Mexico they feature prominently during the Day of the Dead celebrations, known as 'flor de muerto' (flower of the dead). Here, they serve as a beacon to attract and guide the souls of the deceased, marking a time when the veil between worlds is thin, allowing the living to honour their ancestors and the gifts they've bestowed.

Botany: *Calendula officinalis*, Asteraceae, display multiple bright orange or yellow ray florets and flower heads that respond to sunlight, opening in the morning and closing in dark or overcast conditions. They grow easily from seeds and can flower in as a little as eight weeks, before developing numerous robust seeds. Harvesting flowers before they seed encourages the plant to keep flowering abundantly. While many cultivated varieties of Marigold exist, particularly in the *Tagetes* genus, few possess the medicinal potency of *Calendula officinalis*. It's important not to confuse Marigold with Marsh Marigold, a completely different and toxic plant.

Safety: Generally regarded as safe in moderate amounts and often used in salads. Some are allergic to the Asteraceae family so should avoid.

Correspondences: ᚾ Nied – protection, healing, strength, resilience, creativity.
ᚾ Nuin – (Ash tree) shielding from negative influences, growth and transformation, adaptability, link between physical world and spiritual worlds, strength, resilience.
☉ Sun – divine power, protection and healing, illumination, warmth, power, sovereignty.

Meeting Marigold: Start with a simple 15-minute meditation of holding a Marigold flower in your palm and inviting yourself to receive. Notice where on your body you would like to move this Marigold closer and where, perhaps, they feel too close.

Herbalists and ritual: In some ways, Marigold is an easy plant to work with – the flowers are so bright they tend to elicit immediate and mixed responses. However, as we truly invite their medicine in, the process can become more complex. An invitation to embrace greater brightness often challenges our identification with hidden-ness, an identity that may be deeply rooted in trauma, defended with anger, and cloaked in shame.

Inevitably, all of this will surface as we let Marigold draw us out, and to support this requires having done this journey yourself and being skilled in supporting others as they step into initiation. The bolder and brighter the invitation, the more sensitivity and awareness is needed on the part of the facilitator to ensure all feel included, wherever they are on the journey into their own brightness. One student reflected that they found our Marigold ceremony stronger and more catalytic than a Peyote ceremony they'd attended. I think this is where deep respect and humility with regard to the herbs is so important – they all can move us in ways beyond our imagination, that indeed is why I'm a herbalist. The journey, when taken at this level of willingness to turn up to what is being asked, is rarely easy.

Marsh Mallow

How is your relationship with your sensual body? The deeply flowing waters of you, the warming lifeblood, the pulsing aliveness of you?

Over the years of my practice, I've increasingly questioned the value of dialogue. Of course, at points it is essential – to be heard, to reframe inner narratives, to name unnamable things; yet the non-verbal, the embodied threads that simply cannot be named hold some of the most fundamental clues to healing. I work with touch in all my sessions as a way to let the body speak directly. It wasn't a surprise then that the initial dialogue with a new client reveals little to me, but once we start to invite in touch, the landscape gradually becomes clearer. Six decades of chronic insomnia, a lifetime of wakefulness, are written within her body.

Inviting you to remember,
Your warm-bodied sensuality,
The sweet meandering rhythms,
Of warm living waters.

There are a hundred ways to touch, and in this moment, my touch is guided by Mallow. As is generally helpful for people who tend to be overly in their heads, I spend a long time at her feet and lower legs. It is hard to find her there; in place of warmth there is a sense of cold and absence.

I'm used to spending half an hour or more simply holding one part of the body, waiting for it to soften and arrive to the touch; but in her case this hardly scratches the surface. With a little practice in touch you can quickly tell if you are being received – there's a sense of a softening, warming, dropping and opening. The felt sense is like the difference between the warm connection of a good hug and the distance of an awkward, cold hug. Your hands no longer feel like they are merely on the surface of the person, but feel in dynamic relationship with the body and all it holds. I wait, assured in my patience by Mallow, for this welcome sense of connection and warmth to arrive.

Mallow persists. The plants have a patience humans often lack. I notice my own transference – the subtle ways, familiar to any therapist or healer, in which we are affected by the presence of another. If I don't attend to it, my breathing would tighten, my jaw would set, my belly harden. These somatic transferences, skilfully navigated, can offer the most potent insight into both oneself and the other.

I'm deeply glad for the companionship of Mallow, it is not just this client receiving Mallow, it is also me. I'm not the healer or teacher here, Mallow is teaching both of us. I'm just sitting between the tension of my transference and Mallow's invitation.

> Sensual aliveness,
>
> Sweet surrender,
>
> Releasing the grip,
>
> into pulsating warmth

Almost an hour in, I start to feel the slightest murmur of a tide, an inner flow, a momentary rush of warmth, a part of her awakening to this offer of touch. It is uncertain, tentative, questioning … "What is this? What is happening to me? I think I like it but I don't know it …"

My hands stayed steady, answering with constancy, gentleness, delicacy, invitation. In a moment of gnosis I saw that this woman hardly ever dropped into this place, this place of deep, flowing, pulsing, sensual aliveness, this place of soft surrendered body and restful heavy warmth. She didn't know it, and sleep did not take her there.

There are few plants that can guide you back to this place as reliably and gently as Mallow. Valerian, Guelder Rose and Clary can all help unlock this place, but I find myself often returning to Mallow, the gentlest teacher in the flowing joys of embodiment. Mallow offers patience and tenderness as the body finds its way through the maze of forgotten tensions and remembers the way of softness and surrender.

Pulsating warmth

Flowing bliss

Safe holding

Letting go

Letting flow

Embracing humanity

Kind forgiveness

Soft embrace

Embodied tides

Surrendered embrace

Soul soothing

Pulsating river

Grip yielding

Coming home

Warm sensuality

How does it feel to cultivate times and spaces in my life that invite deep relaxation and joyful connection to my sensual body?
How do I numb or disregard these calls and needs from my body?

How do I listen to my body? How does it feel to respond to its wisdom?
How and why do I dissociate from my body?

What does surrender mean to me?
Where am I holding on too tightly, and why?

Traditional: Mallow root has been a staple in herbalism for thousands of years on account of their soothing, mucilaginous qualities. The most known effect is as an anti-inflammatory and demulcent for the digestive tract (mouth, throat, stomach and intestines) and lungs (often used for dry coughs), as well as topically, as a poultice for inflamed and damaged skin. The demulcent effect is also found in the leaves and flowers.

Botany: *Althea officinalis*, family Malvaceae, is a perennial with a large rubbery root, growing all over Europe. The stems can grow to two metres, with soft leaves covered in fine hairs and large white-pink flowers. We harvest the substantial, rubbery roots in November, taking some for medicine and replanting the many new shoots emerging from the root. Once, I helped establish fifteen new plants from a single root, whilst also having plenty for use in teaching and my clinic. This feels a deeply respectful way to honour a plant when harvesting – to give back by nurturing more plants.

Safety: Mallow is generally considered safe with few side effects or interactions. Some confusion has emerged due to a traditional use of the long root as a *physical* intervention to terminate a pregnancy. The tea in moderate doses is considered gentle and safe in pregnancy.

Correspondences: ᛯ Ur (Heather) – healing, protection, nurture, wild beauty. ᚢ Ur (Urez, Ox) – strength, vitality, untamed wildness, sovereignty, freedom, physical health. ☽ Moon – rhythms of life, water.

Meeting Marsh Mallow: If you have access to a living plant, stand close, close your eyes, and let the wind brush the leaves and flowers of Marsh Mallow across your skin. Equally, the soft tenderness of Mallow can be experienced drinking the infusion of the leaf and flowers, or a gentle decoction of the root, both easily available.

Herbalists and ritual: Mallow leaves and root are wonderfully tactile – I encourage working with the physical plant, ritually harvesting and replanting root cuttings together. Mallow is generally very easily received, invoking a soft, open and receptive consciousness which is ideal for deeper somatic enquiry work or touch-based exercises. Mallow tends to be an excellent plant for fostering group coherence and helping everyone drop into a deeper parasympathetic state together.

A simple touch exercise

As I wrote this chapter I remembered a recent moment in a supermarket. I bumped into a friend and gave them a warm hug, and as we went our different ways, an elderly woman, crouched over her trolley, semi-jokingly said, "I was hoping to be next." I readily gave her a warm hug. As we parted she said, "No-one's touched me since my husband died." These words stayed with me for weeks.

Many people, particularly the elderly, are profoundly touch deprived. British culture has always been somewhat touch-phobic, and I fear this contributes to a significant amount of isolation and unhappiness. My years working as a bodyworker, along with numerous developmental research studies, have shown me that touch is fundamental to our wellbeing.

I'd like to offer a simple exercise in self-touch.

Close your eyes. Gently, with one hand, explore the contours of your face as if you were touching a lover. Move with tenderness and slowness, pausing often. Experiment with the lightest touch possible, and be open to discovering your face in a new, tactile way. Let the qualities of Mallow inform your touch. As you do this, tune into your feelings. How do you feel? What is touched in your heart? Who is this person, if all you know of them comes from the sensations in your fingertips? How might you bring more touch into your own life and the lives of others?

Meadowsweet

In June, the Horsley valley, where the Apothecary resides, overflows with lush midsummer abundance. Along the edges of the lakes and streams that once powered woollen mills and bore witness to the valley's historic trade, Meadowsweet gracefully unfurls. The sweet creamy blossoms beckon with their full and uplifting scent. Amidst the reeds and irises that adorn these banks, Meadowsweet offers a sweet summer embrace.

I'm reminded of two other midsummer flowers that cast spells with their fragrance: Elder and Valerian. In the dreamlike embrace of these plants, it's easy to lose one's bearings, to feel subtly affected in ways that defy easy articulation. At times, the only frame of reference is to compare one state of intoxication with another. Where Valerian envelops me in a sweet warm sleep spell, and Elder evokes an other-worldly sense of the Fae, Meadowsweet invites a sweet melodious dance, a dreamy summer lyricism accompanied by the joyful hum of a thousand insects.

I struggle with labels like 'client' and 'patient'. Those who seek my guidance are on a quest to delve deeper into themselves and the realm of plants, and I accompany them on this transformative journey. Tara, a young trainee herbalist, sought extra support from me in a one-to-one session. Her eagerness to plunge into this exploration radiated as brightly as her luminescent white hair. Before we knew it, Meadowsweet was beckoning to us with their expansive, fragrant call.

There is a theme that frequently emerges when dancing with Meadowsweet; the reclaiming of lost youth, particularly where innocent playfulness was lost in puberty. I often hear it shared that this plant touches the Maiden-Mother threshold, the possibility of stepping into full adulthood without losing the luminous playfulness of childhood. In a culture profoundly lacking healthy initiatory thresholds, my experience is that this particular threshold is often incomplete, marked by scars, burdened with shame or bearing subtle bruises.

Tara spent several of her teenage years within the confines of Marlborough House, an adolescent mental health hospital close to Stroud. Emerging from this experience, she carried with her a resolute determination and an unyielding drive to instigate change, weaving new myths into the fabric of our fractured culture. Witnessing her commitment was truly inspiring. Yet within this fierce dragon energy, reflected in Meadowsweet's soft dream, I sensed the quiet call of a delicate innocence that had been tucked away deep in her unconscious.

"The moment I open to Meadowsweet, there's a soft expansive heart space, a softening and grounding, a feeling that it's entirely possible to be grounded *and* in connection with my seership. I'm reminded of the bright blue dragonflies and the joy they bring on a summer's day. Meadowsweet whispers to me, 'Stop trying to grow up – enjoying being where you are at, it's exactly where you need to be.'"

There is a softening; a letting go is invited here. A deep breath and surrender to a comforting languorous sweetness. A gentle awakening, a moistening of edges, a freedom to dance your desires. And at the same time there is an intoxicating, chaotic, mischievous chaos in the mix, stirring unexpected dreams and shadowy visions. The blossoms to me are like the bubbles in a champagne glass, spiralling upwards and outwards, brightly playful and euphoric. To spend time with Meadowsweet at dusk, in the liminal half-light, is to feel the world come alive, to sense the animate in the stones and the shadows.

I've written here of the bright invitation of Meadowsweet, yet there is another doorway that can open for people into a darker, more confusing place; chaotic, overwhelming and out of our control. In this work with the plants, the darker doorways often lead to more potent medicine. Within the confused dreams that can emerge here are to be found many places within ourselves that we have judged, shamed, learned to fear and cast into shadow.

Unless you already have a strong inner framework for your own shadow work, this sort of exploration is best done with another human companion – a herbalist, therapist or healer who you feel you can trust to companion you on the journey.

150

Meadowsweet's presence, particularly when in flower, is potent and evocative, sometimes light and joyful, sometimes musty and full of shadows. Just as they can teach us how to dissolve into the playful mystery of our innocent sensual aliveness they can also reveal the shadows and fears we didn't even realise we held here.

Summer scent

Shadow medicine

Heart softener

Bubbling euphoria

Dream dancer

Maiden's threshold

Whispering mysteries

Musty dreaming

Reclaiming innocence

Water meadow's gift

First kiss

Maiden's magic

Shame revealer

Dusk's companion

Dark liminal doorways

Reclaiming innocence

Invitation: A fragrant loosening of self, a freeing up of the joy and innocence in our play and sensual enjoyment of the world.

How do I honour the thresholds and initiations calling me now?
Have I adopted ideas about how to be an adult that don't feel true to me?

Do I feel anything was lost or missed at my threshold of adulthood?
Am I denying myself my dreams and if so why?

How do I find and enjoy flow, play and ease?
What holds me back from engaging in life and play?
Where have I become too rigid?

Traditional: 'Queen of the Meadow', a member of the rose family, was popular in the Middle Ages as a 'strewing herb' – aromatic herbs that were 'strewn' across the floor to cover other unpleasant smells, some with deodorising properties and as repellents for invasive household bugs such as moths and fleas.

Meadowsweet was once the source of salicylic acid from which aspirin was made. However, unlike aspirin (acetylsalicylic acid), Meadowsweet contains salicylic acid, which, without the acetyl group, does not have the stomach ulcer risk that aspirin carries. It also differs in not having the blood-thinning effect.

Meadowsweet has often been used for inflammatory conditions such as arthritis, acidic indigestion and reflux, and for other gastro-intestinal issues that call for soothing and calming, such as IBS and digestive issues in children. Due to the salicylate content, they can be used much in the way one would use pharmaceutical painkillers, to relieve the pain of headaches, toothache, and the discomfort of colds and flu. Meadowsweet is also a diuretic and promotes sweating, therefore useful in times of illness. Historically, they were also a traditional herb used to flavour mead and are one of the three plants (along with Oak and Broom) from which the Celtic goddess Blodeuwedd was created.

Botany: *Filipendula ulmaria*, Rosaceae family. Meadowsweet is native to Britain and Europe and likes to grow in damp places: along rivers, canals and low-lying fields and marshes. They spread easily and rapidly and have distinctive cloud-like clusters of hundreds of tiny white flowers, which when inspected up close are the distinctive five petals of the Rose family. Grows up to 1.5m tall and harvested in the summer between June and August when the flowers are fully open. Meadowsweet seeds have a distinctive spiral shape, which inspired the name for aspirin (from the older Latin name 'Spiraea ulmaria' which was derived from the latin 'spira', meaning coil).

Safety: Do not take Meadowsweet if you are allergic to aspirin or if you are currently taking aspirin or other salicylate-containing plants, as Meadowsweet is naturally high in salicylates. Additionally, it is advised not to consume Meadowsweet during pregnancy.

Correspondences: ᛝ Ngetal (Reed) – flexibility, adaptability, resilience, remain grounded, protection, flexibility, protection, times of change, creating boundaries, embracing new opportunities. ᛜ Ing – internal growth, potential, transformational process, introspection, incubation, trust, fulfilment, new beginnings, fertility. ♃ Jupiter – expansion, abundance, growth, wisdom, optimism.

Meeting Meadowsweet: Seek out streams, rivers, wetlands or canals in June, particularly around dusk when the flowers take on a luminescent glow. The scent alone is deeply evocative, and liminal time spent swimming in these musty aromatic waters is a rich doorway.

Herbalists and ritual: I think of Meadowsweet as a plant of high summer and prefer to take groups outside, near water, on a hot day (if possible) to meet this plant. Allowing people to find a Meadowsweet-scented spot to drift and journey in for a while is all that is needed with this evocative being. Gentle dusk sharings, inviting storytelling and myth making are well suited here, as are rituals, such as menarche rituals, intended to tend to people's missing initiations of adulthood. Sleeping with a cluster of flowers near one's bed tends to evoke rich dreaming.

Mistletoe

Mistletoe thrives on trees surrounded by light and space, Oaks, Apples and Poplars, those at the edges and those standing alone. The translucent white berries, eaten by birds, allow the seeds to be deposited soon after on the next tree the bird visits; in this way, Mistletoe never touches the earth, but travels from bird to tree to bird to tree.

Born of bird and tree,

Never touching earth,

Of sky and stars,

And dark solstice light.

In Norse mythology, there is a tradition that should enemies meet under a Mistletoe, it is a space of truce and the laying down of arms. In Britain the tradition of – perhaps otherwise prohibited – Christmas kisses under the Mistletoe has a sure place in popular culture. Both speak of a moment in an alternate reality, where animosities and defences can be put aside, and new connections nurtured. Mistletoe's habits invite these mythological weavings; their evergreen nature, the mystery of their 'virgin' tree birth, their un-earthly celestial structure and the sticky white 'Oak-Sperm' of the berries.

Mistletoe plays a pivotal role in the mythological murder of Baldr. Frigg, Baldr's mother, extracted an oath from all living things not to harm her son. However, Mistletoe was fatally overlooked – a detail Loki exploited. He crafted a weapon from the Mistletoe and guided Höðr, Baldr's blind brother, to strike Baldr down.

"There stood on the plains, slender and passing fair,
the mistletoe, the menacing arrow.
From that fair shrub sprang a fatal shaft;
Höðr shot it, but Frigg wept in Fen Halls."

'The Poetic Edda' trans.
Carolyne Larrington
Oxford World Classics

Baldr was prophesied to be reborn after Ragnarok, the cosmic cataclysm. Mistletoe, the weapon of his demise, thus also becomes a symbol of renewal.

Every encounter I've had holding Mistletoe ritual spaces has invited experiences of a quiet expansive light. Not the penetrating, summer solstice sunlight of St. John's Wort, but a cooler and more spacious celestial light. A light that can feel more resonant with distant sun-stars than our local one.

There is often a solitary quality to people's meetings, paradoxical invitations into the vast inner spaciousness of oneself and the timeless infinity of a clear starry night. For me, the association with winter solstice is perfect. Mistletoe is a companion for journeys into vastness, into a place of remembering beyond human drama and worldly concerns, a place beyond birth and death, a place of a deep renewal.

Though we might not be literally at arms against each other, we all can find ourselves stuck in places of conflict. It is difficult to put aside our armour, to take the shielding from our hearts, and for good reason. We've put it there to protect ourselves from being hurt again, and to set it down feels vulnerable. And yet a deeper part of us knows that this armour doesn't really offer a path forward. There is something in the broader perspective Mistletoe offers that might show us doorways to peace. Perhaps, just for a short while, under the Mistletoe, it is possible to step back, see our human dramas for what they are, an eternal replaying of relational dualities, and remember the quiet, bright love that lies beyond this.

Rose, Vervain and Mistletoe, three different plants of truce, each offer a different invitation. Rose unlocks the softness of mother love. Vervain can help untangle our confusion. Mistletoe takes us high up the mountain and reconnects us with the ancient part of us who has seen this all before, and even in grief, pain, confusion and animosity, still chooses a path of love.

Spherical geometries

Of bright celestial emanation

Lay down the arms of our knotted conflict

Remembering for a moment

A greater geometry, a more ancient dance

Invitation: To open realms of dreaming and journeying. To consider a broader perspective.

How would it feel to step back and take a wider perspective?
Where might seeking vision be spiritual bypassing?

How does it feel when I allow time for inner, dreaming time?
How often do I spend time alone under a starry sky?
How do I sabotage this?

How might Mistletoe help me find truce in conflict?
Where might I be holding on to anger or resentment?

Traditional: Mistletoe has a traditional reputation for supporting the circulatory system, hypertension and for anxiety. In Europe, Mistletoe tea can often be found in health food shops. Unfortunately there is very little research regarding any uses of the plant as an infusion or tincture, though there are numerous trials exploring Iscador ⚹, an injectable form of Mistletoe for a variety of cancers. This is a well-known remedy in anthroposophy, well established in Germany and often prescribed by anthroposophical doctors. Within anthroposophy, Mistletoes growing on different trees is understood to have affinities for different types of cancer.

Botany: *Viscum album*, family Loranthaceae, is hemiparasitic and grows on a variety of trees. They have evergreen yellow-green leaves, yellow flowers and milky white berries. Mistletoe is unusual in that they are both parasitic on the host tree, but can also photosynthesise.

Safety: All parts of the plants contain viscotoxins, which can be toxic to humans so caution and skill are needed using Mistletoe. Fortunately, viscotoxins are not easily extracted in an infusion ⚹ and Mistletoe tea is widely available over the counter in much of Europe. Use only in small doses and with caution, not in pregnancy, and preferably with professional supervision.

Correspondences: ⌇ Quert (Apple) – regeneration, vitality, generosity, love, beauty.
‹ Kenaz – knowledge, illumination, enlightenment, inspiration, fire of creativity.
☉ Sun – purpose, will, vitality, authority, confident ego.

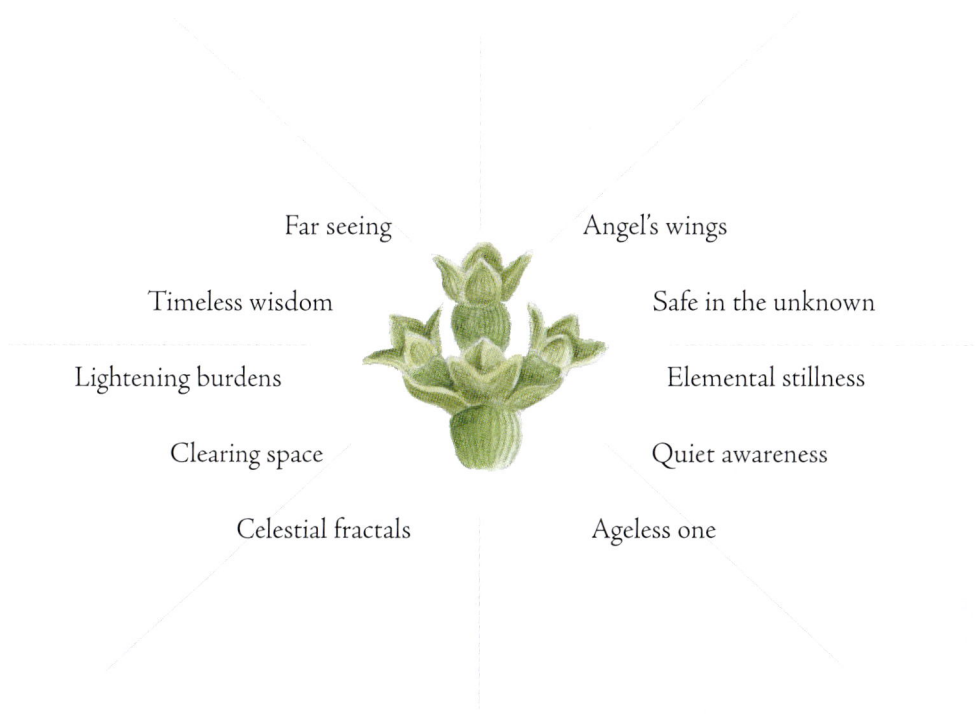

Far seeing

Angel's wings

Timeless wisdom

Safe in the unknown

Lightening burdens

Elemental stillness

Clearing space

Quiet awareness

Celestial fractals

Ageless one

Meeting Mistletoe: Take time in deep winter to be still underneath Mistletoe, using this as a time of expansive inner meditation.

Herbalists and ritual: Mistletoe is a beautiful plant to work with around winter solstice. My experience is that many would like to drop into a quieter dreaming place at this time of year, and rituals that involve a respectful and ritual harvesting of Mistletoe, the careful transportation (not touching the ground!) and the suspending above a dreaming space all help invite participants into a deep, quiet space of dreaming and reflection. I've noticed people often come out of these experiences feeling 'washed by light' and with their thoughts calmer and clearer.

Mugwort

Of all plants, the doors Mugwort opens in ceremony are the least predictable. The response in the circle may be that people are enlivened into chaotic wild drumming and dance; the same circle, another day, can become profoundly inward, each individual silently traversing deep, dark underground journeys.

Dissolve illusions of control
Show me what I cannot see
Stir the cauldron
Mugwort, mother of herbs

In the cauldron of our consciousness, that which we know would be the ever-shifting surface of the warm waters. Beneath this surface lies our dream life and unconscious mind, a deep fluid mass with its own currents and eddies.

At the bottom of this cauldron is a thick sludge, deeply hidden, the forgotten threads of knowing and feeling. Mugwort will stir this sludge, if we let them.

What this means in practice is so individual as to defy generalisation, yet there are certain things I see again and again. Mugwort invites the possibility of opening up our dream world, accessing memories that go beyond anything we've seen in this life, feeling the presence of our ancestors and remembering a more primal way of experiencing the world.

Unfreezing ancient spells
Awakening the witch wound
Inviting the untethered fullness
Of womb and woman's power

As the voices of our deep unconscious surface and flow into awareness, often in unexpected moments, it can feel confusing, bewildering, overwhelming. And at the same time, there can be a sense of doors opening, important memories activated and the possibility of reclaiming lost parts of our power.

"For the first time in a year, my womb feels unfrozen. I can feel its fullness and ache."

Sara Ghanchi (2022)

Deeply maternal

Inviting power

Death dreaming

Wisdom of my bleed

Deep drumbeat

Composting renewal

Powerful darkness

Beating earth heart

Softly sensual

Downward pull

There is an awakening fire here, an arousal of life force, a restoration of movement where before there was numbness. Do we dare invite our wildness? Our madness? Our arousal to life? Do we dare believe the visions of our mythic selves are real, that we can walk towards our dreams, however impossible they seem?

It took me seven years from first meeting (and being mystified by) Mugwort to feel the glimmerings of any real understanding. They taught me the art of slow, patient courtship with plants – that when we show up year after year, we gradually develop an understanding of what plants have to teach us. The Latin name given to Mugwort is *Artemisia vulgaris*. The genus name, *Artemisia*, comes from Artemis, the goddess of the wild and childbirth, whose name may trace back to the ancient Greek word *árktos*, meaning 'bear', suggesting a connection to ancient bear cults.

Many old herbals speak of Mugwort to revive the traveller on their journey. This gave me the first hint that a Mugwort foot bath could be a powerful way of working with this herb. I quickly made two discoveries. The first was that a hot Mugwort foot bath can have powerful effect for women feeling disconnected from their womb's voice.

The second was a surprising discovery. Sometimes the protection, or 'armour' someone surrounds themselves with has become so fixed and rigid that the usual range of naturopathic treatments do not seem to touch them. I found that if I start a bodywork session with a Mugwort foot bath, it seems to both loosen this armour and significantly help catalyse the rest of the work we do. A little Mugwort smoke on a hot coal can also do this. People's ability to hear and speak from their body opens up in this space, as well as the capacity to journey into the deeper stories they hold there.

Mugwort can plunge hands deep into our unknown psyche, unlock our dreams and draw out strengths and fears we have long forgotten. As these gems are revealed, Mugwort shows neither malice nor sympathy, but gentle unassailable confidence and loving warmth.

Traditional: Mugwort has long been considered a herb beneficial to women, bringing blood and aliveness to the womb and acting as an emmenagogue. They are widely regarded as potent in activating dreaming, taken as a tea before bed or by having the plant close to your bed. Other common traditional uses are as a digestive tonic, on account of the bitter and aromatic qualities, and as a fine dried powder in Moxibustion, a technique common in East Asian medicinal practices [*], where Mugwort powder is burnt over meridian points to bring warmth and activation into these energy pathways.

Botany: *Artemisia vulgaris*, Asteraceae. Mugwort is a robust perennial, spreading both through a network of rhizomes and as abundant seed in early autumn. They are sometimes considered invasive due to the ease with which they spread, and are commonly found on pathways, river and canal paths, and brownfield sites. The plant can grow two metres tall with many stems and deeply lobed leaves. These have a distinctive silvery appearance on the underside due to many fine hairs. The flowers, in late summer, are small and of a similar colour to the leaves; the seeds are minuscule and travel easily on the wind.

Safety: Mugwort has a potent action on the womb as an emmenagogue, activating menstrual flow, so should not be used in pregnancy and only used in late pregnancy with the support of an experienced herbalist or midwife. The 'deep stirring' effect on

164

the unconscious means I would advise caution and professional support working with Mugwort with those with deep and unprocessed trauma, anyone with a history of psychosis or borderline personality disorders, and anyone with addictions (medicinal *or* recreational) to psychoactive substances. Mugwort pollen is known to cause allergies in some. There are many species of *Artemisia*, among which *Artemisia absinthium* (Wormwood) and *Artemisia annua* (Sweet Wormwood) are particularly widely used. While these species share some overlapping qualities, it is crucial to distinguish between them due to their distinct medicinal properties and applications.

Correspondences: ᛘ Ruis (Elder) – Fae and the ancestors, magic, witching, crone, healing, transformation. ᚱ Raidho – a journey, movement, spiritual and physical travel, protection and choice in the journey. ♀ Venus – depth of magic and beauty in relationships, feminine power, creativity and artistic expression. ☽ Moon – cycles of life, water, the unconscious, dreams.

Meeting Mugwort: The first step in knowing Mugwort is to meet the living plant in the wild. Once you start to recognise them, you will likely see them everywhere – they have a remarkable capacity to become invisible to us. Dusk meditations, burning a little dried leaf on a coal, is a potent and simple way to invite conscious dreaming and journeying.

Herbalists and ritual: I tend to recommend that student herbalists only start sharing Mugwort once they have travelled a significant distance on their own journey with this plant. Mugwort has a capacity to unlock deep rememberings, unexplored power and ancient wounds, meaning a high degree of experience and integrity is needed to hold a Mugwort space well. I find that the places Mugwort touches often keep unfolding for days and weeks after deeper work, meaning that this deeper work benefits from the holding of an ongoing container, e.g. a well-held group, community or course.

Honouring the Witch Wound

The long term impact of the Witch persecutions is often keenly felt amongst herbalists. Through supporting many apprentice herbalists as they meet deeply internalised fear of persecution, I've come to understand that the traumatic impact of these events wasn't just on those directly persecuted. The deeper shadow and wound is to be found in the collective memory of being complicit, and the fear (at the time pragmatic) of speaking out against injustice, torture and murder.

Mullein

Aaron's Rod, Jacob's Staff, Candlewick, Hag's Taper – these are some of the many names for Mullein, a plant that always captivates the attention of visitors in the herb garden. This year their vibrant seven-foot stems soar brightly into view, standing tall above any other plant. Despite their visibility, I never explored this plant in depth until a couple of years ago. My own bias and projections had caused me to overlook them.

In a culture that often prioritises the brightest and loudest voices, I had associated visible prominence with vacuousness. In many ways it is this very perception that guided me toward the plants 30 years ago, as I sought to turn away from human noise and redirect my focus to the subtler voices of the plants. This same bias hindered my engagement with Mullein, a reflex to turn away from what was bright and prominent.

Mullein's stems and leaves are coated with thousands of tiny hairs, giving the plant a beautiful velvety feel. These contribute to the plant's absorbent capacity when dried; dipped in wax they have been used for millennia as torches and candles. Soft yellow flowers and their buds adorn the entire stem, with a unique 360 degree gesture of flowering.

In the herb garden they are lighthouses, radiating warm yellow light in all directions.

To shine bright and stay centred seems an advanced skill in this day and age. In my own journey of letting go of the protective masks I'd built to try and protect myself from constant overwhelm, Mullein has been an essential ally. They inspire me to stand tall, to be bright, to be constant in purpose – to do all of this with gentleness but without appeasement. Mullein has been a teacher for me in living an unfiltered, unmasked life, letting go of the caretaker role that was an unconscious feature of so much of my life.

Ben, a student, plant lover and lead in Earthsong Seeds, a small organic seed company, shared his wonder and frustration with Mullein.

> "It will never grow where you put it, but emerge exactly where it wants to grow – often on a path, often exactly in the way; yet it is so beautiful it's hard to dig it up and try and move it. I've given up trying to shepherd it into one part of the seed garden. It is such a joy and incredible in its generosity of seeding – one stem gives hundreds of thousands of seeds."

To spend time with this plant is to be inspired to stand tall in your own light, to find an unwavering commitment to yourself, to let your voice speak brightly and gently, and to live with both determination and softness.

Mullein has an unrivalled reputation in herbalism as a gently healing demulcent for the lungs, clearing old phlegm and restoring the moist, fluid aliveness of these delicate tissues. They ease the throat and the voice, both as a tea and, traditionally, as a smoke. This is a use that goes back centuries; in Britain they were often favoured to bring comfort to the lungs in 'consumption' (tuberculosis).

This is a plant whose unique stem I prefer not to harvest, so when I introduce people to them, it is generally in situ. There is always a quiet respect that unfolds in people, as if they themselves are drawn inwards to their centre line, and a brightness and wonder in their eyes and voice when they speak of what Mullein touches in them. They feel to me like a plant that individuates, that helps us know ourselves, know our brightness.

There is a deep connection between breath and self-worth; so often it seems to me that as people contract into themselves in doubt, fear, grief or shame they also contract their breathing. The freeze response – when a layer of trauma within us is touched – often looks like this, a contracting and even momentary stopping of the breath.

This micro-freeze response is familiar to anyone working to support people therapeutically and is often a significant clue to unlocking the embodied memories that lie behind so much ill health. Plants touch us with their brightness and the possibilities they present, but in this they also touch the shadows where our brightness has been dimmed.

In Mullein there is an invitation to soften our breath and soften into ourselves, not with passivity, but with uprightness and determined brightness.

It can take a lot of strength to remain soft, and the human role models for this seem few and far between. It is precisely here, where we have lost our way, where we have lost our archetypes that guide us, that plants can remind us of forgotten ways of being in the world.

Still centre · Soft illumination · Pathway pioneer

Where do I find bold, bright dignity and strength in myself?
How do my posture and breath reflect this?
Where might I have dimmed my light?

How visible am I?
Is the person I present (e.g. on social media) truly me?
Where might I be hiding myself, through glamour or masking?

Where could I bring more softness and gentleness to my boundaries?
Where do I tend to fight, react or antagonise?

Traditional: Mullein, with their striking stature and soft, woolly leaves, have long been cherished in herbal medicine. The leaves and vibrant yellow flowers are particularly renowned for their efficacy in treating respiratory ailments. They serve as a soothing balm for dry coughs, bronchitis, and tracheitis, helping to ease congestion and promote better breathing. Mullein is also valued for their gentle sedative properties that can enhance sleep quality and as a gentle, soothing remedy for cystitis. Their mucilaginous nature combines with astringent effects to soothe the digestive system, making it a supportive remedy for diarrhoea. The dried leaves are often used as a base in herbal smoking mixes. The magical and ritual qualities of Mullein are highlighted during the German 'Kräuterweihe'–a traditional herb blessing held in mid-August, where they are often included in herb bundles used to protect, heal, and ward off evil and illness.

Botany: *Verbascum thapsus*, Scrophulariaceae (Figwort) family, known commonly as great Mullein or common Mullein. They are biennial, germinating in the spring and summer, but able to germinate in the autumn and overwinter if the plant is sufficiently mature. Leaves grow in large rosettes close to the ground, and they flower in their second or third year of growth before dying back. The leaves are soft and hairy, giving them a distinctive light green appearance, and each plant has a tall single spike of bright yellow flowers. Mullein prefers bare open soil to growing with other plants, where they can act as pioneer plants. They are native to southern and central Europe, and to western Asia, but have naturalised globally in temperate regions, growing on open uncultivated land and along roadsides.

Safety: When harvesting take care not to confuse with Agrimony, which is similar but far smaller and without hair on the leaves. Mullein leaf and flower are generally recognised as safe in moderate doses.

Correspondences: ✝ Ailim (Pine/Fir) – endurance and clear vision, clarity, inner strength, clarity of thought, courage, rebirth and protection. ᚨ Ansuz – clear communication and divine inspiration, revelation from the gods, inner guidance, clear thought, connection between earthly and divine realms, wisdom. ♄ Saturn – discipline, sacred responsibility, limitations, structure, maturity, hard work, growth, diligence.

Meeting Mullein: This is such a magnificent plant to meet in person, but might be tricky to find. The leaf tea is easily available and offers a simple accessible way to meet Mullein through a tea meditation.

Herbalists and ritual: I've always been struck by the quiet respect that settles within a group when meeting living Mullein. These plants seems to invite everyone to stand a little more upright, return to their centre and potentially explore themes around sovereignty and dignity. I've discovered that movement exercises, exploring our posture and how it reflects our relationship with our body and ourselves, is a potent doorway here.

Nettle

There is very little that can be compared to starting the day covered in Nettle stings. Every year, on a fresh morning in March, I invite the training group to start their day with the quintessential ritual of the Nettles.

At dawn, each person waits in quiet contemplation to be invited up to our Nettle temple (a sheep-carved hollow under a small Oak in a Bramble hedgerow). I nervously wait until the end for my own annual initiation. Even after 15 years of repeating this ritual I still carry a certain trepidation, for myself, for those in the group entering this threshold for the first time. Yet, the moment the Nettles kiss my skin, all my hesitations dissolve into a radiant, pulsating warmth that blankets my being, a potent reminder of aliveness in this human body.

Even those who were initially hesitant soon surrender into the fire offering of Nettle; many go back the next morning for more. In this space of viscerally feeling our glowing edge there's a persistent call:

How do you choose to inhabit

This body, the sacred earth of you?

Our societal and personal traumas often bury our connection to our bodies, leading to layers of numbness and dissociation. I have come to understand that some degree of somatic disassociation is endemic in our culture and that, by opening up a space of listening to our bodies, new, unforeseen, wisdoms often emerge.

Many drawn to train as healers and herbalists have a high sensitivity to outside energies –a double-edged sword that can lead to overwhelm. Yet it also offers profound empathy and a unique ability to connect with others. In many ways this very sensitivity is their gift, the gift of deep empathy and the ability to meet others in their truth; but it's rarely an easy gift. Many of the people I've worked with struggle with constant sensory overwhelm.

To be in the body is to feel. To be in the body is to experience the multiplicity of sensations the body is capable of, both its pleasure and the pain. Most of us find a level of numbness that suits, and sometimes it is only through these intentional initiations that we remember what is possible. Nettle sting is one that awakens this remembering, mirroring the initiation of cold water immersion in both the initial ambivalence and the profound, warming emergence of life.

The Nettle's sting ignites a fire within, challenging us to confront the subtle infringements upon our boundaries, to acknowledge the multitude of violations we've experienced, and to reclaim our power. Towards the end of this ritual, Lucie, a herbal trainee, reflected, "*I can't help but feel all that I've stomached, that all that I am no longer prepared to.*"

Nettle's gifts and embrace extend far beyond the sting. An overnight infusion of the young leaves offers a different warmth; in the morning you'll be greeted by a deep emerald green potion, a sweet mother's-milk broth that

> "I realise that I unconsciously believed that it was safer for
> me *not* to be in my power. Nettle challenges that in me."

> *Emily Taylor (2023)*

instantly fills the stomach and offers a feeling of satiation. Yet, revisiting the primal breast-nourished satiety of infancy invites complex emotions; for some, these early memories are marred by feelings of scarcity, abandonment, and distrust, challenging us to confront and heal these foundational wounds. Nettle can be a sweet and constant ally on this, all too common, journey of healing.

The infused oil, rich in nourishment, mirrors this depth. By slow-cooking fresh Nettles in cold-pressed sesame oil for eight hours, a luxurious, dark green oil emerges. This is a beautiful oil for anointing, a conscious ritual of touch where the oil is offered to places in the body that have first been invited into awareness though somatic meditation.

Where the sting awakens, the tea and the oil gently fill, nourish and calm. I've seen groups become soporific quickly even as we smell the tea; and people drop into deep states of parasympathetic relaxation in response to the touch of the warm oil. All of healing is a cycle of awakening and integration, enlivening and rest, and Nettle, in these two aspects offers both.

" Deep rest is needed for deep aliveness
… Nettle offers both … "

Ellen Voges (2024)

Later in the day, as the glow and sting slowly subside, there's a sense of camaraderie within the circle that feels determined, awake, purposeful. Some plants that help us individuate also seem to invoke a solitary place in us; Nettle is the polar opposite, somehow they engender both individuation *and* togetherness, they help us remember both who we are *and* reweave the purposeful tribe and sense of belonging that many today crave.

Many now consider that the realms of healing and therapy have today become too individualistic. In this Nettle offers a different path, one that invites both individual sovereignty and healthy interdependence.

175

Boundary fire · Tribe weaver · Earth's milk

What helps me be more fully in my body?
How do I habitually dissociate from my body?

What helps me feel nourished in a way that enlivens?
To what degree is the food I eat not truly nourishing me?

How clearly do I know my edges and boundaries?
Where are my boundaries too loose?

Where is my tribe, my community?
Where do I struggle with this?

What does it feel like to be in my power?
How do I make myself small?

Traditional: Valued by humans for millennia for their nourishing qualities, the leaves are often used as a tea or decoction during pregnancy, postpartum, and for anaemia. There is research into the use of the roots being beneficial in conditions of the prostate, and as a male sexual tonic.※ The seeds are even more potent than the leaves, rich with nourishing oils and mildly stimulating. Flagellations with freshly picked stems of the leaves is an old remedy for arthritis, and is thought to originate as a Roman practice to help cope with the damp cold of Britain. Nettle has anti-allergic properties, useful for hay fever, asthma, itchy skin conditions and bites.※ There have been some control studies into the boosting of milk supply in mothers of pre-term babies, with positive results.※ Nettle is also a diuretic and can have blood sugar stabilising effects in type II diabetes.※

Botany: *Urtica dioica,* Urticaceae family. Found throughout Europe and America, Nettles grow prolifically where humans dwell, particularly on human-wasteland, reviving damaged soil.※ Jagged leaves growing in pairs from a square stem, with unmistakable fine needle-like silica hairs which contain the sting. The leaves are harvested in spring when they are young and fresh and always before the plant begins to flower. Seeds and roots are harvested in autumn.

Safety: Some people are hypersensitive to the sting, something I check carefully before any Nettle sting ceremonies. I personally would not advise working with the sting by yourself or on anything more than a small area of skin (e.g. forearm) initially, since without experience it is impossible to know how strong the effect will be. Likewise, this approach is not suitable for those with fragile skin, the young or the elderly, or anyone with severe inflammatory skin conditions. Professional advice should be sought if considering combining with blood-thinning drugs, diuretic or lithium. Some sources on the internet suggest Nettle is unsafe in pregnancy, though there is little substantiating clinical evidence for this, whilst there is a long herbal tradition of Nettle being used in pregnancy – if considering this I would recommend consulting a herbalist and exploring it as part of an entire pregnancy support plan.

Correspondences: ᚃ Fearn (Alder) – protection, defence, path finding, endurance, resilience, growth, a bridge in conflict, shield. ᚠ Fehu – wealth, nourishment, fertility, abundance, generosity, spiritual protection, flowing energy. ♂ Mars – action, courage, initiation, purpose, passion, fire.

Herbalists and ritual: Nettle flagellation is a powerful ceremony and I would absolutely not recommend holding this yourself unless you've had extensive personal and group experiences with it, due to the strong effect (and long lasting, it can be 48 hours before all sign of the stings has gone). This is not only the effect on the physical, which can vary from minimal to really strong, but also the emotional processes this might activate. Whenever we bring this in I ensure that we have at least another two full days in ceremony together to process whatever has been touched. Fortunately Nettle tea (as a guided meditation) and Nettle oil (as an anointing ceremony) are both far gentler ways into ritual meeting, no less profound, but somewhat less provocative. Harvesting all parts of the Nettle, juicing, decocting roots and sieving seeds are all thoroughly enjoyable group activities.

Poppy

I am transfixed in stillness as I walk past one of these Poppies, sucked into their world. The delicate, striking petals draw me in, inviting me into a sweet melodious dream. For a moment everything quietens and it's just me and Poppy. The breeze whispers softly, and the sun on my skin feels like a gentle loving touch. There is an undeniable allure here that's hard to define, a playful seduction that is hard to turn away from.

Humans reach for opium, as we have done for thousands of years, for curiosity, pleasure and to soothe our pain. And sometimes, used skilfully and wisely, Poppy might teach through our dreams, become an ally and healer.

However, more often, we fall for opium's charms. We succumb to *this* particular pleasure without realising how we might be sacrificing our wider, more innate capacity for pleasure. We are seduced by the sweet numbing of those pains that we feel are beyond our ability to tend.

> A plant of pleasure and pain, an evocative muse, a
> cautionary tale, a dangerous curiosity.

Between the pursuit of pleasure and the quieting of pain, Opium Poppies and their many synthetic opioid descendants have woven themselves deeply into cultures worldwide. They have become emblems of how our desire for simple solutions to suffering can sometimes lead to greater pain.

In the US, three million people are addicted to opioids, while a baby is born every 15 minutes with neonatal opioid withdrawal syndrome. Each year 80,000 people die of opioid overdose, which is double the amount of those who die in road accidents.

Inducing sweet deep sleep, Poppy removes almost any form of pain and distress, and wraps us in a milky latex dream. This is a plant of rich colourful dreams, of beautiful fantasy, of profound relaxation of the body and soul. A friend once returned from Thailand having spent some time smoking opium there and assured me, *"I'm not addicted, but I'd really like a little more …"*

In my first lecture in Pharmacology at Edinburgh University, a melon-sized ball of opium was passed around the room. As I held it, something opened up in me: a sense of profound wonder at the dance between plants' biochemistry and our own, and the first glimpses of a dawning realisation that our evolution has always taken place alongside plants.

Dale Pendell, writing about another potent plant, *Salvia divinorum*, shares this provocative understanding: *"It is plants that have consciousness. Animals get consciousness by eating plants."* * Opium, throughout human history, has been a muse for dreaming, art and poetry. Opium has for some, for a moment at least, been an ally that lets the light of consciousness in.

Morphine (from Morpheus, God of Dreams), the best known of 80 alkaloids * found in Poppy, is an opioid receptor agonist, binding to μ-opioid receptors throughout our nervous system. It effectively mimics our naturally produced endorphins, known to be released through laughing, touch, sex and food. As morphine binds to these receptors, nerve impulses that we interpret as pain are blocked, but this is only part of the picture. Morphine also switches off GABAergic neurones * in the midbrain, allowing dopamine to flood the brain, potentially giving pleasure via the nucleus accumbens *, and quieting anxiety and fear by acting on the the amygdala. In addition to blocking pain and releasing pleasure, morphine also unlocks our dreaming. Despite the capacity to unlock potent and colourful dreams being known for millennia, the neuropharmacology of opium-induced dreaming is still little understood.

To open to Poppy is to reflect on our relationship to pleasure and pain, and to question how free our dreams are to fly.

How might it feel to be in sensual responsive relationship with our own endorphins, our own pleasure? On a recent online class, inviting in the presence of Poppy simply through painting and intention, Meltem shared:

> "Losing the edges of the I of me and I that is the being of the plant. Everything becomes a celebration, utterly delightful lightness of being. Fluttering excitement as if floating through a dream."
>
> *Meltem (2024)*

Do we truly listen to the voice of our pain and seek to listen more, follow its paths of wisdom, or do we numb it? Where do we sit on the edge between life-serving creative imagination and dissociative fantasy? Where do we live, lost within our dreams and where do we let our dreams give us the purpose to live?

> "To be free of weight and burden, remain fluid and soft. Most things are out of my control anyway, so surrender to what unfolds."
>
> *Glenn (2023)*

On one side, life can become numbed and flattened with the loss of playful fantasy. On the other, an epidemic of spiritual bypassing becomes anti-life. Pleasure nourishes us and feeds us, yet separation and trauma-driven hedonism – often dressed in spiritual robes – alienates us from our souls.

Our dreaming and our pleasure are crucial and enrich our lives, but if, in the allure of our dreams, we neglect the multiplicity of our relationships (inner and outer), we all end up even more alone and even more lost.

In the Poppy field

Mad Patsy said, he said to me,
That every morning he could see
An angel walking on the sky;
Across the sunny skies of morn
He threw great handfuls far and nigh
Of poppy seed among the corn;
And then, he said, the angels run
To see the poppies in the sun.

A poppy is a devil weed,
I said to him – he disagreed;
He said the devil had no hand
In spreading flowers tall and fair
Through corn and rye and meadow land,
By garth and barrow everywhere:
The devil has not any flower
But only money in his power.

And then he stretched out in the sun
And rolled upon his back for fun:
He kicked his legs and roared for joy
Because the sun was shining down:
He said he was a little boy
And would not work for any clown:
He ran and laughed behind a bee,
And danced for very ecstasy.

James Stephens, *The Hill of Vision*, 1912

Sleep whisperer · Pleasure's shadow · Death doorway

How does my dreaming nourish my life?
*Where might short-lived pleasures be keeping me
stuck or addicted?*

Which places in nature open up my dreaming?
How does connection to nature give me pleasure?
Which situations in life lead me to to feel numbed?

How do I find sensory pleasure in my life?
*Where might this slip into addiction? Might I ask a friend's perspective on
this? (We can be remarkably good at denial in such matters!)*

Traditional: Opium Poppies have been cultivated by humans for at least 4000 years. They are widely used in modern medicine to make morphine, codeine and numerous derivatives. These substances are powerful analgesics, often used in palliative end-of-life care. Opium Poppy is often referenced in Assyrian herbals; the Assyrians' contribution to ancient medicine was the establishment of organised medical care in their society, the echoes of which we can still see today in modern government-run medical systems.

Field Poppy, also know as Red Poppy (*Papaver rhoeas*) contains many similar alkaloids to Opium Poppy but is a much milder plant and has long been used in European medicine, particularly for children and in the elderly, notably as a mild analgesic and for irritable coughs. Recreational use of Poppy is often traced back to the British attempt to balance their trade deficit with China by importing opium from India to China. This resulted in much social instability in China, leading to the Opium Wars. In Britain, laudanum (opium tincture) was legal and cheaper than alcohol, leading to widespread use and addiction in the 19th century.

Botany: *Papaver somniferum*, Papaveraceae. The distinctive spherical-shaped seed capsule of poppy contains latex, from which the Opium is derived. Member of the Papaveraceae family, an annual that grows up to one metre tall, with dull green leaves and a solitary pink, purple or white flower atop. They are native to western Asia and are now cultivated commercially around the world as a source for Opium in the medical industry, and as an illegal crop to produce opium and heroin. Red Poppy or Field Poppy, is an annual, native to Europe and North Africa and temperate regions of Asia. They have a delicate hairy stem with a basal rosette of lance-shaped leaves. The red flowers have four petals with black anthers, and small spherical seed capsules.

Correspondences: ᚼ Huathe (Hawthorn) – careful steps in the face of obstacles, hidden knowledge, respect of boundaries, Fae doorway, protection. ᚼ Hagall (Hail) – resilience against adversity, sweeping clean, uncontrollable forces of nature, opening to flow. ☽ Moon – deep unconscious, dreaming, intuition, mystery, inner world.

Safety: Aside from a flower essence and Poppy seeds, all other forms of preparation are illegal/scheduled in UK. High risk of addiction. Poppy seeds, which are edible, are non-psychoactive and found in many foods.

Meeting Poppy: Poppies have such a bold presence, simply being in their flowering presence and taking time to receive them is enough for initial meetings. Drawing, sketching and the unique touch of the petals on skin are good ways into connection.

Primrose

Nestled below Dartington Hall, there's a beautiful brook cradled at the base of a small valley, adorned with Primroses. In this delicate haven I find solace, allowing the gift of grief and rage to settle within me.

Less than an hour ago, on the lunch break, I could tell that something was surfacing in Lara, one of the students on the Holistic Science programme. We sit together and she tells me a poignant story of the loss of her fiancé who died suddenly in an avalanche just a few weeks ago.

Such conversations often begin at a threshold, where words are delivered with a measured distance and restrained emotion. In this sacred space, whether influenced by the tender embrace of the Primroses or the receptive presence of a fellow human, a transformative crack appears in the composed veneer of grief. The atmosphere shifts, thickening with a profound energy reminiscent of deep regression or the enchantment spun by a gifted storyteller.

Her rage starts to surface and before I know it, I'm holding her as a rage with the force of an avalanche fills the room with resounding yells that surely echo halfway across the campus. Though accustomed to holding ritual spaces and expanding my capacity to accommodate whatever emerges, the sheer intensity of this outpouring leaves me momentarily shaken.

The anguished cries eventually subside, replaced by a palpable exhaustion and the quiet sobbing that follows. Grief permeates the room, the same current of sorrow experienced universally for love lost. The earlier rage now a distant memory, swept away by the overwhelming tide of mourning for love that once was.

Grief, a paradox of individual and shared experiences, is profoundly personal while also serving as the most powerful gateway to empathy.

To grieve is to swim in an ocean of our ancestors' tears. Grieving allows us to navigate the potent currents of love and loss, currents that transcend cultural, religious and temporal differences. To grieve is to surrender to these depths, releasing our grasp on certainty, allowing ourselves to be temporarily pulled under, unfreezing the barriers and permitting the tears to flow.

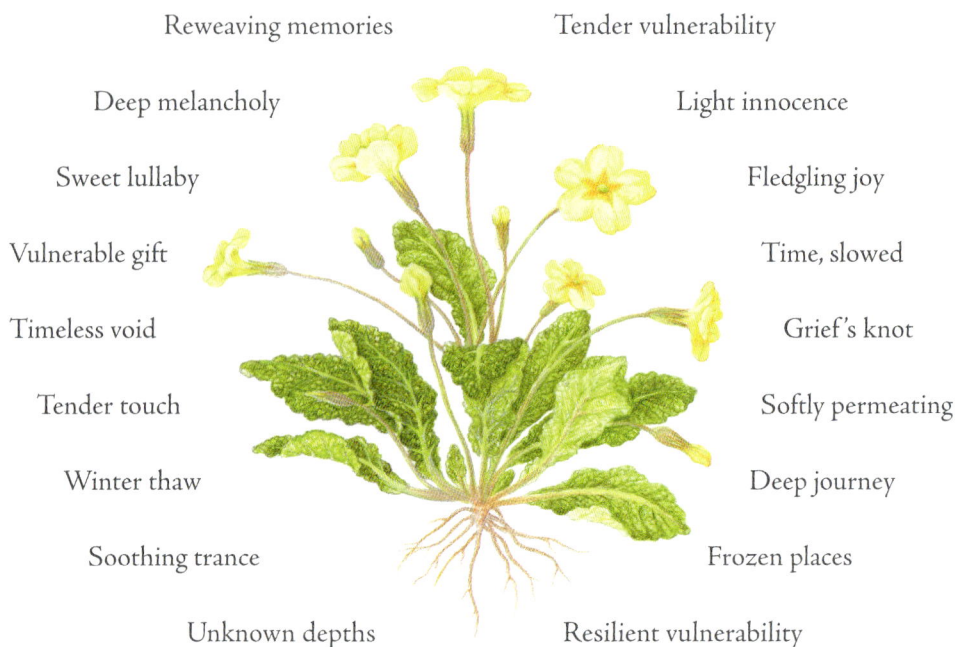

Reweaving memories   Tender vulnerability

Deep melancholy   Light innocence

Sweet lullaby   Fledgling joy

Vulnerable gift   Time, slowed

Timeless void   Grief's knot

Tender touch   Softly permeating

Winter thaw   Deep journey

Soothing trance   Frozen places

Unknown depths   Resilient vulnerability

The frozen places inside us, often hidden and wrapped in shame, are reservoirs of untapped life waiting to be lived. But before they can receive the warm breath of life, they need to be found. Before they can bask in the soft, warm light of spring, they must choose to welcome this warmth, choose to trust, and ultimately, choose to embrace life anew.

Primrose brings in a quiet presence, an unexpected gravity. Time slows and it feels as if the busyness of life is paused momentarily. In these pauses a delicate dance unfolds, weaving together profound beauty and profound grief. These pauses offer the opportunity to gaze into ancient pools of ancestral pain, discovering the tender resilience in our hearts, enabling us to hear both our own cries and the echoes of those who came before us.

The infusion of the flowers has a soft yellow hue, offering a delicate sweetness. Sipping it feels like being enveloped in ethereal veils, a gentle embrace that simultaneously nurtures a sense of security and delicately touches the edges of our wounds – some of which we may have long forgotten.

I've called on Primrose when supporting those navigating deep grief, individuals gradually integrating painful historic trauma and and others finding their way amidst realisations about early-life experiences of sexual or emotional abuse. The gift of Primrose lies in its ability to unlock the door to feeling.

They are gentle plants, yet remarkably potent in effect. A friend in the thawing of the frozen places of ourselves.

The healing of these inner spaces is not a swift process, nor does it occur within mere weeks or months. Instead, with the passage of time and gentle companionship, these frozen places may gradually soften, allowing the bright, concealed aspects of ourselves, beneath the pain, to surface.

How do I welcome the frozen parts of myself?
What insights, creativity, needs and perceptions do those parts bring?
Are there parts of myself I have forgotten or even given up on?

How does grief feel in my body?
How have I hidden my grief, and why?

Might time and space be the most needed medicine just now?
Why do I not give myself this?

Where might I express my love more through tenderness and patience?
Where have I hardened myself?
Where has my care slipped into caretaking and co-dependency?

Traditional: Primrose flowers (and root) have been traditionally recognised as a relaxant and an anxiolytic, whilst the leaves are known to make a good green wound salve. Historically, Primrose was often recommended for gout and paralysis whilst today, Primroses are mostly well regarded for their effect on nervousness and anxiety as a simple flower infusion.

Botany: *Primula vulgaris*, Primulaceae, is closely related to Cowslip and Oxlip. They are perennial, sometimes decades old, love to grow in shady banks. Flowering February to April; do notice the pin and thrum forms! There are many cultivars (often found at garden centres and municipal planting schemes), and I would not recommend taking any of these internally; some *Primula* species are known to trigger contact dermatitis.

Safety: Primrose has few safety concerns, and Primrose flower tea, though little known in Britain, has a rich tradition of use in Europe. Caution – sometimes internet searches will bring up Evening Primrose when searching for Primrose; they are very different plants. Do not consume other cultivated Primula species.

Correspondences: ᚇ Duir (Oak) – sovereignty, resilience, perception of the invisible, growth, protection, crossing of boundaries. ᛚ Daeg (Dawn) – awakenings, new beginnings, hope, positive change, clarity, things coming to light. ♀ Venus – beauty, creativity, relationship, harmony.

Meeting Primrose: In late February, when there is little in flower aside from the Hazel catkins, Winter Honeysuckle and the occasional brave Plum tree, Primrose is such a welcome friend to mark the tentatively emerging spring. Often growing on woodland edges or by the banks of streams, spending time lying amongst them, ideally soaking up a little of the early year sunshine, is one of the seasonal rituals I most look forward to.

Practitioners and ritual: Primrose, as a fresh or dried petal tea, can be brought into many emotionally delicate spaces, particularly when working with grief or historical trauma. They invite a spacious slowness, allowing the delicate unmasking of our survival self and the slow discovering of a truer self. There is no rush with Primrose, and the space invited, without any judgment or pressure to heal, does itself catalyse the healing process. They can help open sensitivity to the non-physical layers of us – those boundaries of self that exist inches or feet away from us, which, through not knowing them, we inadvertently (and often repeatedly) allow to be violated. Tied in with this is their gentle meeting of the freeze (trauma) response in us, itself often an old response to violated boundaries. For journeying and regression work, Primrose is a wonderful ally when working with inner children, and is particularly suited to supporting winter to spring inner transitions. As a practitioner, these awakenings can be delicate, thus the companionship of both plant and practitioner is invaluable here; there is always the chance of a late frost.

Rose

Many of our deepest wounds are double wounds. The first, feeling stung, violated or neglected, sent us into shock, into disassociation. But if it were just this, we would return to ourselves, renew and heal, as is the way of nature.

However, if there is a second wound, a more subtle one, part of us may stay disassociated. This second wound is the one where we are not seen in our distress, where there was no one there to have our back, where we felt alone in the world with our pain. This can feel too much, the aloneness and isolation of it unbearable. Alone, we abandon part of ourselves, numb it and in time, often entirely forget it.

Yet our body, our heart, our soul longs for all of us. There is a calling deep inside for the scattered parts of ourselves to return home, for our fragmented self to find its own loving ecosystem of belonging in this fragile human body. Rose has been at the core of the school I founded since we began, and this is the reason.

Few herbs have quite the power,
to gather scattered parts of ourselves as Rose,
to soften, warm and open our hearts,
to the very things we are most scared of.

Rose doesn't do this alone; we have to follow the invitation, choose to go seeking, choose to walk into the unknown of ourselves, call ourselves back and feel the forgotten pain of our lost fragments. To be wrapped in Rose for a moment is a balm and in this there is healing for sure. But to take the doorway offered and walk a deeper path with Rose brings a more profound healing. A coming home to ourselves and a life guided by the innate trust and love that the depths of our hearts know.

I find that most people are very receptive to Rose. Few remain untouched by the delicacy of *Rosa canina*, the wild Rose in the painting. These delicate, thorned beauties can be found weaving themselves through hedgerows with an agile brightness, robustness and beautiful five-petalled flowers. Some of the more scented Roses we meet, *Rosa damascena, Rosa gallica*, can be overpowering if prepared too strongly, though sometimes there is a more subtle reason for the overwhelm and repulsion here. Sometimes, in a Rose ceremony, the person who initially had the strongest revulsion to Rose will, in the following months, receive the strongest initiation.

These Rose initiations are often related to the maternal attachment wound, the pain of not receiving the tenderness so crucial to our development. This wound is often a complex mix of emotional or physical absence alongside an overbearing presence (a care-giver who unconsciously tries to meet their emotional needs through the child), leading to a complex rift of insecure-attachment patterns. Exploring these wounds can feel like navigating a minefield of blame and guilt. These wounds are always deeply ancestral, cultural, systemic and often rooted in patriarchy. Understanding this, stepping back a little from the rawness of our individual experience to the recognition of a collective wound, can help bring compassion and

Permeating love   Softly enveloping

Making space   Infinite trust

Tender grief   Deep sigh

Gentle touch   Unravelling sorrow

Loving embrace   Re-mothering

kindness to the healing here. Furthermore, it can help save us from dead-end individualism and thrust us into a more collective movement, lifting everyone. My work in herbalism is inspired by seeing that, if we tend to our earthly-attachment wound, that to the land, some of our attachment needs can be eased and partially met through our relationships with myriad non-human beings.

When opening a Rose ceremony we often start with a simple, yet powerful exercise. In pairs, within a framework of consent, one person offers a palm to the back of the other's heart. I've come to notice that our attachment wounds often affect our ability to receive love more than to give it. In fact, some of the most loving people I've met deeply struggle to receive; perhaps because the wound that is touched in the vulnerability of receiving is too painful to approach. The lack of a secure-attachment foundation sends ripples through every relationship, including our relationship with ourselves.

The dense, thorny thickets of *Rosa canina* offer a similar ecological paradise to their close relative Bramble, providing pollen for countless insects and safe nesting for small birds. The fleshy rose hips give good winter fodder to all manner of small creatures whilst their adaptability and genetic variability lies behind the tens of thousands of cultivars, testament to thousands of years of creative human co-evolution.

We have around 15 varieties of Rose growing in the school herb garden, some thriving with incredible abundance and some struggling in the north-facing, somewhat exposed environment here. Roses tend to thrive when very well fed and somewhat protected from the extremes of wind and cold, leading

to a rich British tradition of walled Rose gardens. Though entirely captivated by the scent of these cultivars, I find myself touched in a different way if I unexpectedly encounter a climbing wild Rose on a woodland's edge or in a hedgerow.

Something stills in me, a delicacy touches my heart, a quiet reminder of the possibility of being both toughly resilient and holding my heart open in exquisite tenderness. Rose has spoken to us humans for millennia; their medicine and their invitation are no less needed now than they have ever been.

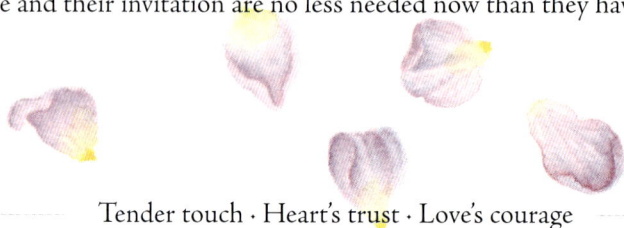

Tender touch · Heart's trust · Love's courage

How does my heart feel right now? What helps me open it?
How does Rose help me to feel uncomfortable feelings?

Where am I being asked to trust life?
Where have I hardened my heart to protect myself?

How does my heart make decisions? Do I trust these decisions?
How do I sabotage my heart's knowing?

How resilient and strong are the boundaries I need to keep my heart open?
Where do I neglect to defend my heart's own needs and boundaries?

Traditional: Many of the traditional uses of Rose relate to an understanding of their cooling quality and thus have been used for conditions related to excess heat and inflammation. The petals of wild Rose have cooling and astringent qualities that have been used to support conditions such as diarrhoea, menstrual cramps, fevers and inflammation. Rose hips have very high quantities of vitamin C, leading to the popularity of Rose hip syrup during the Second World War in Britain to help enhance immunity. They are nutrient rich, bioavailable, astringent and anti-inflammatory, and have been used traditionally in diarrhoea and arthritis. The oil from the seeds is valued topically on the skin as an anti-inflammatory. Research points towards potent anti-inflammatory, anti-oxidant and anti-cancer effects as well as healing effects for various Rose preparations for pain, anxiety and UTIs following caesarian section.

Emotionally and mentally, Rose has long been valued for soothing and uplifting the nervous system, in anxiety, insomnia and for an emotionally bruised heart. Spiritually, Rose holds a sacred place in many cultures around the world, and very much for me and the school, as a gateway to divine love and the path of the heart.

Botany: *Rosa canina*, Rosaceae. Dog Rose is a rambling deciduous shrub found in hedgerows, with thorny stems and five-petalled white or pink flowers. There are at least 14 varieties of wild Rose that grow native in Britain. Flowers are gathered in midsummer and the deep red hips collected in the autumn. The name Dog Rose may have been given for a number of reasons, possibly because the root was believed to be useful in treating dog bites, a remedy that dates back to Pliny, or that 'dog' derives from 'dag', referring to the dagger-like thorns of the plant.

Safety: When using the hips, ensure that the hairy seeds are removed as they are irritating. Many sources list Rose's use as contraindicated in pregnancy though the evidence for this is far from convincing; recent research suggests Rose oil can be safe and useful for lower back pain in pregnancy.

Correspondences: ᚻ Huathe (Hawthorn), community and connection, protection and vulnerability, fertility, growth, and transformation, spiritual. ᚺ Hagall, growth, renewal, devotion, transformation, balance and harmony, acceptance of change. ♀ Venus, love, beauty, fertility, abundance, reverence for the natural world.

Meeting Rose: Spend time with the living plant, both the wild Rose of the hedgerows and a cultivated Rose that speaks to you. All Roses carry a different energy, let yourself be drawn to one. I'd advise caution around Rose preparations unless from a good supplier, as there are a lot of synthetic Rose waters and oils on the market.

Herbalists and ritual: Rose has been the axis around which the School of Intuitive Herbalism grew, and my respect for them has only deepened over two decades of sharing and working with Rose. Rose can reliably touch the heart, often in a gentle, easy-to-receive way, but not always. I find that in around one in five to ten people they can touch something deeply painful, something that may provoke a revulsion, strong emotions or an overwhelm response. Deep care, compassion and tenderness are needed to support people in this journey of meeting their heart, since deep wounds, particularly mother-wounds, are easily touched here. Distilling Rose in midsummer is a joy.

St. John's Wort

The most powerful teachings from plants often come to us in our darkest times. St. John's Wort was the first plant to reveal to me that plants can be more than just remedies, they can be teachers. They don't just affect us physically; they can also show our hearts, bodies and minds new ways of being. They awaken visions drawn from our deep collective unconscious, reminding us of who we are and who we might become. A few years ago, in the quiet darkness of night, overcome by terrifying flashbacks, St. John's Wort came to me again.

> Radiant sword, seer of light,
>
> Holy anointment, piercing rays
>
> Shrinking mental demons to their true size

Sadly, I'm sure many of you can relate to the portals of cold fear that can open in the small hours of the morning. At that time, when the dream world and reality blur, I found myself frozen in terror – viscerally reliving early life experiences of abandonment. I reached for a jar of blood red oil. Touching it to my heart, St. John's Wort's warmth penetrated and spread, bringing life and fire where a moment ago there was only cold.

There is no better way to meet St John's Wort than to seek them out at midsummer and make an infused oil. Carefully collect the bright yellow flowers and those flower buds just on the verge of opening, and add them to cold-pressed sesame oil. As far as I'm aware, this is the only plant where direct sunlight is essential for its preparation – leave this jar of oil somewhere warm and exposed to sun, checking it daily as the greens and yellows slowly turn deep red.

The oil is just as much a preparation of the sun as it is a preparation of the plant. Depending on the weather, the oil will become thick and blood-red over two to three weeks. For many trainee herbalists, this is their first experience of alchemy in action, discovering the deep joy in tending to this alchemical process whilst knowing how to welcome this stored sunshine later in the year when the sun is low and scarce.

St John's Wort is a well-known plant 'for depression'; I have come to understand them far more broadly as a plant of vision and warmth. As we rediscover our inner seeing, our inner sun, our inner warmth and our vision for ourselves, the heavy fog of depression lifts. Amongst a myriad of pharmacological actions *, this is a plant that helps lift serotonin, which is, perhaps, our body's own expression of internalised sunshine.*

I'm not sure how useful it is to think of depression as an individual problem. In these times of massive environmental and social jeopardy and upheaval, we all need a vision we can believe in. In the process of writing this book, as I take a little time out from my teaching, clinic and even to some degree, my friendships, I'm being reminded again and again – the warmth of our hearts, our deep empathy, our ability to surrender to life and love – all of these need to dance hand in hand with our vision. It is not easy to find the balance, to be true to all these aspects of ourselves.

Our vision is important – it isn't just for ourselves, but also for the human-plant-earth ecosystem we are part of. We are in a time where many long-established visions and cultural mythologies are collapsing, and new ones, born from relationship with each other and the earth, are desperately needed.

To move forward in confidence, we need our vision to heed our hearts, just as our hearts heed our vision. We need clear purpose and direction as much as we need to meet each other in deep and equitable acceptance.

I've seen many students exploring St John's Wort feel the presence of the sun and light in this plant, often touching their own internalised father archetypes. There's an invitation to come into relationship with a certain clarity of light, purpose and vision in oneself, an invitation that can sometimes be overwhelming but is more often restorative, inspiring

and reassuring. Sometimes those who are already overstimulated in the realm of ideas and vision find this plant can amplify the overwhelm, whilst those feeling lost, numbed or lacking direction find them a valuable ally.

For many, our inner mother and father archetypes carry deep wounds, both from personal experiences growing up, as well as ancestral and systemic threads of neglect, abuse and pain. Where, in an ideal world, there might be a harmonious loving dance here, these internalised aspects of ourselves fight, bruised and battered, berating each other from corners of the room of life, at times dominating in superficial machismo, at times shrinking in fear, distrust and uncertainty.

Finding mutual love and respect may take a lifetime, but it is vital for healing both personal and cultural wounds.

> Ennobled in heart's forge
> Brightening our radiant brow
> Choosing to trust in
> The sometime hidden,
> But never fading light.

A beacon of midsummer fire, St. John's Wort can make visible our nascent vision, kindle our inner fire and light the way for that fragile next step ahead of us. They are the only plant where I've had the experience of people looking away from them, turning their gaze aside from an overwhelming bright intensity and pressure on the area of their third eye. This bright midsummer plant speaks to me of Gwion, who became Taliesin, legendary bard of Welsh mythology, a name than can be translated 'shining brow'; Taliesin, who inadvertently sipped a drop from Ceridwen's cauldron of wisdom and, in that moment, received the gift of wisdom and prophesy.

Whilst I can't quite promise that, a little of St. John's Wort's liquid sunshine, be that as oil, tea or tincture, can carry us far on the journey of letting our brows shine and our hearts radiate with midsummer's warmth.

What ideas and vision do I need to take action on?

What gives me a sense of joyful purpose?

Do I struggle with this and if so how might St. John's Wort help?

How do I receive light and inspiration?

Where do I feel blocked in this? What is sabotaging this?

What do I see and feel when I envision the future?

What might St. John's Wort bring to this seeing?

Traditional: St. John's Wort has been valued for millennia, sometimes as a panacea (cure-all) and more recently as a treatment for depression. The name St. John's Wort is a Christianisation of an older summer solstice festival, and where we live in the UK, they seem to (fairly reliably) flower on summer solstice, true to their name. Many of the names given to this plant, for example 'devil's scourge' and 'demon-flight' reference a deep tradition of hanging them on doors, above shrines and burning them as offerings in bonfires to drive away evil influences. The deep red oil is a valuable for treating wounds and burns, as well as for its antiviral effects on herpes simplex. It can also be used for nerve pain such as sciatica.

The use in depression is well researched [*], widely accepted and considered to have fewer adverse effects than equivalent pharmaceutical antidepressants. The antidepressant action is thought to be mediated by many different compounds including hyperforin, hypericin and pseudohypericin. These compounds are believed to reduce the re-uptake of several mood-regulating neurotransmitters, including serotonin, dopamine, norepinephrine (noradrenaline), GABA, and glutamate.[*] By reducing re-uptake within the synaptic cleft, greater quantities of these neurotransmitters are available to diffuse into the postsynaptic surface, thereby enhancing their effects. Research has also indicated value in reducing menopausal symptoms.[*] Whilst the pharmacological discoveries are fascinating, our understanding of depression remains incomplete. Neurological models are just one part of a broader picture, one that recognises and addresses damaging cultural and systemic forces [*] which often lead to depression.

Botany: *Hypericum perforatum*, I Iyperiaceae. Native to Britain and Europe, but often considered a weed where they have been introduced (such as in Australia and New Zealand). This is a perennial plant, growing to around 0.5m, with strong erect stems, small elliptical leaves and bright yellow flowers with five petals and numerous long yellow stamens. Our experience is that they only grow for a few years in the herb garden, though are quickly replaced by volunteers growing from seed. This particular *Hypericum* (and there are many) is distinguished by the tiny holes in the leaves, which can be seen when holding up a leaf to the sky. The flower buds are rich in a dark red oil that can be seen if you squash one between your fingers. This is the most potent part of the plant, meaning there can be a short harvesting window for this, often around summer solstice. In some countries, sale of St John's Wort is restricted.

Safety: St. John's Wort has many drug interactions, the most common of which are listed in the end notes.[*] Don't use in combination with other pharmaceutical medications (including the contraceptive pill) unless you have reviewed this thoroughly for yourself or are working with an experienced herbalist. Both internal and external preparations can also cause photosensitivity, so be particularly aware of excess exposure to UV light if taking this. The plant is toxic to many grazing animals, though they will generally ignore it unless it becomes accidentally mixed in with hay or silage. This is a potent plant, but worked with appropriately, with respect and care, is safe.

Correspondences: ᚛ Duir (Oak) – steadfast, protection, strength, truth, door to wisdom. ᛞ Daeg – enlightenment, awakening, non-duality, vision, day, ideals, moments of illumination and change. ☉ Sun – vision, activation, purpose, direction, healthy ego.

Meeting St. John's Wort: Preparing a little of your own oil around midsummer solstice is a beautiful way to get to know this plant. Even if you don't have access to many plants you can still start small, even half a jam jar works well. Cover the fresh (but not damp) flowers and buds with oil (I prefer cold-pressed sesame oil, but almond or olive oil can also be used – I'd avoid sunflower oil as it goes rancid quickly). Cover with a light cloth so the moisture can evaporate and check daily. If the weather is cloudy, it can help to give the process a little boost by warming the jar up a little in a water bath for a few hours, allowing any excess moisture to evaporate.

Herbalists and ritual: Of all the plants, St. John's Wort is met well through a simple quiet sitting meditation, bringing awareness to the forehead and pineal gland, which are often activated by this plant's presence when in flower. A slow, conscious, anointing with the oil is a rich way to meet this later in the season.

Silver Birch

Merlin, a name given to the Welsh prophet, Myrddin Wyllt, was a fatherless child, wild bard and magician, born of the forest. One of his earlier names was Merlin Sylvestris, Merlin of the woods. It is in these woods Merlin received the gift of prophecy.

Deep in the ancient Caledonian forest, a realm of the trees, of Oak, Pine, Birch, Rowan, Aspen and Juniper, he learnt to channel the wisdom of the land, the wisdom of the trees and the wisdom of the beasts.

Silver Birch is the brightest of these trees, emanating liquid light, the white of their bark reflecting and amplifying the light of the sun and moon; the light canopy of leaves whispering an ancient watchfulness. That Merlin is fatherless is significant, freeing him from human ties, emissary of a deeper wisdom of the earth and the stars.

Tree of new beginnings
Bright woodland pioneer

Birch is the first of the Ogham, a tree of new beginnings, a first coloniser of land amongst trees. Merlin is a key figure within the Celtic mythic masculine, but the key here is this masculine is born of the Goddess, of mythic feminine, of the womb of the land.

The rekindling of deeper masculine archetypes, beyond the corruptions of patriarchy, feels urgent; so many male-identified people I know struggle to find purpose and meaning in this collapsing world, and I believe that it is in the wisdom of the wild that we can find this again.

203

To step into Birch woodland is to be invited to step into dreaming. To rest within the gentle holding and potentised silence of this bright presence. Fiona's painting speaks to a time of deep hibernation, of stillness and from this regenerative stillness the possibility of the emergence of the new.

Birch has a long folklore related to cleansing and renewal; bundles of Birch twigs, the original broomstick, have been used to beat out old spirits, 'beating the bounds' of land and 'switching' with fresh Birch 'vihta' in a sauna.

Birch is the companion to the Birch polypore (mostly saprophyte, growing on dead trees) and *Amanita* (symbiotic, in relationship with the living roots), both important allies to me. Every October I collect a few of the satisfyingly smooth Birch polypores which we dry above the fire and brew up with ginger to support my family's immunity through the winter. An infusion, made from young Birch leaves, feels cleansing, bright and clear.

Tapping Birch trees for the abundantly flowing sap is a well-known skill of bushcraft, but I've become wary of the damage this likely causes the tree, damage that only shows years later, so it's not a practice I encourage. Birch is not as resilient to tapping as Maple.* Taking a small amount of bark which is already flaking off does not harm the tree. This bark has been used for many things; as a material to write on, for making fine bark boxes, and as the lining of canoes. Fiona, as part of her apprenticeship, made a ritual cloak from it.

Birch invites in a time for rest and clarity, revisioning and reconfiguring. Birch's bright spaciousness offers the possibility of new perspectives, new visions, new directions and the safe holding to rest and hibernate, shedding something of the old in this letting go. Birches tend to be young, rarely more than 100 years old. They are a tree of beginnings and pioneering. Among a stand of Silver Birch, allow this presence to help the threads of the old to loosen, making way for the quiet emergence of the new.

Dream gateway · Forest hermit · Deep rest · Bright wisdom

Invitation: Take time out to rest, to remember the holding and refuge to be found in nature.

What new beginnings are calling me?
Where might I be holding on to the old?

How do I value my need for hibernation?
Where am I overriding my needs for rest and stillness?

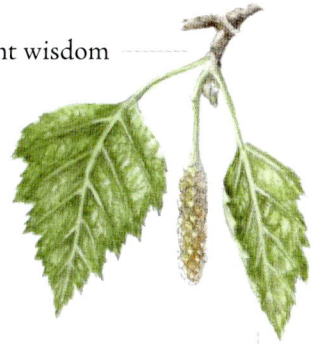

Traditional: Birch leaf tea has a traditional reputation for arthritis and oedema, and as a spring tonic. The tea can also be used as a cooling astringent wash for inflamed skin. The wood of Birch contains betulin, which is found in Birch polypore as betulinic acid and is now being explored for immunomodulatory and anti-cancer [*], effects. Birch polypore is known to have been used by humans over 5000 years ago.[*]

Botany: *Betula pendula*, family Betulaceae, is one of various species of Birch found in Britain. They are well known as short-lived woodland pioneers (100 years or so) and prized for their distinctive silver-white bark and bright canopy.

Safety: Birch sap and young leaf tea are generally considered safe in culinary quantities, though tapping Birch sap can damage the tree. Leaf tea is diuretic so professional advice should be taken if already taking diuretics. Possible allergy to Betulaceae family.

Correspondences: ᛒ Beith (Birch) – purification and renewal, Celtic divine feminine, cycles of life, clarity and vision. ᛒ Beorc (Birch) – rebirth, new beginnings, patience, fertility, clearing old energies, initiation. ♀ Venus – beauty, harmony, elegance, love, renewal, sensory awakening.

Meeting, herbalists and ritual: Silver Birch invites long, slow nature immersions, ideally overnight, with time for solitude. I particularly enjoy and recommend hammocking amongst the trees for a full immersion. Birch woodland carries such a presence little additional ritual is needed, indeed too much can take away from the experience. Simple frameworks such as finding sit-spots, stilling breath meditations and time for gentle group reflections can all add to the experience. Birch, Oak or Conifer woodland can all offer a good contrast – a night spent in each very effectively shows up their profoundly contrasting presences.

Valerian

How can a plant simultaneously invoke the repulsion felt towards the pungent odour of a urine-soaked male goat and, in the next breath, inspire a desire to crawl inside the same plant and make a cosy nest?

I've come to expect such marked contradictions in groups meeting Valerian, yet with time, nearly all initial aversions transform into something else. Sometimes the smell repulses, sometimes it softens us into a warm, peaceful nest of deep convalescence, sometimes it excites and unlocks a mischievous playfulness, sometime it causes people to catch their breath with a reminder of their own capacity for deep sensuality and pleasure.

This is a plant that needs to be called on judiciously and wisely. The key lies in sensitivity to both dosage and the method of meeting. A drop of root tincture has the potential to overwhelm an individual who might otherwise find a gentle spritz of Valerian flower hydrosol a welcome and inviting experience.

The root, although better known in herbalism, can be a heavy-handed way into meeting. The flowers, with their mist of hazy fragrance, offer an invitation few refuse. As we distil this white-pink blossom, the room becomes soft and quiet, as if the air thickens and the sharp edges of sounds are buffered. It becomes increasingly difficult for me to maintain a thought to the end of a sentence. In fact, thought just generally feels far too much effort.

Breath deepens, muscles soften. Each person becomes both more internal and more connected at the same time; their edges appear soft and malleable, flowing gently into each other. A ripple of laughter follows its path through these softened, merged energies, followed by a wave of tender sadness. Few remain sitting; bodies feel the force of gravity in a way that quietly whispers, "Why fight me? Just give in to gravity".

There's a warmth here, like the embers of a fire. Deep, penetrating, reminding us of our animal warmth. The scent, like a healthy aura of body odour, un-scrubbed and un-sanitised, wraps each person in themselves like a second skin, like an etheric version of the waxy vernix that coats newborn babies. These warming embers echo with those deep within our body, softly stirred by the warm breath of life-affirming oxygen.

In this embodied warmth are many possible un-foldings. For some, deep rest calls, Valerian offering a reminder of the tiredness they carry and an invitation to let go of the weight of the world on their shoulders. Others may find a whimsical companionship emerging, marked by laughter and a playful, Pan-like mischievousness. Meanwhile, for others still, this inner warmth unfurls gradually, activating their sensual body, tenderly easing their muscles and gradually revealing a pulsing awakening throughout their entire being. It becomes a remembrance of embodied pleasure, a recognition that this experience is uniquely ours; though it may be shared or unlocked by others, at its core, it belongs to us to savour and enjoy.

I take a break from the room to fetch some spring water and am struck by the softness in my vision, the play of light and sound all around. I feel buffered from the breeze, peaceful. I almost forget my task, enjoying the warm sun, pausing long enough for any previous thoughts to disintegrate.

Ten minutes later I return. Opening the door, the thickness of Valerian's scent hits me. The room is quiet. Everyone drifts happily in their own meetings with this potent plant. I feel called to sing a little – a gentle lullaby, wordless, flowing simple melodies to a slow heartbeat. The sound touches this thickened air and lands softly on each person, their bodies receiving these vibrations as a gentle balm of homecoming.

In the ethereal realm of Valerian's gentle embrace and playfulness, sound transcends mere auditory perception. It becomes a tactile presence, lapping at the edges of our skin, moving within us, dancing in synchrony with the living pulsing being of our bodies. The inherent truth of music as vibration is felt viscerally, offering an experience of these vibrations as regulators, re-balancers, and restructuring forces. Valerian extends an invitation to dissolve into this rhythmic vibrational landscape, discovering profound nourishment and sustenance in its embrace.

Valerian can be many things, and in my work as herbalist and edge-walker I invite them as a gateway plant, a being possessing the power to soften the edges and unveil doorways to other plants and experiences. Used with skill, they can soften the most rigid and frozen of us, guiding us towards a realm of playful, sensual freedom.

Weighted blanket

Deep massage

Slow motion

Sweet hypnosis

Feline ecstasy

Softly sensual

Awakened eros

Calm ocean

Thickly heady

Liquid spine

Earthy richness

Deep purr

Stuck in the mud

Animal self

Elastic limbs

Rhythmic release

Feral dancer

Delicately ethereal

Weaver of dreams

Heavy honey

Liminal liberation

Dissolving thoughts

Mysterious mistress

Elegant power

Letting go · Sensual surrender · Playful dissolution

When do I fully surrender and let go?
What helps me to do this?
Where am I holding myself in a state of tension? Why?
Where in my life are my attempts to relax actually a form of numbing?

How do I awaken my soft, sensual being?
How have I armoured this or hidden this from myself?

Where can I allow playful merging with others, a soft dissolving in relationship and connection?
Where do I feel distrust and keep distance?

Traditional: Valerian has a firm reputation as a relaxant and sedative in traditional and modern herbalism. They are used widely for anxiety, stress, poor sleep and as an antispasmodic, particularly for the gut, lungs and womb. Valerian has been extensively researched [*], a brief overview of this research can be found in the endnotes.

Botany: *Valeriana officinalis*, Valerianaceae, is a perennial thriving in full sun and damp rich soils. The white-pink, strongly scented flowers appear in early summer, and the root is generally harvested in late autumn.

Safety: Valerian can have rather unpredictable effects on different individuals, so any internal use should start at a very low dosage so as to better gauge individual response. Professional advice should be taken if combining with any psychoactive medications such as tranquillisers, antidepressants or mood stabilisers (in all these cases the effect of the combination may be unpredictable) and in pregnancy and breastfeeding. Avoid combining with alcohol and do not drive or operate machinery for several hours after taking Valerian.

Correspondences: ᛚ Luis (Rowan) – enchantment, protection from harmful influences, insight, intuition. ᛚ Lagaz (Sea) – intuition, emotion, unconscious, flow, adaptability. ☿ Mercury – alchemical transformation, the trickster, harmony between intuition and intellect, exploration of the unknown, insight.

Meeting Valerian: Seek out the flowering plant around midsummer and let yourself dream and journey with the scent. Valerian preparations can be found easily; if meeting through this I'd recommend buying dried root and starting with a pinch of dried root infused in boiling water, building up from this if it feels appropriate. Alternatively, you could try a few drops of tincture in hot water.

Herbalists and ritual: Valerian is a powerful plant to bring into ritual. My experience is that the flower, fresh or as a hydrosol, is a gentle way to introduce this plant. The fresh root is extremely evocative, often provoking very immediate and strong responses, whilst the dried root or tincture has the most varied and unpredictable responses, sometimes euphoric and sometimes powerfully sedative. This variance is possibly due to the difficulty finding a suitable dose for all since whilst one individual might respond strongly to a single drop of tincture, another might be hardly touched by 10ml. The effect of Valerian is often both immediate and prolonged, sometimes lasting for several hours. The sphere of consciousness invited by Valerian can lend itself well to exploring embodied practice, somatic meditation and guided journeys, though navigating these dreamy, soft landscapes as a practitioner takes experience and skill – definitely not for a beginner. Worked with skilfully, Valerian can give profound experiences of deep parasympathetic relaxation, sometimes an offering so profound that people comment that it is the most relaxed they ever remember feeling. This is a strong plant and should only be used with others when you have extensive experience with Valerian yourself.

Vervain

In the days leading up to writing about Vervain I felt such a sense of relief. This plant is such an old friend, an ally for 25 years, and to write about them feels like sharing something deeply sacred. They invite in me a deep out-breath and a reminder of the quiet beauty of life. Simply thinking of Vervain instantly brings a smile and the feeling of a brushing a cool, calming comb through the busy chaos of my brain.

I've known cultivated Vervain for a long time, but the first time I met Vervain in the wild was in Italy, whilst on a writing and painting retreat with Fiona. It was hot and dry, and the woods buzzed with cicadas. Lizards darted out from the side of the road as I followed the mountain trail in the hills of Arcevia. Suddenly, on a curve in the path, the view opened up to a clearing with some ruins and a bench. Vervain grew all around, seemingly not challenged by the hard-baked ground and lack of moisture. The place had a potency to it, a gravitas, and a grief. All things I feel a deep draw and affinity to. There was a plaque near the bench and slowly (with my very limited Italian) I worked out that this was a memorial; the building remains had been intentionally left to remember an entire family that was lined up and shot by Nazi soldiers in the Second World War. A shiver went down my spine as I started to understand why this place had a feeling of such depth. It was the same feeling I'd had visiting a concentration camp-turned-memorial close to Berlin when I was 18.

There are times when we are so lost, so deep in hopeless despair or exhausted depression, that it feels like nothing can touch us. Witnessing people in this place in my practice is heartbreaking, with every part of me wanting to reach out and make the world safe for them again. In these times, many of the usual approaches and herbs feel like they hardly touch the surface of their pain.

It is here that Vervain reveals their unique ability to dive deep with us, to companion us in the depths of darkness, to gently and steadily bring tiny specks of light to the path. This isn't something that happens immediately, but over weeks and months. Vervain slowly finds their way into the cage of our confusion and can untangle the threads of perception and memory that hold us there.

> "A beauty so fine it moves me to tears."
>
> *Sara Ghanchi (2022)*

In the same way that talk therapy is rarely a quick solution to deep wounds, Vervain's magic reveals itself slowly, as they somehow help to unstick the stories of trauma with the experiences of the moment. They enable us to undertake the underworld journey that has been too painful, too hard to previously consider.

Trauma, un-met, can make every experience subtly layered with fear and awaken constant vigilance to every encounter. Perhaps worst of all, it can make us suspicious of every movement of love towards us. Many of those who find themselves drawn to the path of herbs do so because nature offers a meeting and love that they have struggled to find in the human realm.

No herb can make this pain go away, but some can be allies in the long journey of healing. Vervain can help separate echoes of the past from the present, run a discerning brush through layered, entangled thoughts, and bring spaciousness to a knot of confusion. It is only when we can discern what is happening in the present moment from the echoes of our past wounds that we can build a life beyond those wounds.

> "This is place full of stillness, the most sacred room in the temple. There is permission to rest here, spaciousness in the density. Nothing is left unforgotten."
>
> *From my notes of words shared in Vervain ritual (2022)*

Clear pool

Precious life

Timeless reverence

Melancholy history

Light in the darkness

Silent retreat

Still centre

Death's friend

Peaceful sadness

Quiet illumination

Within Vervain's weavings, I see everyone enter a spacious, reflective place in themselves, a quiet inward motion, a remembering of old hurts with new perspective.

"Vervain gives rest to the part of me that has been walking a really long time."

Denise Rowe (2022)

Once in the school we came into ritual meeting with Vervain soon after a day with Clary. This juxtaposition was striking and dramatically heightened the experience for everyone involved. People spoke that it was as if we were coming from a raucous colourful party to a melancholic meditation on death, from a human realm of colour, warmth and play to the quiet sitting with the skeletons of our ancestors. In this place, it is as if the confusion in our thoughts and our brain is slowly combed out, disentangling one narrative from another, bringing simplicity and space to a muddy entanglement.

Vervain leads us underground, into the deep caves of our often painful human story, and lines the path with a gentle light that helps us remember that we can walk this walk.

I call on Vervain often for those people who are the most lost in the depth of their healing journey, those bed-bound in exhaustion and fatigue. This is a place few plants can touch; many, even in their gentleness, are too provocative, too stimulating here. I've worked with people finding their way out of chronic fatigue, fibromyalgia and, more recently, long Covid, and the experience of significant setbacks if they overstretch themselves is common. The path out of these places is slow and gradual, and Vervain is a true companion on this difficult path.

Our hearts are strong enough to love, forgive and embrace all that we find as we walk these difficult roads. The challenges we face are never ours alone. The love we discover within ourselves while facing these challenges doesn't just heal us; it ripples outward, lifting up everyone around us.

Sweet stillness · Untangling knots · Inner-world journey

Invitation: To drop into a place of stillness, deep underground as if in meditation in a cave, held by the weight of rock all around you.

How do I make time for this stillness?
Where and why do I find it difficult to be still in the busyness of life?

How do I untangle the threads of grief and trauma within?
How do I turn away from or hide from this?

Where do I experience reverence, humility and wonder?
Where have I lost my sense of the sacred?

Traditional: Vervain has a long traditional use in ceremonies, as a plant of peace, respectful negotiation and allyship. Consider having a sprig of Vervain or drinking some before a difficult meeting – they bring a quality of spacious reflectiveness that can help us find a mutually beneficial outcome. Medicinally, Vervain is mostly used today for their calming, anxiolytic effects and for the bigger, digestive stimulating effects. This combination is useful when stagnation and anxiety are found together, Vervain gently easing the body and digestion into movement, whilst also easing anxiety. Many herbalists will call on Vervain for supporting depression, grief and those struggling with long, chronic illness.

Safety: Vervain is considered generally safe in moderate doses, though if pregnant or taking blood-thinning drugs, consult with a herbalist before taking.

Botany: *Verbena officinalis*, Verbenaceae is a strong, small, fine perennial plant with tiny lilac flowers. The branching form has a beautiful geometry and flowers in midsummer.

Correspondences: ᛖ Coll (Hazel) – wisdom and knowledge, divination, creativity, illumination, resilience and renewal, lost initiations. ᚲ Kenaz (Fire) – a torch in the darkness, creative expression, insight, dispelling illusions, skill in creative manifestation, knowledge. ♀ Venus – creativity, beauty, balance, harmony, intuition, love.

Meeting Vervain: Vervain is a beautiful plant to give time and space to when you feel the need to come inwards, be still and reflect. The infusion is bitter and is ideal to drink before a long solitary walk or time of meditation. I also recommend sketching the living plant, they are so fine and beautiful it is easy to become absorbed in the detail and character of Vervain this way.

Herbalists and ritual: I always enjoy bringing Vervain into a ritual space - perhaps something in me half-remembers lifetimes of curating deeply reflective ritual. This is a plant that invites a lot of space for still reflection, solitary work and deep quiet inner-underworld journeying. Of all the plants, Vervain can touch the deepest places, yet I often find people need very little support when receiving it, as if this plant calls them toward their own inner resources. This depth opens a door to our ancestors, their pain, and their gifts – perhaps the potency of Vervain lies in how it helps us find a sense of belonging in this shared, ancestral field of consciousness.

Wild Garlic

The woods are quiet in late winter. Ferns, Holly and Ivy provide the only green in the Beech woodlands near where I live. Squirrels quietly dart above, and for a moment, I sense a deer, alert in the distance. Birds squabble in the leafless canopy and in the cool moist air there's a satisfying musty scent of the soft decomposing leaves. However, veering off the path, every footstep releases an almost imperceptible scent of Garlic. Underfoot, thousands of bulbs are awakening. Here and there the first tiny leaves push through the layers of last year's fallen leaves.

This evocative scent is a harbinger of spring, a gentle kindling of the fires of the year yet to be. Allicin, a significant part of the distinctive scent of Garlic, owes much of its potency to the sulphur atoms that lie at the heart of this molecule. This is a well-researched molecule, thanks to the ubiquity of garlic in food and medicine throughout the world, and has numerous medicinal properties, not least as a potent antimicrobial, antiparasitic, aid to the cardiovascular system and immune modulator. In all these aspects, Garlic is a dynamic catalyst, invigorating and revitalising, helping us transition from the introspective stillness of winter to the vibrant, flourishing vitality of spring.

Returning to the woods with a small group of students a couple of weeks later, the ground is entirely carpeted with waxy dark green leaves. We lie down amongst them, gently so as not to damage the floor of Garlic, and close our eyes.

It feels that the earth is humming beneath us, a persistent energising, magnetic buzz. I look around and have the impression that each person has let themselves be held and wrapped, deeply earthed, as if being plugged in to our earthly energy source to be recharged. Time passes and no one feels inclined to move. Later people share that they felt a deep warmth permeate

their body and a profound sense of being connected to the aliveness of the soil; a restoration and nourishment after the long winter.

Rubbing a leaf between fingers leaves an oily residue that soaks deep into the skin, lingering for hours unless vigorously scrubbed away with soap. Eaten, the effect is even more prolonged, as Garlic works through our bodies, eventually released through our sweat and breath. Penetrating, permeating, lingering, awakening – Wild Garlic is insistent and demanding, determined to fill us with their sulphurous presence should we let them in. The mossy damp of the woods and fiery pungency of Garlic are striking in their contrast.

Often, students are so enthused by their experience they opt to bivvy out in the woods that night. It only feels right to warn them, "Don't expect to get too much deep sleep." People's dreams amongst the Garlic are often wild and intense – the smell, so welcome in a small dose, can quickly become overwhelming, even delirium inducing.

There's medicine here, if you are ready to ride your dreams, but it's a potent medicine. The wild goat-god Pan is awake and will quite likely want to play. The aliveness in the ground evokes a massive snake, stirring and coiling. Bodies and dreams may want to respond, as if to a sulphurous Bacchus.

> "A sticky, pungent mist permeates me. The perfume is calling, an insistence to play with the carnality, frivolity and trickery of life. Time tumbles and merges. I wake from this turbulence with glinting euphoria."
>
> *Crispin (2016)*

In the morning they return, a little wide-eyed and wired, the lack of sleep competing with the desire to run, dance or fight, to yield to passionate impulses, to push outwards into the bigness of themselves.

Sulphur's secret · Serpent stirring · Earth hum · Pan's playground

Where is my sulphur, my snake-dragon energy, my fire?
How have I dampened and put out my own fire?
How does my fire express itself erratically?

How can I invite greater aliveness into my breath?
How might I be compromising my lungs?

Where do I need to walk towards the fire of my passions?
Where am I turning away from this?

Traditional: Garlic (though not Wild Garlic) is well-regarded and researched with anti-microbial, anti-parasitic, anti-cancer, anti-diabetic, cardio-protective, anti-neurogenerative, anti-inflammatory and anti-obesity properties. Wild Garlic is a much-loved folk medicine, often favoured to help clear congestion and respiratory infections and enliven the blood and circulation.

Safety: There are safety concerns around harvesting. Wild Garlic is known to be confused with Lords and Ladies which looks similar in early growth and is toxic. Some people are sensitive to Garlic plants, overconsumption can cause digestive upset and heartburn. Garlic can thin the blood so may not be suitable for those taking blood-thinning medications such as warfarin or aspirin.

Botany: *Allium ursinum*, family Amaryllidaceae, is found mostly in woodlands and is highly recognisable by the strong and distinctive Garlic smell. They have star-like white flowers growing in umbels from a triangular stem amongst the broad, vibrant green elliptical leaves. Flowers from April into June and widespread over Europe.

Correspondences: ᛞ Duir (Oak) – strength, endurance, protection, leadership, gateway to mysteries, ability to cross boundaries, truth. ᛗ Daeg – enlightenment, transformation, clarity, awakening, new beginnings. ♂ Mars – our survival capacity, fire, passion, anger, ambition, warrior. 🜍 Sulphur – expansion, fire, soul, consciousness.

Meeting Wild Garlic: Wild in the woods, nibbling on the fresh plant – I particularly recommend the unopened flower buds. Garlic macerated in apple cyder vinegar is a great way to preserve this for later in the year. Enjoy eating the leaves and flowers in salads.

Herbalists and ritual: I've found a range of ways of inviting people into relationship with Wild Garlic – the gentlest is to simply give people the space and invitation to lie down amongst the Garlic when at any stage of their growth and listen for the aliveness of the bulbs beneath them. Any work with juicing or eating Wild Garlic tends to strongly awaken something of a fiery, chaotic energy so it's good to plan the ritual in a way that allows this to express itself. Some people will undoubtedly find this plant too strong, which might express itself as a repulsion or shut down; finding gentler ways for these people to come into connection, such as sketching, can help everyone feel included.

223

Wood Anemone

In the rolling green hills around Stroud, there are places that defy even the flattest, most overcast day with their own light. The light green of tender young Beech leaves. The ever-shifting colour tones of Bluebells filling the air with their sweet heady scent. And brightest amongst the soft woodland colours, white Anemones, breaking the sea of Bluebells, each solitary flower delicately poised on a fine stem.

The flowers close in rain, lending themselves the common folklore as sheltering spaces for the smaller of the woodland Fae, though some might argue it is merely to protect the pollen. But step back a little and we notice that as the rain starts, the insects, the winged pollinators of the woodland, themselves take shelter, and as it dries, the woodland is once again enlivened with their flight.

I suspect that ecological diversity and experiences of the Fae intertwine; we encounter wonder and magic when we immerse ourselves in these ancient ecosystems, the very woodland ecosystems signified by the presence of these flowers and their sometimes centuries-old root systems. Language matters. Language becomes the threads of the mythologies we choose to weave.

Spiralling light

Windflower

Thimbleweed

Forest guardian

Many people describe a quiet lifting of the heart in Anemone's presence, a subtle current of hope and brightness in times when lost in confusion. In their brightness they seem able to shine through our terror and darkness in a way that feels as if they have roots beyond this lifetime, systemic, ancestral, ecological roots beyond our conscious knowing. I have no doubt that

generations of ancestors have been touched and have
taken a moment to stop and be still in this
woodland presence.

In many traditions of Scandinavia, a small
wreath of Wood Anemones placed on a doorstep
was understood to ward off trolls. Norse
mythology tends to present trolls as dangerous only when
defending their home or treasure; they don't generally
venture, unprovoked, into human lands and attack, but rather pose a
danger to humans who trespass into theirs.

Trolls represent the unknown, the primal, the shadow and the deep dark
forest; they are territorial guardians of pre-human wildness. They are the
wild's fierce resistance to our trespass, our greed and our shadow, our
aggressive desire for a level of control and colonisation beyond necessity.

The troll hides under the bridge that separates our civilised self from our
wild self. If we turn away from that bridge in fear, how do we ever truly meet
the unconscious that drives us? But crossing the bridge is perilous, we need
allies, we need a thread or trail of breadcrumbs for fear that we become forever
lost in our unconscious, in madness and psychosis.

This is where the plants, and in this case Wood Anemone, as we venture
deep into the woods alone, offer us something unique. Unlike human allies
who often share our myopic views and shadow, or technological allies that
serve as mere extensions of our will, plant allies are beyond our
comprehension. This is precisely why they are so important, they are beyond
our ken and will challenge our shadow, but only if we let them.

I wake up, the spring sun dappling the wood with shafts of light. The
Anemones glow bright, like floating Lilies on a sea of ever-shifting Bluebells.
Their three deeply lobed leaves, just as delicate as the flowers, gesture upwards
to the light. I feel I've been a long way away, in woods deeper and darker than
the relatively benign ones of Stroud. As I slowly meander home, it's with a
deep quietness and humility, a gentle heart and quiet respect for the magic of
the woodland Fae.

Forest guardian · Light bringer · Fae invitation

How do I honour and thrive (or not) on the roots of my ancestry?
How and why do I turn away from my ancestry?

Where do I find light when all around is in shadow?
Where have I lost my faith and trust?

Traditional: Wood Anemone is highly poisonous, so not now used in herbalism, despite Culpeper's suggestion in 1650 of snuffing the juice. They are often found in flower essence collections, often offered with themes around bringing fresh lightness and trust to old ancestral issues.

Botany: *Anemone nemorosa*, a member of the Buttercup (Ranunculaceae) family can be found growing in British woodlands from April-June and may still flower in shaded areas into August. Anemone has an unusual strategy of reproduction. Myrmecochory is seed dispersal by ants, although Anemone mostly spreads by extending their rhizomes underneath the forest floor. This long-established rhizome and the time it takes to grow (six feet every 100 years) is why they are considered an indicator of ancient woodland.

Safety: All parts of the plant are toxic and should not be consumed. Can cause blistering to those with sensitive skin, when picked and crushed onto the skin.

Correspondences: ᚴ Beith (Birch) – fresh starts, potential, renewal, cleansing ritual, purification, honouring of nature, youthfulness, vitality, flexibility, protection, new beginnings. ᛒ Beorc – feminine principle, harmony, balance, rebirth, renewal, protection, inspiration, fertility, life-giving, compassion, rites of passage. ♀ Venus – rejuvenation, harmony, inspiration, beauty.

Ritual: Solitary time in sunny woodlands when they are flowering, drawing and movement practices inspired by their form. Liminal journeying into ancestral connection with their gentle support. I find people often come away from working with Wood Anemone with a quiet and simple brightness about them.

Wormwood

There are unexpected moments, profound pivot points in our lives. The sudden crumbling away of the old, a diagnosis, an accident, the moment you know you need to leave your job, your partner, your home. And equally, the dawning of a the new, a new path, a new love, the moment of conception.

It can feel as if your skin is ripped away.

In this exfoliation lies the possibility of knowing the small flickering flame beneath, a delicate warmth and truth that feels truer, clearer, than any truth we've known before. Some call it the soul, and perhaps it is. It feels unimportant what we call it, what matters is that we know it.

Many journeys of inner enquiry eventually present us with a choice, the choice between the known and the unknown. The greater the wounds we carry, the more likely we feel fear facing into the unknown. Yet escaping the imprisoning ego-identity of the known often requires a leap of faith into uncharted lands, a stepping into darkness.

Wormwood has the capacity to call in the winds of life.

They will both rip away at all that is not you *and* carry you forward. It takes being churned a lot to fully trust that these are one and the same.

They are fierce teachers, uncompromising, asking you to be uncompromising. Asking you to shed your conditioned layers of internally colonised cultural appeasement in favour of a raw truthfulness. They offer in equal measure the strength to be vulnerable and the strength to be in power. They can be the powerful waterfall that calls to you, "Are you here to observe me from a safe distance, and are you ready for my medicine? Are you ready to be pounded and reborn whole?"

Wormwood's reputation for clearing parasites goes far beyond the physical, with a capacity to purge all that is not us. This is not a gentle medicine.

> Stepping outside into the biting wind
> Welcoming its teeth, its rawness.
> Tear away all that is not me,
> I do not need it any more.

Working with Wormwood may well invite our rage and a heightened awareness of the ways in which we've allowed ourselves to be trampled on. If we've accumulated too many false skins, the medicine will be potent and needs to be titrated slowly, within our resilience. First initiations with Wormwood are often profound – and challenging – awakenings, but once this plant has become a true ally, it is a consciousness we can call on evermore to help us shed the layers of our unconscious appeasement.

"Sword of truth, cuts away all of the patterning and bullshit, drawing my energy inwards to the centre of my being and focusing me. My inner sight and my outer sight become clear."

Charlotte Gordon (2022)

"Touches the deep, ancient, dreaming part of me."

Lucy Turner (2023)

"Reminds me that we can't grow if we don't know our edges."

Emily Taylor (2022)

"Gives me the grounded confidence to take my path at my pace ... cuts through and shows me what I do to myself and it inverts from self-hatred and misery to an embodied lightness and a moving to action."

Hettie Peplow (2020)

Courageous will · Clear boundaries · Fierce determination

What is emerging in me?
Which old ways of being am I ready to let go of?
Which behaviours and interpersonal dynamics are harming me?

How do I find the courage to walk unknown paths?
What holds me back?

What really matters in my life?
How do I create more space for this?

Traditional: Wormwood has a strong traditional and modern use as a cholagogue, activating the liver, helping improve digestion and is being researched for use in Crohn's disease.* As the name suggests, they have often been used as an anthelmintic, to clear intestinal worm infections. Wormwood is a key component of the potent spirit absinthe, and though the compound thujone found in Wormwood has often been considered neurotoxic, it is also being researched for its neuro-protective qualities, potentially of value in Parkinson's and following a stroke. Wormwood's close relatives, Mugwort and Sweet Annie (famous as a highly effective antimalarial) have their own quite distinct qualities, but with some overlap with Wormwood.

Botany: *Artemisia absinthium*, family Asteraceae, has distinctive aromatic silvery grey leaves which can be harvested from April right through to October.

Safety: Wormwood is an extremely strong plant and should only be taken internally with care; the compound thujone, which gives the strong bitter taste is considered neurotoxic in high doses or prolonged use, though the dosage typically found in food and medicine is generally considered safe. The plant should be avoided in pregnancy, breastfeeding, and those with kidney disorders or epilepsy. Seek professional advice if on any anticonvulsants. Allergy risk if Compositae/Asteraceae allergy. If in any doubt about suitability, this is a plant to be extra cautious with and seek the guidance of a skilled herbalist.

Correspondences: ᛁ Ioho (Yew) – perseverance, resilience, new ventures. ᛉ Eolh – stag/elk, new influence, protection. ᚱ Ruis – warrior, reddening, protection, banishing, exorcism. ☉ Sun – penetrating light, truth, clear identity.

232

Herbalists and ritual: Wormwood is only suitable for use by those with extensive personal and client experience, since the effects can be quick, strong and varied. It is not usual that Wormwood will initially invoke strong revulsion, negative projections, fear and distrust and it is only through knowing how to navigate these that we can help guide others into working with Wormwood constructively as an ally. In both ritual and 1:1 client work, Wormwood is likely to unlock hidden anger. If working with Wormwood over a moon cycle, they are highly likely to lead to people becoming significantly more reactive as they discover and establish new boundaries around what they do and do not want to invite into their life. It is important that anyone choosing to work with Wormwood internally is resourced and supported appropriately in this process. In our Insight Herbalism training, we would only recommend people work with Wormwood in their final year of training once they have sufficient experience to support the potent processes that can unfold here.

"Breaking open like a landslide,
shell of dry lava breaking away,
cracking off under a new eruption,
a power orgasm."

Annabel Pinker (2019)

233

Working with plants safely

This book is intentionally written to inspire you to desire to get to know a plant better, to start a journey of exploration. It is not designed or written to give advice about dosage or appropriateness of any plant for any medical condition. There are no lack of excellent books that cover this in depth – I've included a few of my favourites in the bibliography.

Many may be curious how this work of building relationship with plants relates to working systematically with health conditions. That, I hope, will be the topic of another book (quite likely many years away) as I slowly compile and review many of my own, my students' and graduates' hundreds of experiences of supporting people and the journeys that emerge when we truly take the invitations and teachings of the plants on board.

Listen to your own body

This is one of the most important considerations. If you want to start to take a plant, check it is safe and appropriate for you, and then start with small quantities, perhaps even with the smell alone. Always honour your own body's response, overriding this can lead to unexpected effects.

Correct identification

Only harvest and consume a plant if you are 100% sure of the identity. If in doubt please consult a good field guide or a herbalist. Some herb mis-identifications can potentially be fatal and people frequently find themselves in hospital on account of this.

Dosage and side effects

Dosage varies across different plants and different people. I would advise checking multiple reliable sources before taking any plant internally. There is always the possibility of side effects and rare, unusual responses with any plant. I do not give doses in this book as it would be impossible to honour the range of individuals' responses to different dosages – again, often this comes back to listening to your own body. Many side effects are mild and pass quickly – if you are concerned about a possible side effect, stop taking the plant and seek advice from a herbalist.

Drug interactions

There are many possible herb-drug interactions, and it is possible to check these on online databases such as RxList. If you are taking any prescription medications, do **always** check for this first. If you feel out of your depth assessing if a herb is suitable for you, given the medication you are taking (including the contraceptive pill), please seek advice from a herbalist.

Appropriateness

Appropriateness depends on many factors such as age, vulnerability, pregnancy, proximity to surgery, medical and mental health conditions. If in doubt consult a herbalist.

The boxes below categorise the plants in this book into: (1) Those widely found and used in traditional herbal medicine and are generally considered safe enough to buy over the counter. (2) Those that I consider particularly strong acting and should only be used with care and experience or with professional supervision. (3) Those plants that may be subject to legal restrictions in some countries and those that are potentially highly toxic or dangerous.

Chamomile, Cleavers, Dandelion, Blackberry fruit, Marigold, Mallow, Meadowsweet, Mullein, Nettle, Elder, Fennel, Hawthorn, Horsetail, Lady's Mantle, Lemon Balm, Primrose, Rose, Silver Birch leaf, Vervain, Wild Garlic	These plants are all widely available over the counter throughout Europe or as foods and, used sensibly, with an awareness of possible drug interactions and individual suitability, are safe as regular infusions/foods.
Angelica, Borage, Clary Sage, Mistletoe, Mugwort, Wormwood, Valerian, St. John's Wort	Caution and more research are needed before working with these plants, either because they are strong, have serious potential side effects or have highly complex drug interactions. Not suited for on-going, long-term use without professional supervision.
Poppy, Fly Agaric Bluebell, Fern, Wood Anemone	These plants are either subject to legal restrictions in some countries, very strong or should never be taken internally apart from as flower essences. Potentially dangerous if misused.

Safety and self-care:
Navigating trauma activation in plant work

Working with plants in the way we introduce in this book can be a profound experience, offering insights, healing, support and guidance. However, this journey – as with any form of inner work or healing process – may touch old wounds and embodied trauma. Any plant (as with any human relationship) can potentially evoke memories (sometimes pre-verbal, somatic memories) that have been buried deep within us.

If you notice additional signs like heightened distress, anxiety, dissociation, or physical discomfort such as muscle tension, headaches, or shaking, these may also be indications of trauma activation. These responses can vary widely from person to person. It is crucial to approach these moments with gentleness and self-compassion. Recognise that this is neither a sign that something is wrong, nor a failure on your part, nor a signal to push forward. Most importantly it is an opportunity for you to honour your own pace and your own limits.

Avoid pushing through strong emotions, know your limits and stay within your own resilience. If a particular plant activates something challenging in you that you do not want to step into, simply thank that plant and put it aside. This could be an ideal time to call on those plants that you know and skills you already have to support and resource you. There is no rush to get anywhere with these plant meetings – much as in a human relationship, trying to force the process will often backfire. These relationships flourish when taken at your own pace.

Grounding techniques, such as working with your breath, your body and simple movement, are really useful to bring you back into the present moment.

Getting support

No one needs to walk a path of healing on their own. If you find yourself struggling with emotions that feel too intense, seek support. Here are a few suggestions:

• **Talk to a friend** who has some experience with trauma and feels able to hold a space for you to feel supported and understood.

• **Seek professional support** with someone who has experience working with trauma to help guide and support you. This could be within many possible healing disciplines – I would suggest organising a chat with a potential new therapist to see how you might feel working alongside them. I particularly recommend Somatic Experiencing as an approach as it works with the body's memory, though this is a very quickly developing field and there are many other excellent approaches.

• **Assess your own support network:** How does this currently look and feel? What might help you build a stronger support network for yourself? The strength of an individual's support network is often a key factor in how deep people feel able to go into their own process of healing. Places in nature, classes, meditation practices, somatic and movement practices, online resources, books, community, family, friends, your workplace and professionals can all potentially be sources of support. I have listed a selection of good books on trauma in the bibliography.

There is no rush in healing journeys, since the journey is about honouring yourself along the way. Healing is a non-linear process. If you feel frustrated or as though you are not progressing 'fast enough', know that this is a natural part of the journey.

By respecting your own boundaries, your own resilience and finding the support you need you create a strong container for your healing to unfold at its own pace.

Endnotes

These endnotes have been compiled to offer doorways for further exploration of each of the plants, derived from things I myself find fascinating. The intention here is not to establish an evidence base, but to give doorways for the curious. Whilst I've included some of the clinical research typical to a herbal, I've also woven in research to do with ecology and the wider aspects of health (e.g. the relationship between emotions and inflammation in the Borage chapter), feeling that this gives a wider perspective on the potential of plant to human health and culture in the widest sense.

I have chosen **not** to include animal experiments in these references. This has meant being very selective and dismissing much that you might find on a web research trawl. I am somewhat limited in my attempts to do this – whilst I can filter out original research, reviews, which generally draw on hundreds of research papers, rarely exclude this so need to be read with care to be sure where information is derived from. The reasons for this position on animal experiments are twofold: (1) An ethical position where we believe that effort should be put into research models that do not involve causing suffering to animals. (2) The highly questionable validity of 'findings' that derive from animal research. Instead, we have favoured *in vitro*, human clinical trials and research reviews.

Citations also appear online (for hyperlink ease) via: WildEnchantments.org.uk

---

Introduction We stand on the shoulders of our ancestors. Though many of the insights, approaches and concepts introduced in this book have emerged entirely through a process of slow discovery – and a refinement of this over many years – I doubt any of the concepts are truly new. Some of the simple models that have shown themselves to be most powerful, for instance working with the Triskele as Plant-Pilgrim-Server, went through countless iterations (e.g. Plant-Invitation-Shadow) before finally landing in its current form, which was then tested over many years. As it landed within the school I felt a deep remembering of the value of pilgrimage and service and the many who have walked these paths. The bibliography also gives a taste of the many authors who have inspired me over the years. There is not a single book here I wouldn't want to read again.

I am particularly grateful to those who translated the *The Cauldron of Poesy*, in particular Erynn Rowan Laurie, whose translation is available at: Obsidianmagazine.com/Pages/cauldronpoesy.html. I am also indebted to the work of John and Caitlin Matthews: Hallowquest.org.uk who have helped me dive deeper into my own roots. I would like to thank the 'Radical Herbalism Gatherings' and the team that put this together, which ran from 2014-2018 and brought a much-needed depth of political dialogue to herbalism. I highly recommend the 'Wort Journal' edited by Leo Qawas: Wortjournal.com, which publishes regularly to give a voice to 'radical, rooted and relational herbalism'.

Angelica Despite a long history of use, there has been no human clinical research on Angelica for pulmonary conditions. This is surprising, given its well-established antiviral, antibacterial, and antifungal properties. Initial clinical research on Angelica, particularly in the form of the product 'Feru-guard' indicates potential benefits in reducing neuroinflammation and aiding dementia. In my practice, I often work with Angelica to help people come into deeper relationship with their breathing, whether addressing specific pathologies or improving overall breath quality. For those interested in the significance of breathing to health, I highly recommend James Nestor's very accessible book, *Breath: The New Science of a Lost Art*.

‣ Rajtar B, Skalicka-Woźniak K, Świątek Ł, Stec A, Boguszewska A, Polz-Dacewicz M. Antiviral effect of compounds derived from Angelica archangelica L. on Herpes simplex virus-1 and Coxsackievirus B3 infections. Food Chem Toxicol. 2017 Nov;109(Pt 2):1026–31.

‣ Kaur A, Bhatti R. Understanding the phytochemistry and molecular insights to the pharmacology of Angelica archangelica L. (garden angelica) and its bioactive components. Phytother Res. 2021 Nov;35(11):5961–79.

‣ Aćimović MG, Pavlović SĐ, Varga AO, Filipović VM, Cvetković MT, Stanković JM, et al. Chemical Composition and Antibacterial Activity of Angelica archangelica Root Essential Oil. Nat Prod Commun. 2017 Feb;12(2):205–6.

‣ Kimura T, Hayashida H, Murata M, Takamatsu J. Effect of ferulic acid and Angelica archangelica extract on behavioral and psychological symptoms of dementia in frontotemporal lobar degeneration and dementia with Lewy bodies. Geriatr Gerontol Int. 2011 Jul;11(3):309–14.

Bluebell Bluebells have seen limited medicinal use, likely due to their toxicity. However, Mrs. M. Grieve noted that dried and powdered roots were historically used as a styptic to stop bleeding. Although there is no research specifically on the effects of Bluebells on humans, some interesting preliminary research has been conducted, and there is rich folklore surrounding them. Thanks to Emily for collating the folk names, which were drawn from many sources, including *Agar-Zenry* by Ron Freethy, Crowwood Press, 1920, *A Modern Herbal* by Mrs M Grieves, Tiger Book, 1996 and the website of the Woodland Trust and RHS.

‣ Thoss V, Murphy PJ, Marriott R, Wilson T. Triacylglycerol composition of British bluebell (Hyacinthoides non-scripta) seed oil. RSC Adv. 2012;2(12):5314.

‣ A. Mulholland D, L. Schwikkard S, R. Crouch N. The chemistry and biological activity of the Hyacinthaceae. Natural Product Reports. 2013;30(9):1165–210.

‣ Richardson R. Britain's Wild Flowers: A Treasury of Traditions, Superstitions, Remedies and Literature. National Trust; 2017. 323 p.

‣ Gledhill D. The names of plants. 3rd ed. Cambridge [England]; New York: Cambridge University Press; 2002. 326 p.

Borage In the chapter on Borage, I explore how this remarkable plant can support us in our grief and help moderate excessive passion and anger. I am intrigued by how our emotional lives profoundly impact health outcomes, and several studies highlight the link between anger and inflammation. Much of the research on Borage focuses on its oil which exhibits notable anti-inflammatory effects, particularly in conditions such as dermatitis, asthma, arthritis, and menopause. Borage oil likely mediates its anti-inflammatory effects through pathways involving increased prostaglandin E and cAMP levels, resulting in a reduction of TNF-alpha, a key pro-inflammatory compound in many autoimmune conditions.

Thanks to the 2024 Foundation training group for part of the poem 'Standing strong in ritual tight', a response to Borage unlocking some of the depths of the sisterhood bond and an ancient remembering of what it was to be held within this.

• Marsland AL, Prather AA, Petersen KL, Cohen S, Manuck SB. Antagonistic characteristics are positively associated with inflammatory markers independently of trait negative emotionality. Brain Behav Immun. 2008 Jul;22(5):753–61.

• Barlow MA, Wrosch C, Gouin JP, Kunzmann U. Is anger, but not sadness, associated with chronic inflammation and illness in older adulthood? Psychol Aging. 2019 May;34(3):330–40.

• Suarez EC, Krishnan RR, Lewis JG. The relation of severity of depressive symptoms to monocyte-associated proinflammatory cytokines and chemokines in apparently healthy men. Psychosom Med. 2003;65(3):362–8.

• Kast RE. Borage oil reduction of rheumatoid arthritis activity may be mediated by increased cAMP that suppresses tumor necrosis factor-alpha. Int Immunopharmacol. 2001 Nov;1(12):2197–9.

• Ghasemian M, Owlia S, Owlia MB. Review of Anti-Inflammatory Herbal Medicines. Adv Pharmacol Sci. 2016;2016:9130979.

• Mirsadraee M, Khashkhashi Moghaddam S, Saeedi P, Ghaffari S. Effect of Borago Officinalis Extract on Moderate Persistent Asthma: A Phase two Randomized, Double Blind, Placebo-Controlled Clinical Trial. Tanaffos. 2016;15(3):168–74.

• Foster RH, Hardy G, Alany RG. Borage oil in the treatment of atopic dermatitis. Nutrition. 2010;26(7–8):708–18.

• da Costa Hime L de FC, Carvalho Lopes CM, Roa CL, Zuchelo LTS, Baracat EC, de Andrade J, et al. Is there a beneficial effect of gamma-linolenic acid supplementation on body fat in postmenopausal hypertensive women? A prospective randomized double-blind placebo-controlled trial. Menopause. 2021 Feb 1;28(6):699–705.

Bramble Whilst the fruits are well recognised for their nutritional benefits, there has been virtually no clinical research concerning Bramble. Below I've included a couple of papers describing the ecological benefits of Bramble with regard to woodland regeneration.

• Kuiters AT, Slim PA. Tree colonisation of abandoned arable land after 27 years of horse-grazing: the role of bramble as a facilitator of oak wood regeneration. Forest Ecology and Management. 2003 Aug;181(1–2):239–51.

• Harmer R, Kiewitt A, Morgan G, Gill R. Does the development of bramble (Rubus fruticosus L. agg.) facilitate the growth and establishment of tree seedlings in woodlands by reducing deer browsing damage? Forestry: An International Journal of Forest Research. 2010 Jan 1;83(1):93–102.

• Wignall VR, Arscott NA, Nudds HE, Squire A, Green TO, Ratnieks FLW. Thug life: bramble (Rubus fruticosus L. agg.) is a valuable foraging resource for honeybees and diverse flower-visiting insects. Insect Conservation and Diversity. 2020;13(6):543–57.

• Harmer R, Kiewitt A, Morgan G, Gill R. Does the development of bramble (Rubus fruticosus L. agg.) facilitate the growth and establishment of tree seedlings in woodlands by reducing deer browsing damage?

Chamomile The range of conditions for which Chamomile has been investigated is impressive. I've included a snapshot below which includes research looking at Chamomile's effect on sleep, depression, anxiety, diabetes, obesity, skin repair, inflammation, cancer complications, side effects of chemotherapy, pain following caesarian section, lower back pain, PMS, rhinosinusitis, migraine, peristomal skin lesions, carpal tunnel syndrome, nausea and vomiting and oral lichen planus and phlebitis following IV infusion. Extensive as it is, this list is far from exhaustive!

• Zemestani M, Rafraf M, Asghari-Jafarabadi M. Chamomile tea improves glycemic indices and antioxidants status in patients with type 2 diabetes mellitus. Nutrition. 2016 Jan;32(1):66–72.

• Zargaran A, Borhani-Haghighi A, Faridi P, Daneshamouz S, Kordafshari G, Mohagheghzadeh A. Potential effect and mechanism of action of topical chamomile (Matricaria chammomila L.) oil on migraine headache: A medical hypothesis. Med Hypotheses. 2014 Nov;83(5):566–9.

• Zardosht R, Basiri A, Sahebkar A, Emami SA. Effect of Chamomile Oil on Cesarean Section Pain in Primiparous Women: A Randomized Clinical Trial. Curr Rev Clin Exp Pharmacol. 2021;16(4):369–74.

• Tan CSS, Lee SWH. Warfarin and food, herbal or dietary supplement interactions: A systematic review. Br J Clin Pharmacol. 2021 Feb;87(2):352–74.

• Shirzad-Siboni V, Nobahar M, Ghorbani R. Effect of chamomile oil on the intensity of nonspecific low back pain in prehospital emergency technicians. Am J Emerg Med. 2022 Oct;60:200–3.

• Sharifi-Ardani M, Yekefallah L, Asefzadeh S, Nassiri-Asl M. Efficacy of topical chamomile on the incidence of phlebitis due to an amiodarone infusion in coronary care patients: a double-blind, randomized controlled trial. J Integr Med. 2017 Sep;15(5):373–8.

• Sarecka-Hujar B, Szulc-Musioł B. Herbal Medicines – Are They Effective and Safe during Pregnancy? Pharmaceutics. 2022 Jan 12;14(1):171.

• Sanaati F, Najafi S, Kashaninia Z, Sadeghi M. Effect of Ginger and Chamomile on Nausea and Vomiting Caused by Chemotherapy in Iranian Women with Breast Cancer. Asian Pac J Cancer Prev. 2016;17(8):4125–9.

• Paulsen E. Systemic allergic dermatitis caused by sesquiterpene lactones. Contact Dermatitis. 2017 Jan;76(1):1–10.

• Niazi A, Moradi M. The Effect of Chamomile on Pain and Menstrual Bleeding in Primary Dysmenorrhea: A Systematic Review. Int J Community Based Nurs Midwifery. 2021 Jul;9(3):174–86.

• Nemati S, Yousefbeyk F, Ebrahimi SM, FaghihHabibi AF, Shakiba M, Ramezani H. Effects of chamomile extract nasal drop on chronic rhinosinusitis treatment: A randomized double blind study. Am J Otolaryngol. 2021;42(1):102743.

• Maleki M, Mardani A, Manouchehri M, Ashghali Farahani M, Vaismoradi M, Glarcher M. Effect of Chamomile on the Complications of Cancer: A Systematic Review. Integr Cancer Ther. 2023;22:15347354231164600.

• Lopez Jornet P, Aznar-Cayuela C. Efficacy of topical chamomile management vs. placebo in patients with oral lichen planus: a randomized double-blind study. J Eur Acad Dermatol Venereol. 2016 Oct;30(10):1783–6.

• Lin TK, Zhong L, Santiago JL. Anti-Inflammatory and Skin Barrier Repair Effects of Topical Application of Some Plant Oils. Int J Mol Sci. 2017 Dec 27;19(1):70.

• Lefort ÉC, Blay J. Apigenin and its impact on gastrointestinal cancers. Mol Nutr Food Res. 2013 Jan;57(1):126–44.

• Khalesi ZB, Beiranvand SP, Bokaie M. Efficacy of Chamomile in the Treatment of Premenstrual Syndrome: A Systematic Review. J Pharmacopuncture. 2019 Dec;22(4):204–9.

• Keefe JR, Mao JJ, Soeller I, Li QS, Amsterdam JD. Short-term open-label chamomile (Matricaria chamomilla L.) therapy of moderate to severe generalized anxiety disorder. Phytomedicine. 2016 Dec 15;23(14):1699–705.

• Hashempur MH, Ghasemi MS, Daneshfard B, Ghoreishi PS, Lari ZN, Homayouni K, et al. Efficacy of topical chamomile oil for mild and moderate carpal tunnel syndrome: A randomized double-blind placebo-controlled clinical trial. Complement Ther Clin Pract. 2017 Feb;26:61–7.

• Eskandari F, Mousavi P, Valiani M, Ghanbari S, Iravani M. A comparison of the effect of Swedish massage with and without chamomile oil on labor outcomes and maternal satisfaction of the childbirth process: a randomized controlled trial. Eur J Med Res. 2022 Nov 25;27(1):266.

• El Mihyaoui A, Esteves da Silva JCG, Charfi S, Candela Castillo ME, Lamarti A, Arnao MB. Chamomile (Matricaria chamomilla L.): A Review of Ethnomedicinal Use, Phytochemistry and Pharmacological Uses. Life (Basel). 2022 Mar 25;12(4):479.

• Ebrahimi H, Mardani A, Basirinezhad MH, Hamidzadeh A, Eskandari F. The effects of Lavender and Chamomile essential oil inhalation aromatherapy on depression, anxiety and stress in older community-dwelling people: A randomized controlled trial. Explore (NY). 2022;18(3):272–8.

• de Lima Dantas JB, Freire TFC, Sanches ACB, Julião ELD, Medrado ARAP, Martins GB. Action of Matricaria recutita (chamomile) in the management of radiochemotherapy oral mucositis: A systematic review. Phytother Res. 2022 Mar;36(3):1115–25.

• Charousaei F, Dabirian A, Mojab F. Using chamomile solution or a 1% topical hydrocortisone ointment in the management of peristomal skin lesions in colostomy patients: results of a controlled clinical study. Ostomy Wound Manage. 2011 May;57(5):28–36.

• Chang SM, Chen CH. Effects of an intervention with drinking chamomile tea on sleep quality and depression in sleep disturbed postnatal women: a randomized controlled trial. J Adv Nurs. 2016 Feb;72(2):306–15.

• Bayliak MM, Dmytriv TR, Melnychuk AV, Strilets NV, Storey KB, Lushchak VI. Chamomile as a potential remedy for obesity and metabolic syndrome. EXCLI J. 2021;20:1261–86.

Clary Sage   There is a fascinating scatter of research into Clary, touching on a wide range of uses in hypertension, increasing oxytocin, increasing testosterone, positive effect on mood, antispasmodic effect, pain reduction, anti-viral and anxiolytic effects.

• Yarosh AM, Tonkovtseva VV, Grigoriev PE, Batura IA. [Impact of essential oil vapors inhalation on blood pressure in patients with hypertension]. Vopr Kurortol Fizioter Lech Fiz Kult. 2023;100(2):22–30.

• Tarumi W, Shinohara K. The Effects of Essential Oil on Salivary Oxytocin Concentration in Postmenopausal Women. J Altern Complement Med. 2020 Mar;26(3):226–30.

• Sienkiewicz M, Głowacka A, Poznańska-Kurowska K, Kaszuba A, Urbaniak A, Kowalczyk E. The effect of clary sage oil on staphylococci responsible for wound infections. Postepy Dermatol Alergol. 2015 Feb;32(1):21–6.

• Seol GH, Lee YH, Kang P, You JH, Park M, Min SS. Randomized controlled trial for Salvia sclarea or Lavandula angustifolia: differential effects on blood pressure in female patients with urinary incontinence undergoing urodynamic examination. J Altern Complement Med. 2013 Jul;19(7):664–70.

• Randjelović M, Branković S, Jovanović M, Kitić N, Živanović S, Mihajilov-Krstev T, et al. An In Vitro and In Silico Characterization of Salvia sclarea L. Methanolic Extracts as Spasmolytic Agents. Pharmaceutics. 2023 Apr 29;15(5).

• Mitic M, Zrnić A, Wanner J, Stappen I. Clary Sage Essential Oil and Its Effect on Human Mood and Pulse Rate: An in vivo Pilot Study. Planta Med. 2020 Oct;86(15):1125–32.

• Lee MK, Hur MH. Effects of the Spouse's Aromatherapy Massage on Labor Pain, Anxiety and Childbirth Satisfaction for Laboring Women. Korean J Women Health Nurs. 2011 Sep;17(3):195–204.

• Ghiasi A, Bagheri L, Haseli A. A Systematic Review on the Anxiolytic Effect of Aromatherapy during the First Stage of Labor. J Caring Sci. 2019 Mar;8(1):51–60.

• Choi HJ. Chemical Constituents of Essential Oils Possessing Anti-Influenza A/WS/33 Virus Activity. Osong Public Health Res Perspect. 2018 Dec;9(6):348–53.

• Amirhosseini M, Dehghan M, Mangolian Shahrbabaki P, Pakmanesh H. Effectiveness of Aromatherapy for Relief of Pain, Nausea, and Vomiting after Percutaneous Nephrolithotomy: A Randomized Controlled Trial. Complement Med Res. 2020;27(6):440–8.

• Wataru Tarumi, Chizu Kumagai, Kazuyuki Shinohara. Exposure to Essential Oil Odors Increases Salivary Testosterone Concentration in Perimenopausal Women. Acta Med. Nagasaki. 2019. 62: 49–54

Cleavers   There is very little research into Cleavers, though in vitro work points to an immune-modulating effect via the increase lymphocyte proliferation, anti-oxidant effect and scavenging. I've also included a interesting paper exploring Cleavers' climbing mechanism.

• Ilina T, Skowrońska W, Kashpur N, Granica S, Bazylko A, Kovalyova A, et al. Immunomodulatory Activity and Phytochemical Profile of Infusions from Cleavers Herb. Molecules. 2020 Aug 14;25(16):3721.

• Ilina T, Kashpur N, Granica S, Bazylko A, Shinkovenko I, Kovalyova A, et al. Phytochemical Profiles and In Vitro Immunomodulatory Activity of Ethanolic Extracts from Galium aparine L. Plants (Basel). 2019 Nov 25;8(12):541.

• Bokhari J, Khan MR, Shabbir M, Rashid U, Jan S, Zai JA. Evaluation of diverse antioxidant activities of Galium aparine. Spectrochim Acta A Mol Biomol Spectrosc. 2013 Feb;102:24–9.

• Bauer G, Klein MC, Gorb SN, Speck T, Voigt D, Gallenmüller F. Always on the bright side: the climbing mechanism of Galium aparine. Proc Biol Sci. 2011 Jul 22;278(1715):2233–9.

Dandelion Dandelions are a well-established traditional remedy with regard to their digestive and diuretic effects; both of these have been fairly well studied. Recent research points to interesting anti-cancer, anti-diabetic and anti-bacterial effects.

• Zhu H, Zhao H, Zhang L, Xu J, Zhu C, Zhao H, et al. Dandelion root extract suppressed gastric cancer cells proliferation and migration through targeting lncRNA-CCAT1. Biomed Pharmacother. 2017 Sep;93:1010–7.

• Xu P, Xu XB, Khan A, Fotina T, Wang SH. Antibiofilm activity against Staphylococcus aureus and content analysis of Taraxacum Officinale phenolic extract. Pol J Vet Sci. 2021 Jun;24(2):243–51.

• Wirngo FE, Lambert MN, Jeppesen PB. The Physiological Effects of Dandelion (Taraxacum Officinale) in Type 2 Diabetes. Rev Diabet Stud. 2016;13(2–3):113–31.

• Ovadje P, Ammar S, Guerrero JA, Arnason JT, Pandey S. Dandelion root extract affects colorectal cancer proliferation and survival through the activation of multiple death signalling pathways. Oncotarget. 2016 Nov 8;7(45):73080–100.

• Martinez M, Poirrier P, Chamy R, Prüfer D, Schulze-Gronover C, Jorquera L, et al. Taraxacum officinale and related species – An ethnopharmacological review and its potential as a commercial medicinal plant. Journal of Ethnopharmacology. 2015 Jul 1;169:244–62.

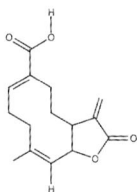

Taraxinic acid, a well known sesquiterpene lactone found in Dandelion, is the key contributor to Dandelion's bitter taste, which is a significant part of Dandelion's action on the digestive system. Recent research has found that Taraxinic acid has a significant effect on human leukemia cells, with the authors encouraging further research about possible clinical applications.

• Li Y, Chen Y, Sun-Waterhouse D. The Potential of Dandelion in the Fight Against Gastrointestinal Diseases: A Review. J Ethnopharmacol. 2022 Apr 8;15(293):115272.

• Kenny O, Brunton NP, Walsh D, Hewage CM, McLoughlin P, Smyth TJ. Characterisation of antimicrobial extracts from dandelion root (Taraxacum officinale) using LC-SPE-NMR. Phytother Res. 2015 Apr;29(4):526–32.

• Fan M, Zhang X, Song H, Zhang Y. Dandelion (Taraxacum Genus): A Review of Chemical Constituents and Pharmacological Effects. Molecules. 2023 Jun 27;28(13):5022.

• Clare BA, Conroy RS, Spelman K. The diuretic effect in human subjects of an extract of Taraxacum officinale folium over a single day. J Altern Complement Med. 2009 Aug;15(8):929–34.

• Choi JH, Shin KM, Kim NY, Hong JP, Lee YS, Kim HJ, et al. Taraxinic acid, a hydrolysate of sesquiterpene lactone glycoside from the Taraxacum coreanum NAKAI, induces the differentiation of human acute promyelocytic leukemia HL-60 cells. Biol Pharm Bull. 2002 Nov;25(11):1446–50.

Elder Elderberry has always been a popular influenza remedy, and research revolves around the actions of Elder for respiratory illnesses. Elderberry has been found to inhibit the ability of viruses to enter into cells (and thus reduce viral replication), stimulate cytokine production, enhance the activity of macrophages and natural killer (NK) cells whilst also having an anti-inflammatory effect which can help prevent excess inflammation. The verses included in this chapter are from the old Scottish ballad 'Thomas the Rhymer' I first read in R.J. Stewart's *The Underworld Initiation*.

- Zakay-Rones Z, Thom E, Wollan T, Wadstein J. Randomized study of the efficacy and safety of oral elderberry extract in the treatment of influenza A and B virus infections. J Int Med Res. 2004;32(2):132–40.
- Wieland LS, Piechotta V, Feinberg T, Ludeman E, Hutton B, Kanji S, et al. Elderberry for prevention and treatment of viral respiratory illnesses: a systematic review. BMC Complement Med Ther. 2021 Apr 7;21(1):112.
- Stich L, Plattner S, McDougall G, Austin C, Steinkasserer A. Polysaccharides from European Black Elderberry Extract Enhance Dendritic Cell Mediated T Cell Immune Responses. Int J Mol Sci. 2022 Apr 1;23(7):3949.
- Stępień AE, Trojniak J, Tabarkiewicz J. Health-Promoting Properties: Anti-Inflammatory and Anticancer Properties of Sambucus nigra L. Flowers and Fruits. Molecules. 2023 Aug 24;28(17):6235.
- Harnett J, Oakes K, Carè J, Leach M, Brown D, Cramer H, et al. The effects of Sambucus nigra berry on acute respiratory viral infections: A rapid review of clinical studies. Adv Integr Med. 2020 Dec;7(4):240–6.

Fern Many Ferns are toxic and potentially carcinogenic, which is why they are rarely used medicinally today, despite some traditional recorded uses. The primary toxic compound in certain ferns, such as Bracken, is ptaquiloside. Interestingly, Ferns also possess bioremediation properties, enabling them to accumulate toxic elements like arsenic, particularly in areas contaminated by gold mining activities.

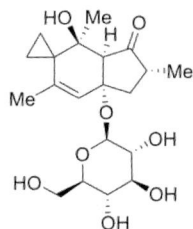

- Alonso-Amelot ME, Avendaño M. Human carcinogenesis and bracken fern: a review of the evidence. Curr Med Chem. 2002 Mar;9(6):675-86.
- Potter DM, Baird MS. Carcinogenic effects of ptaquiloside in bracken fern and related compounds. Br J Cancer. 2000 Oct;83(7):914–20.
- Besedin JA, Khudur LS, Netherway P, Ball AS. Remediation Opportunities for Arsenic-Contaminated Gold Mine Waste. Applied Sciences. 2023 Jan;13(18):10208.

Ptaquiloside is an unstable compound found in certain Ferns, particularly Bracken. Due to its chemical instability, ptaquiloside can form reactive intermediates, which act as DNA alkylating agents. This alkylation can lead to mutations, and it has been associated with an increased risk of cancers such as mouth, oesophageal, and gastric cancer in humans.

Fennel Fennel seeds have long been recognised for their benefits for breastfeeding mothers, and research has explored this as well as a range of other effects, including reducing menopausal symptoms, aiding in polycystic ovary syndrome (PCOS) and hirsutism, and calming infantile colic. Anethole, a constituent in Fennel, is considered to be estrogenic.

• Wagner CL, Boan AD, Marzolf A, Finch CW, Morella K, Guille C, et al. The Safety of Mother's Milk® Tea: Results of a Randomized Double-Blind, Controlled Study in Fully Breastfeeding Mothers and Their Infants. J Hum Lact. 2019 May;35(2):248–60.

• Rahimikian F, Rahimi R, Golzareh P, Bekhradi R, Mehran A. Effect of Foeniculum vulgare Mill. (fennel) on menopausal symptoms in postmenopausal women: a randomized, triple-blind, placebo-controlled trial. Menopause. 2017 Sep;24(9):1017–21.

• Mohebbi-Kian E, Mohammad-Alizadeh-Charandabi S, Bekhradi R. Efficacy of fennel and combined oral contraceptive on depot medroxyprogesterone acetate-induced amenorrhea: a randomized placebo-controlled trial. Contraception. 2014 Oct;90(4):440–6.

• Manouchehri A, Abbaszadeh S, Ahmadi M, Nejad FK, Bahmani M, Dastyar N. Polycystic ovaries and herbal remedies: A systematic review. JBRA Assist Reprod. 2023 Mar 30;27(1):85–91.

• Javidnia K, Dastgheib L, Mohammadi Samani S, Nasiri A. Antihirsutism activity of Fennel (fruits of Foeniculum vulgare) extract. A double-blind placebo controlled study. Phytomedicine. 2003;10(6–7):455–8.

• Ghaffari P, Hosseininik M, Afrasiabifar A, Sadeghi H, Hosseininik A, Tabatabaei SM, et al. The effect of Fennel seed powder on estradiol levels, menopausal symptoms, and sexual desire in postmenopausal women. Menopause. 2020 Nov;27(11):1281–6.

• Alexandrovich I, Rakovitskaya O, Kolmo E, Sidorova T, Shushunov S. The effect of fennel (Foeniculum Vulgare) seed oil emulsion in infantile colic: a randomized, placebo-controlled study. Altern Ther Health Med. 2003;9(4):58–61.

• Albert-Puleo M. Fennel and anise as estrogenic agents. J Ethnopharmacol. 1980 Dec;2(4):337–44.

• Alazadeh M, Azadbakht M, Niksolat F, Asgarirad H, Moosazadeh M, Ahmadi A, et al. Effect of sweet fennel seed extract capsule on knee pain in women with knee osteoarthritis. Complement Ther Clin Pract. 2020 Aug;40:101219.

• Abdi F, Rahnemaei FA, Roozbeh N, Pakzad R. Impact of phytoestrogens on treatment of urogenital menopause symptoms: A systematic review of randomized clinical trials. Eur J Obstet Gynecol Reprod Biol. 2021 Jun;261:222–35.

• Aarshageetha P, Janci PRR, Tharani ND. Role of Alternate Therapies to Improve the Quality of Life in Menopausal Women: A Systematic Review. J Midlife Health. 2023;14(3):153–8.

• Zeng H, Chen X, Liang J. In vitro antifungal activity and mechanism of essential oil from fennel (Foeniculum vulgare L.) on dermatophyte species. J Med Microbiol. 2015 Jan;64(Pt 1):93–103.

Fly Agaric Muscimol and ibotenic acid (IA) are considered key constituents in Fly Agaric (*Amanita muscaria*). Ibotenic acid is converted to muscimol via decarboxylation when dried or cooked. The concentration of ibotenic acid is highest in the cap skin, and cultures familiar with the mushroom often peel the skin before processing to reduce its content. Muscimol, an agonist for the GABA$_A$ receptor, is likely to be the main neuroactive constituent, responsible for both the psychoactive effects of Fly Agaric and their analgesic effect on neuropathic pain.

There has been extensive exploration of the idea that Fly Agaric may be the Soma mentioned in the Rig Veda. Feeney's PhD thesis thoroughly reviewed and supports the idea that Amanita muscaria could be Soma, based on various anecdotes and traditional methods of processing the mushroom that resemble descriptions in the Rig Veda.

- Winkelman MJ. Amanita muscaria: Fly Agaric history, mythology and pharmacology. Journal of Psychedelic Studies. 2022 Apr 19;6(1):1–4.
- Voynova M, Shkondrov A, Kondeva-Burdina M, Krasteva I. Toxicological and pharmacological profile of Amanita muscaria (L.) Lam. – a new rising opportunity for biomedicine. Pharmacia. 2020 Nov 26;67:317–23.
- Ramawad HA, Paridari P, Jabermoradi S, Gharin P, Toloui A, Safari S, et al. Muscimol as a treatment for nerve injury-related neuropathic pain: a systematic review and meta-analysis of preclinical studies. Korean J Pain. 2023 Oct 1;36(4):425–40.
- Ordak M, Galazka A, Nasierowski T, Muszynska E, Bujalska-Zadrozny M. Reasons, Form of Ingestion and Side Effects Associated with Consumption of Amanita muscaria. Toxics. 2023 Apr 17;11(4):383.
- Michelot D, Melendez-Howell LM. Amanita muscaria: chemistry, biology, toxicology, and ethnomycology. Mycol Res. 2003 Feb;107(Pt 2):131–46.
- Łukasik-Głebocka M, Druzdz A, Naskret M. [Clinical symptoms and circumstances of acute poisonings with fly agaric (Amanita muscaria) and panther cap (Amanita pantherina)]. Przegl Lek. 2011 Jan 1;68(8):449–52.
- Jahanabadi S, Amiri S, Karkeh-abadi M, Razmi A. Natural psychedelics in the treatment of depression; a review focusing on neurotransmitters. Fitoterapia. 2023 Sep 1;169:105620.
- Feeney K. Revisiting Wasson's Soma: exploring the effects of preparation on the chemistry of Amanita muscaria. J Psychoactive Drugs. 2010 Dec;42(4):499–506.

Books

- Wasson, RG. Soma: Divine Mushroom of Immortality. Harcourt, Brace & World; 1968.
- Baba Masha Microdosing with Amanita Muscaria: Creativity, healing, and recovery with the sacred mushroom. Rochester, VT: Park Street Press; 2022.
- Letcher, A. Shroom: A cultural history of the magic mushroom. HarperCollins; 2008.

Hawthorn   Hawthorn berry, flowers and young leaves have a firm place in herbalism, and are well researched. Focus has been on wide-ranging cardiovascular benefits as well as qualities useful in diabetes and liver pathologies.

♦ Zhang J, Chai X, Zhao F, Hou G, Meng Q. Food Applications and Potential Health Benefits of Hawthorn. Foods. 2022 Sep 15;11(18):2861.

♦ Wang J, Xiong X, Feng B. Effect of crataegus usage in cardiovascular disease prevention: an evidence-based approach. Evid Based Complement Alternat Med. 2013;2013:149363.

♦ Nabavi SF, Habtemariam S, Ahmed T, Sureda A, Daglia M, Sobarzo-Sánchez E, et al. Polyphenolic Composition of Crataegus monogyna Jacq.: From Chemistry to Medical Applications. Nutrients. 2015 Sep 11;7(9):7708–28.

♦ Kim E, Jang E, Lee JH. Potential Roles and Key Mechanisms of Hawthorn Extract against Various Liver Diseases. Nutrients. 2022 Feb 18;14(4):867.

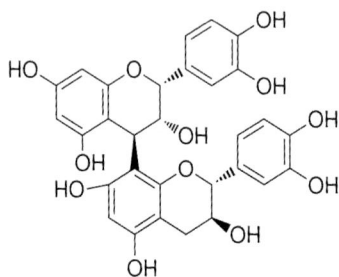

Procyandin B2, one of the most abundant oligomeric proanthocyanidins (OPCs) found in many plants, often as pigment, including Hawthorn, Apple peel, Blueberries, Cacao and Grape seeds. This molecule has been extensively researched, revealing a wealth of health giving properties. In particular it is considered cardio-protective, powerfully antioxidant, wound healing and anti-inflammatory.

♦ Gheitasi I, Savari F, Akbari G, Mohammadi J, Fallahzadeh AR, Sadeghi H. Molecular Mechanisms of Hawthorn Extracts in Multiple Organs Disorders in Underlying of Diabetes: A Review. Int J Endocrinol. 2022;2022:2002768.

♦ Dood KP, Frey AD, Geisbuhler TP. The Effect of Hawthorn Extract on Coronary Flow. J Evid Based Complementary Altern Med. 2013 Oct 1;18(4):257–67.

♦ Dahmer S, Scott E. Health effects of hawthorn. Am Fam Physician. 2010 Feb 15;81(4):465–8.

♦ Cloud A, Vilcins D, McEwen B. The effect of hawthorn (Crataegus spp.) on blood pressure: A systematic review. Advances in Integrative Medicine. 2020 Sep 1;7(3):167–75.

♦ Lu M, Zhang L, Pan J, Shi H, Zhang M, Li C. Advances in the study of the vascular protective effects and molecular mechanisms of hawthorn (Crataegus anamesa Sarg.) extracts in cardiovascular diseases. Food Funct. 2023 Jul 3;14(13):5870–90.

Horsetail   Horsetail grows abundantly in the valley where my apothecary is based and is valued as a spray to protect plants from fungi that thrive in damp environments. The papers below describe the various ways in which silica (in the form of bio-available orthosilicic acid) impacts bone health, modulates immune function, and helps clear aluminium from the body.

Horsetail and fungal infections in plants

• Trebbi G, Negri L, Bosi S, Dinelli G, Cozzo R, Marotti I. Evaluation of Equisetum arvense (Horsetail Macerate) as a Copper Substitute for Pathogen Management in Field-Grown Organic Tomato and Durum Wheat Cultivations. Agriculture. 2020 Dec 23;11:5.

• Guerriero G, Law C, Stokes I, Moore KL, Exley C. Rough and tough. How does silicic acid protect horsetail from fungal infection? J Trace Elem Med Biol. 2018 May;47:45–52.

• Pat Bowen , Jim Menzies, David Ehret, Lacey Samuels and Anthony D.M. Glass. Soluble Silicon Sprays Inhibit Powdery Mildew Development on Grape Leaves. J Amer Soc Hort Sci. 1992;117(6):906-912.

Human health effects - bones, immunity and aluminium

• Rodella LF, Bonazza V, Labanca M, Lonati C, Rezzani R. A review of the effects of dietary silicon intake on bone homeostasis and regeneration. J Nutr Health Aging. 2014 Nov;18(9):820–6.

• Reffitt DM, Ogston N, Jugdaohsingh R, Cheung HFJ, Evans B a. J, Thompson RPH, et al. Orthosilicic acid stimulates collagen type 1 synthesis and osteoblastic differentiation in human osteoblast-like cells in vitro. Bone. 2003 Feb;32(2):127–35.

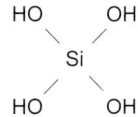

A molecular diagram of orthosilicic acid, found in Horsetail. This has a key role in the human body for bone growth, collagen production and connective tissue repair.

• Jugdaohsingh R. Silicon and bone health. J Nutr Health Aging. 2007;11(2):99–110.

• Jeong SY, Yu HS, Ra MJ, Jung SM, Yu JN, Kim JC, et al. Phytochemical Investigation of Equisetum arvense and Evaluation of Their Anti-Inflammatory Potential in TNFα/INFγ-Stimulated Keratinocytes. Pharmaceuticals (Basel). 2023 Oct 16;16(10):1478.

• Gründemann C, Lengen K, Sauer B, Garcia-Käufer M, Zehl M, Huber R. Equisetum arvense (common horsetail) modulates the function of inflammatory immunocompetent cells. BMC Complement Altern Med. 2014 Aug 4;14:283.

• Gillette Guyonnet S, Andrieu S, Vellas B. The potential influence of silica present in drinking water on Alzheimer's disease and associated disorders. J Nutr Health Aging. 2007;11(2):119–24.

• Davenward S, Bentham P, Wright J, Crome P, Job D, Polwart A, et al. Silicon-rich mineral water as a non-invasive test of the 'aluminum hypothesis' in Alzheimer's disease. J Alzheimers Dis. 2013;33(2):423–30.

Lady's Mantle Despite being valued for centuries for their balancing effect on the womb, this application appears to have never been researched. Recent research highlights some of the topical healing effects (for mouth ulcers and post-operative sore throat) as well as interesting antiproliferative and genoprotective effects against cancer cell lines."

• Chung CJ, Jeong SY, Jeong JH, Kim SW, Lee KH, Kim JH, et al. Comparison of prophylactic effect of topical Alchemilla vulgaris in glycerine versus that of dexamethasone on postoperative sore throat after tracheal intubation using a double-lumen endobronchial tube: a randomized controlled study. Anesth Pain Med (Seoul). 2021 Apr;16(2):163–70.

• Shrivastava R, John GW. Treatment of Aphthous Stomatitis with topical Alchemilla vulgaris in glycerine. Clin Drug Investig. 2006;26(10):567–73.

• Vlaisavljević S, Jelača S, Zengin G, Mimica-Dukić N, Berežni S, Miljić M, et al. Alchemilla vulgaris agg. (Lady's mantle) from central Balkan: antioxidant, anticancer and enzyme inhibition properties. RSC Adv. 2019 Nov 13;9(64):37474–83.

• Jelača S, Dajić-Stevanović Z, Vuković N, Kolašinac S, Trendafilova A, Nedialkov P, et al. Beyond Traditional Use of Alchemilla vulgaris: Genoprotective and Antitumor Activity In Vitro. Molecules. 2022 Nov 22;27(23):8113.

• Ibrahim OHM, Abo-Elyousr KAM, Asiry KA, Alhakamy NA, Mousa MAA. Phytochemical Characterization, Antimicrobial Activity and In Vitro Antiproliferative Potential of Alchemilla vulgaris Auct Root Extract against Prostate (PC-3), Breast (MCF-7) and Colorectal Adenocarcinoma (Caco-2) Cancer Cell Lines. Plants (Basel). 2022 Aug 17;11(16):2140.

Lemon Balm Widely recognised and researched for their anxiolytic and anti-viral qualities, Lemon Balm is also increasingly acknowledged for its potential benefits in dementia and Alzheimer's disease. For further reading on the Puer Aeternus see: The Psychology of The Man-Child (Puer Aeternus): www.eternalisedofficial.com/2022/10/09/puer-aeternus-psychology/.

• Zam W, Quispe C, Sharifi-Rad J, López MD, Schoebitz M, Martorell M, et al. An Updated Review on The Properties of Melissa officinalis L.: Not Exclusively Anti-anxiety. Front Biosci (Schol Ed). 2022 Jun 7;14(2):16.

• Safari M, Asadi A, Aryaeian N, Huseini HF, Shidfar F, Jazayeri S, et al. The effects of melissa officinalis on depression and anxiety in type 2 diabetes patients with depression: a randomized double-blinded placebo-controlled clinical trial. BMC Complement Med Ther. 2023 May 2;23(1):140.

• Nawrot J, Gornowicz-Porowska J, Budzianowski J, Nowak G, Schroeder G, Kurczewska J. Medicinal Herbs in the Relief of Neurological, Cardiovascular, and Respiratory Symptoms after COVID-19 Infection A Literature Review. Cells. 2022 Jun 11;11(12):1897.

• Ghazizadeh J, Sadigh-Eteghad S, Marx W, Fakhari A, Hamedeyazdan S, Torbati M, et al. The effects of lemon balm (Melissa officinalis L.) on depression and anxiety in clinical trials: A systematic review and meta-analysis. Phytother Res. 2021 Dec;35(12):6690–705.

The Psychology of The Man-Child (Puer Aeternus). Available from: https://eternalisedofficial.com/2022/10/09/puer-aeternus-psychology/

‣ Dutta T, Anand U, Mitra SS, Ghorai M, Jha NK, Shaikh NK, et al. Phytotherapy for Attention Deficit Hyperactivity Disorder (ADHD): A Systematic Review and Meta-analysis. Front Pharmacol. 2022;13:827411.

‣ Behzadi A, Imani S, Deravi N, Mohammad Taheri Z, Mohammadian F, Moraveji Z, et al. Antiviral Potential of Melissa officinalis L.: A Literature Review. Nutr Metab Insights. 2023;16:11786388221146683.

‣ Astani A, Reichling J, Schnitzler P. Melissa officinalis extract inhibits attachment of herpes simplex virus in vitro. Chemotherapy. 2012;58(1):70–7.

‣ Ahmad S, Ahmed SB, Khan A, Wasim M, Tabassum S, Haider S, et al. Natural remedies for Alzheimer's disease: A systematic review of randomized controlled trials. Metab Brain Dis. 2023 Jan;38(1):17–44.

Mallow The clinical research on Marshmallow is still fairly preliminary, with investigations spanning various areas. Studies have explored its efficacy in treating dry coughs, dermatitis in children, breast engorgement (using leaf compresses), reducing fevers (as a body wash), and moisturising the mouth in cases of hypo-salivation. In vitro research indicates that marshmallow possesses anti-inflammatory and hypoglycemic effects and can enhance cell viability and proliferation in epithelial cells, aligning well with its traditional use for wound healing. I've also included a few review papers exploring the importance of touch.

‣ Xue TT, Yang YG, Tang ZS, Duan JA, Song ZX, Hu XH, et al. Evaluation of antioxidant, enzyme inhibition, nitric oxide production inhibitory activities and chemical profiles of the active extracts from the medicinal and edible plant: Althaea officinalis. Food Res Int. 2022 Jun;156:111166.

‣ Skrinjar I, Vucicevic Boras V, Bakale I, Andabak Rogulj A, Brailo V, Vidovic Juras D, et al. Comparison between three different saliva substitutes in patients with hyposalivation. Clin Oral Investig. 2015 Apr;19(3):753–7.

‣ Naseri V, Chavoshzadeh Z, Mizani A, Daneshfard B, Ghaffari F, Abbas-Mohammadi M, et al. Effect of topical marshmallow (Althaea officinalis) on atopic dermatitis in children: A pilot double-blind active-controlled clinical trial of an in-silico-analyzed phytomedicine. Phytother Res. 2021 Mar;35(3):1389–98.

‣ Khosravan S, Mohammadzadeh-Moghadam H, Mohammadzadeh F, Fadafen SAK, Gholami M. The Effect of Hollyhock (Althaea officinalis L) Leaf Compresses Combined With Warm and Cold Compress on Breast Engorgement in Lactating Women: A Randomized Clinical Trial. J Evid Based Complementary Altern Med. 2017 Jan;22(1):25–30.

‣ Goodarzi H, Valizadeh F, Ghasemi F, Ebrahimzade F, Seifosadat SH, Delfan B, et al. Comparing the effect of body wash with marshmallow plant and lukewarm water on reducing the temperature of febrile children: a randomized clinical trial. BMC Complement Med Ther. 2022 Nov 12;22(1):293.

‣ Fink C, Schmidt M, Kraft K. Marshmallow Root Extract for the Treatment of Irritative Cough: Two

Surveys on Users' View on Effectiveness and Tolerability. Complementary Medicine Research. 2018 Aug 1;25(5):299–305.

• Deters A, Zippel J, Hellenbrand N, Pappai D, Possemeyer C, Hensel A. Aqueous extracts and polysaccharides from Marshmallow roots (Althea officinalis L.): cellular internalisation and stimulation of cell physiology of human epithelial cells in vitro. J Ethnopharmacol. 2010 Jan 8;127(1):62–9.

• Curnow A, Owen SJ. An Evaluation of Root Phytochemicals Derived from Althea officinalis (Marshmallow) and Astragalus membranaceus as Potential Natural Components of UV Protecting Dermatological Formulations. Oxid Med Cell Longev. 2016;2016:7053897.

• Bonaterra GA, Schmitt J, Schneider K, Schwarzbach H, Aziz-Kalbhenn H, Kelber O, et al. Phytohustil® and root extract of Althaea officinalis L. exert anti-inflammatory and anti-oxidative properties and improve the migratory capacity of endothelial cells in vitro. Front Pharmacol. 2022 Dec 8;13:948248.

• Bonaterra GA, Bronischewski K, Hunold P, Schwarzbach H, Heinrich EU, Fink C, et al. Anti-inflammatory and Anti-oxidative Effects of Phytohustil® and Root Extract of Althaea officinalis L. on Macrophages in vitro. Front Pharmacol. 2020 Mar 17;11:290.

• Amini F, Namjooyan F, Zomorodian K, Zareshahrabadi Z, Shojaei K, Jaladat AM, et al. The efficacy of complementary treatment with marshmallow (Althaea officinalis L.) on vulvovaginal candidiasis: A randomized double-blinded controlled clinical trial. Explore (NY). 2023;19(6):813–9.

• Jablonski NG. Social and affective touch in primates and its role in the evolution of social cohesion. Neuroscience. 2021 Jun 1;464:117–25.

• Pepito JAT, Babate FJG, Dator WLT. The nurses' touch: An irreplaceable component of caring. Nurs Open. 2023 Sep;10(9):5838–42.

• Navyte G, Gillmeister H, Kumari M. Interpersonal touch and the importance of romantic partners for older adults' neuroendocrine health. Psychoneuroendocrinology. 2024 Jan;159:106414.

Marigold The word glamour has its roots in the Scottish term 'gramarye', which itself comes from the Old French and Latin words 'gramaire' and 'grammatica', the art of letters and magical learning. Clearly the meaning has shifted over the centuries, from the recognition of magical power of words and letters, to a specific incantation of allure and attraction. However, it seems, to me at least, that the quality of intentional invocation, of both words and appearance representing reality and thus altering others' perceptions is broadly similar. As a writer this feels a sacred art, to weave words in a way that invites you into a deeper experience of *your* reality.

The references below give a *very* broad set of doorways into the many themes touched on in the Marigold portrait, from social media to lutein and root-knot nematodes to fibroblast activation and eye health.

I'd like to thank Chloë Cacau for her thorough, critical review and suggestions for this chapter, one of the last chapters to find its shape when writing.

Social media and the lure of glamour

• Zsila Á, Reyes MES. Pros & cons: impacts of social media on mental health. BMC Psychol. 2023 Jul 6;11(1):201.

• Barthorpe A, Winstone L, Mars B, Moran P. Is social media screen time really associated with poor adolescent mental health? A time use diary study. J Affect Disord. 2020 Sep 1;274:864–70.

Anti-pathogenic qualities

• Zaki AA, Ashour AA, Qiu L. New sesquiterpene glycoside ester with antiprotozoal activity from the flowers of Calendula officinalis L. Nat Prod Res. 2021 Dec;35(23):5250–4.

• Doligalska M, Jóźwicka K, Szewczak L, Nowakowska J, Brodaczewska K, Goździk K, et al. Calendula officinalis Triterpenoid Saponins Impact the Immune Recognition of Proteins in Parasitic Nematodes. Pathogens. 2021 Mar 4;10(3):296.

• Saffari E, Mohammad-Alizadeh-Charandabi S, Adibpour M, Mirghafourvand M, Javadzadeh Y. Comparing the effects of Calendula officinalis and clotrimazole on vaginal Candidiasis: A randomized controlled trial. Women Health. 2017;57(10):1145–60.

• Huang WH, Hung CY, Chiang PC, Lee H, Lin IT, Lai PC, et al. Physicochemical Characterization, Biocompatibility, and Antibacterial Properties of CMC/PVA/Calendula officinalis Films for Biomedical Applications. Polymers (Basel). 2023 Mar 14;15(6):1454.

Lutein, a carotenoid that occurs frequently in plants, but is not made by animals. It is found in the macula and retina of the human eye and is thought to be crucial to protecting the eye from UV damage.

Wound healing and eye health

• Mares J. Lutein and Zeaxanthin Isomers in Eye Health and Disease. Annu Rev Nutr. 2016 Jul 17;36:571–602.

• Johra FT, Bepari AK, Bristy AT, Reza HM. A Mechanistic Review of β-Carotene, Lutein, and Zeaxanthin in Eye Health and Disease. Antioxidants (Basel). 2020 Oct 26;9(11):1046.

• Dinda M, Dasgupta U, Singh N, Bhattacharyya D, Karmakar P. PI3K-mediated proliferation of fibroblasts by Calendula officinalis tincture: implication in wound healing. Phytother Res. 2015 Apr;29(4):607–16.

• Kandathil AM, Aslam SA, Abidha R, Cherian MP, Soman S, Sudarsanan M. Evaluation of Microbial Adherence on Antibacterial Suture Materials during Intraoral Wound Healing: A Prospective Comparative Study. J Contemp Dent Pract. 2023 Aug 1;24(8):515–20.

• Jiménez-Medina E, Garcia-Lora A, Paco L, Algarra I, Collado A, Garrido F. A new extract of the plant Calendula officinalis produces a dual in vitro effect: cytotoxic anti-tumor activity and lymphocyte activation. BMC Cancer. 2006 May 5;6:119.

Mistletoe   Research on mistletoe focuses on injectable preparations such as 'Iscador,' which are well-established within anthroposophical medicine. However, much of this research is based on animal experiments and is therefore not included here. I have included two reviews of clinical trials and a couple of papers indicating possible mechanisms of action via Mistletoe lectins, which appear to inhibit protein synthesis in ribosomal RNA and have various immunomodulatory activities, including increased activity of natural killer (NK) cells. Mistletoe growing on different host trees is considered to vary in their specific clinical application – one research paper below explores this difference with human bladder cancer cell lines.

Despite a long history of use for aiding blood circulation, migraines and epilepsy, there is little research on orally taken Mistletoe, except for an analysis examining the extraction rates of different compounds. This analysis establishes that viscotoxins are not extracted by simple infusion or maceration. For further reading on 'The Poetic Edda,' a rich collection of ancient Norse poems, see: www.voluspa.org. I've also included a reference to Mistletoe's unique relationship with and impact on its host tree.

Mistletoe toxicity

- Jäger S, Beffert M, Hoppe K, Nadberezny D, Frank B, Scheffler A. Preparation of herbal tea as infusion or by maceration at room temperature using mistletoe tea as an example. Sci Pharm. 2011;79(1):145–55.
- JHall AH, Spoerke DG, Rumack BH. Assessing mistletoe toxicity. Ann Emerg Med. 1986 Nov;15(11):1320–3.

Iscador clinical trial systemic review and possible mechanisms of action

- Kienle GS, Kiene H. Review article: Influence of Viscum album L (European mistletoe) extracts on quality of life in cancer patients: a systematic review of controlled clinical studies. Integr Cancer Ther. 2010 Jun;9(2):142–57.
- Horneber M, Ackeren G van, Linde K, Rostock M. Mistletoe therapy in oncology. Cochrane Database of Systematic Reviews [Internet]. 2008 [cited 2024 Mar 29];(2).
- Büssing A, Suzart K, Bergmann J, Pfüller U, Schietzel M, Schweizer K. Induction of apoptosis in human lymphocytes treated with Viscum album L. is mediated by the mistletoe lectins. Cancer Lett. 1996 Jan 19;99(1):59–72.
- Büssing A, Schietzel M. Apoptosis-inducing properties of Viscum album L. extracts from different host trees, correlate with their content of toxic mistletoe lectins. Anticancer Res. 1999;19(1A):23–8.
- Juengel E, Rutz J, Meiborg M, Markowitsch SD, Maxeiner S, Grein T, et al. Mistletoe Extracts from Different Host Trees Disparately Inhibit Bladder Cancer Cell Growth and Proliferation. Cancers (Basel). 2023 Oct 4;15(19):4849.

Mistletoe and host tree

- Lázaro-González A, Gargallo-Garriga A, Hódar JA, Sardans J, Oravec M, Urban O, et al. Implications of mistletoe parasitism for the host metabolome: A new plant identity in the forest canopy. Plant Cell Environ. 2021 Nov;44(11):3655–66.

Mugwort Research on Mugwort is limited compared to research on other *Artemisia* species, particularly *Artemisia annua*, which is highly valued for treating malaria. For those curious about Moxibustion I've included a couple of trials of this when used for IBS and for helping turn breech babies – the later is a very traditional use of Moxa (dried Mugwort) and requires a lot of experience.

◆ Omar AM, Dibwe DF, Tawila AM, Sun S, Kim MJ, Awale S. Chemical constituents from Artemisia vulgaris and their antiausterity activities against the PANC-1 human pancreatic cancer cell line. Nat Prod Res. 2021 Nov;35(22):4279–85.

◆ Liu T, Dai M, Zhu H, Huang Y, Chen J, Li M, et al. Activity-guided isolation and identification of antiherpesvirus and antineuroinflammatory active terpenoids from Artemisia vulgaris L. based on the LC-MS/MS molecular network. Phytochemistry. 2023 Dec;216:113863.

◆ Ekiert H, Pajor J, Klin P, Rzepiela A, Ślesak H, Szopa A. Significance of Artemisia Vulgaris L. (Common Mugwort) in the History of Medicine and Its Possible Contemporary Applications Substantiated by Phytochemical and Pharmacological Studies. Molecules. 2020 Sep 25;25(19):4415.

◆ Wang Z, Xu M, Shi Z, Bao C, Liu H, Zhou C, et al. Mild moxibustion for Irritable Bowel Syndrome with Diarrhea (IBS-D): A randomized controlled trial. J Ethnopharmacol. 2022 May 10;289:115064.

◆ Cardini F, Weixin H. Moxibustion for correction of breech presentation: a randomized controlled trial. JAMA. 1998 Nov 11;280(18):1580–4.

Mullein Mullein (*Verbascum thapsus*) is an early pioneer plant known for its ability to thrive in cleared lands. It has a rich history of traditional use, particularly for supporting lung health, though systematic research in this area is lacking. However, some clinical and experimental studies have begun to explore its potential health benefits, with one notable clinical trial indicating that Mullein can help reduce the size of uterine fibroids (leiomyomas).

In this chapter I also mention masking. I highly recommend *Unmasking Autism* by Dr. Devon Price for anyone exploring the complexities of masking.

◆ Ghassab-Abdollahi N, Sadeghzade Oskouei B, Asgharian P, Jahanshahi A, Farshbaf-Khalili A. The effect of Mullein capsule on uterine leiomyomas volume and the amount of menstrual bleeding: A randomized controlled trial. Journal of Herbal Medicine. 2020 Apr 1;20:100317.

◆ Gupta A, Atkinson AN, Pandey AK, Bishayee A. Health-promoting and disease-mitigating potential of Verbascum thapsus L. (common mullein): A review. Phytother Res. 2022 Apr;36(4):1507–22.

◆ Gross KL. Colonization by Verbascum Thapsus (Mullein) of an Old-Field in Michigan: Experiments on the Effects of Vegetation. Journal of Ecology. 1980;68(3):919–27.

◆ Dulger G, Tutenocakli T, Dulger B. Antimicrobial potential of the leaves of common mullein (Verbascum thapsus L., Scrophulariaceae) on microorganisms isolated from urinary tract infections.

◆ Dar MA, Bhat MF, Hassan R, Masoodi MH, Mir SR, Mohiuddin R. Extensive Phytochemistry, Comprehensive Traditional Uses, and Critical Pharmacological Profile of the Great Mullein: Verbascum thapsus L. The Natural Products Journal. 2019 Sep 1;9(3):158–71.

Nettle Nettle is a well-researched plant with a substantial evidence base for their use in treating various health conditions. The root of Nettle is effective in managing benign prostatic hyperplasia (BPH). Additionally, research has explored their potential benefits in treating prostate cancer, diabetes, urinary tract infections (UTIs), kidney stones, arthritis, allergies, and as a galactagogue (enhancing breast milk production). They are also recognised for their neuroprotective properties, making them valuable in managing neurodegenerative diseases. In the chapter about Nettle I explore the common experience of nurture and satiation with Nettle leaf decoction and how this often touches early life experiences of nurture. I feel this is very relevant to the psycho-spiritual gifts Nettle can bring and have included a selection of research exploring the significance of early life nurture and the long lasting effect on the HPA axis.

Review and clinical trials regarding BPH, prostrate cancer and diabetes

• Safarinejad MR. Urtica dioica for treatment of benign prostatic hyperplasia: a prospective, randomized, double-blind, placebo-controlled, crossover study. J Herb Pharmacother. 2005;5(4):1–11.

• Santos HO, Howell S, Teixeira FJ. Beyond tribulus (Tribulus terrestris L.): The effects of phytotherapics on testosterone, sperm and prostate parameters. J Ethnopharmacol. 2019 May 10;235:392–405.

• Cicero AFG, Allkanjari O, Busetto GM, Cai T, Larganà G, Magri V, et al. Nutraceutical treatment and prevention of benign prostatic hyperplasia and prostate cancer. Arch Ital Urol Androl. 2019 Oct 2;91(3).

• Namazi N, Esfanjani AT, Heshmati J, Bahrami A. The effect of hydro alcoholic Nettle (Urtica dioica) extracts on insulin sensitivity and some inflammatory indicators in patients with type 2 diabetes: a randomized double-blind control trial. Pak J Biol Sci. 2011 Aug 1;14(15):775–9.

• Kianbakht S, Khalighi-Sigaroodi F, Dabaghian FH. Improved glycemic control in patients with advanced type 2 diabetes mellitus taking Urtica dioica leaf extract: a randomized double-blind placebo-controlled clinical trial. Clin Lab. 2013;59(9–10):1071–6.

Early life experience and the HPA axis

• Moore ER, Bergman N, Anderson GC, Medley N. Early skin-to-skin contact for mothers and their healthy newborn infants. Cochrane Database Syst Rev. 2016 Nov 25;11(11):CD003519.

• Montgomery SM, Ehlin A, Sacker A. Breast feeding and resilience against psychosocial stress. Arch Dis Child. 2006 Dec;91(12):990–4.

• Maniam J, Antoniadis C, Morris MJ. Early-Life Stress, HPA Axis Adaptation, and Mechanisms Contributing to Later Health Outcomes. Front Endocrinol (Lausanne). 2014;5:73.

• Kim AW, Adam EK, Bechayda SA, Kuzawa CW. Early life stress and HPA axis function independently predict adult depressive symptoms in metropolitan Cebu, Philippines. Am J Phys Anthropol. 2020 Nov;173(3):448–62.

• Juruena MF, Bourne M, Young AH, Cleare AJ. Hypothalamic-Pituitary-Adrenal axis dysfunction by early life stress. Neurosci Lett. 2021 Aug 10;759:136037.

• Gonzales AM, Tejero LMS. Concept analysis of maternal-infant attachment during the weaning process. Belitung Nurs J. 2022;8(5):381–8.

• Bergman NJ, Ludwig RJ, Westrup B, Welch MG. Nurturescience versus neuroscience: A case for rethinking perinatal mother-infant behaviors and relationship. Birth Defects Res. 2019 Sep 1;111(15):1110–27.

Other research

• Semwal P, Rauf A, Olatunde A, Singh P, Zaky MY, Islam MM, et al. The medicinal chemistry of Urtica dioica L.: from preliminary evidence to clinical studies supporting its neuroprotective activity. Nat Prod Bioprospect. 2023 May 12;13(1):16.

• Özalkaya E, Aslandoğdu Z, Özkoral A, Topcuoğlu S, Karatekin G. Effect of a galactagogue herbal tea on breast milk production and prolactin secretion by mothers of preterm babies. Niger J Clin Pract. 2018 Jan;21(1):38–42.

• Easton L, Vaid S, Nagel AK, Venci JV, Fortuna RJ. Stinging Nettle (Urtica dioica): An Unusual Case of Galactorrhea. Am J Case Rep. 2021 Dec 8;22:e933999.

• Devkota HP, Paudel KR, Khanal S, Baral A, Panth N, Adhikari-Devkota A, et al. Stinging Nettle (Urtica dioica L.): Nutritional Composition, Bioactive Compounds, and Food Functional Properties. Molecules. 2022 Aug 16;27(16):5219.

• Bhusal KK, Magar SK, Thapa R, Lamsal A, Bhandari S, Maharjan R, et al. Nutritional and pharmacological importance of stinging nettle (Urtica dioica L.): A review. Heliyon. 2022 Jun;8(6):e09717.

• Mittman P. Randomized, double-blind study of freeze-dried Urtica dioica in the treatment of allergic rhinitis. Planta Med. 1990 Feb;56(1):44–7.

• Chrubasik S, Enderlein W, Bauer R, Grabner W. Evidence for antirheumatic effectiveness of Herba Urticae dioicae in acute arthritis: A pilot study. Phytomedicine. 1997 Jun;4(2):105–8.

• Nirumand MC, Hajialyani M, Rahimi R, Farzaei MH, Zingue S, Nabavi SM, et al. Dietary Plants for the Prevention and Management of Kidney Stones: Preclinical and Clinical Evidence and Molecular Mechanisms. Int J Mol Sci. 2018 Mar 7;19(3):765.

Opium Poppy Poppy has been extensively written about; I recommend *Opium: How an Ancient Flower Shaped and Poisoned Our World* by John Halpern as great primer. I've included a few fascinating archeological papers and reviews of the current opioid epidemic below.

• Vincenti F, Montesano C, Ciccola A, Serafini I, Favero G, Pallotta M, et al. Unearthed opium: development of a UHPLC-MS/MS method for the determination of Papaver somniferum alkaloids in Daunian vessels. Front Chem. 2023;11:1238793.

• Lawler A, Cannabis, opium use part of ancient Near Eastern cultures. Science360,249-250(2018)

• Jesus A, Bonhomme V, Evin A, Soteras R, Jacomet S, Bouby L, et al. Morphometrics of waterlogged archaeological seeds give new insights into the domestication and spread of Papaver somniferum L. in Western Europe. PLoS One. 2023;18(5):e0286190.

• Giordano G, Mattia M, Biehler-Gomez L, Boracchi M, Tritella S, Maderna E, et al. Papaver somniferum in seventeenth century (Italy): archaeotoxicological study on brain and bone samples in patients from a hospital in Milan. Sci Rep. 2023 Feb 28;13(1):3390.

• Stoicea N, Costa A, Periel L, Uribe A, Weaver T, Bergese SD. Current perspectives on the opioid crisis in the US healthcare system: A comprehensive literature review. Medicine (Baltimore). 2019 May;98(20):e15425.

• Humphreys K, Shover CL, Andrews CM, Bohnert ASB, Brandeau ML, Caulkins JP, et al. Responding to the opioid crisis in North America and beyond: recommendations of the Stanford-Lancet Commission. Lancet. 2022 Feb 5;399(10324):555–604.

Rose Safety considerations in herbalism are frequently over-expressed or under-expressed. This is where working alongside an experienced herbalist can be essential if you yourself feel uncertain. Rose in pregnancy is a good example of this. The possible reasons why include: (1) potential emmenagogue effects (in theory could provoke miscarriage), (2) the energetic cooling effect of Rose, which may be at odds with the traditional sense of the warmth needed for gestation, (3) overuse of strong preparations such as Rose essential oil, (4) lack of research to confirm safety.

There is no published clinical evidence I could find of Rose used in moderate quantities causing harm in pregnancy. Personally I would always be cautious with essential oils in pregnancy, since they are extremely potent extracts, and always start with small quantities of any herb, listening carefully for your body's response. Individuals differ in their response to herbs and no individual response can be predicted based on generalisations.

The research links below point towards potent anti inflammatory, anti-cancer and anti-oxidant effects of *Rosa canina* preparations, as well as an interesting ongoing research trial for Rose and ADHD. The chemist in me was fascinated to find a paper describing Rose extract effectively used to help synthesise gold and silver nanoparticles. A couple of the papers here concern *Rosa damascena*, one we work with frequently in the school, since this is widely used as an essential oil and hydrosol. Even with *Rosa damascena*, which is heavily scented, it takes a massive amount to make a small quantity of essential oil. *Rosa canina* is so subtle in their scent that essential oil production at scale would be impossible.

• Živković J, Stojković D, Petrović J, Zdunić G, Glamočlija J, Soković M. Rosa canina L.--new possibilities for an old medicinal herb. Food Funct. 2015 Dec;6(12):3687–92.

• Shirazi M, Mohebitabar S, Bioos S, Yekaninejad MS, Rahimi R, Shahpiri Z, et al. The Effect of Topical Rosa damascena (Rose) Oil on Pregnancy-Related Low Back Pain: A Randomized Controlled Clinical Trial. J Evid Based Complementary Altern Med. 2017 Jan;22(1):120–6.

• Seifi M, Abbasalizadeh S, Mohammad-Alizadeh-Charandabi S, Khodaie L, Mirghafourvand M. The effect of Rosa (L. Rosa canina) on the incidence of urinary tract infection in the puerperium: A randomized placebo-controlled trial. Phytother Res. 2018 Jan;32(1):76–83.

• Peña F, Valencia S, Tereucán G, Nahuelcura J, Jiménez-Aspee F, Cornejo P, et al. Bioactive Compounds and Antioxidant Activity in the Fruit of Rosehip (Rosa canina L. and Rosa rubiginosa L.). Molecules. 2023 Apr 18;28(8):3544.

• Jiménez S, Gascón S, Luquin A, Laguna M, Ancin-Azpilicueta C, Rodríguez-Yoldi MJ. Rosa canina Extracts Have Antiproliferative and Antioxidant Effects on Caco-2 Human Colon Cancer. PLoS One. 2016;11(7):e0159136.

• Turan I, Demir S, Kilinc K, Yaman SO, Misir S, Kara H, et al. Cytotoxic effect of Rosa canina extract on human colon cancer cells through repression of telomerase expression. J Pharm Anal. 2018 Dec;8(6):394–9.

• Golsorkhi H, Qorbani M, Kamalinejad M, Sabbaghzadegan S, Bahrami M, Vafaee-Shahi M, et al. The effect of Rosa canina L. and a polyherbal formulation syrup in patients with attention-deficit/hyperactivity disorder: a study protocol for a multicenter randomized controlled trial. Trials. 2022 May 23;23(1):434.

• Cheng BCY, Fu XQ, Guo H, Li T, Wu ZZ, Chan K, et al. The genus Rosa and arthritis: Overview on pharmacological perspectives. Pharmacol Res. 2016 Dec;114:219–34.

• Cardoso-Avila PE, Patakfalvi R, Rodríguez-Pedroza C, Aparicio-Fernández X, Loza-Cornejo S, Villa-Cruz V, et al. One-pot green synthesis of gold and silver nanoparticles using Rosa canina L. extract. RSC Adv. 2021 Apr 15;11(24):14624–31.

• Belkhelladi M, Bougrine A. Rosehip extract and wound healing: A review. J Cosmet Dermatol. 2024 Jan;23(1):62–7.

• Abbasijahromi A, Hojati H, Nikooei S, Jahromi HK, Dowlatkhah HR, Zarean V, et al. Compare the effect of aromatherapy using lavender and Damask rose essential oils on the level of anxiety and severity of pain following C-section: A double-blinded randomized clinical trial. J Complement Integr Med. 2020 Sep 23;17(3).

St. John's Wort One of the most extensively researched medicinal plants, the papers below merely give a snapshot of research into St. John's Wort. I've included a couple of papers first highlighting how depression can be closely related to both systemic and personal experiences of trauma, since it seems critical to me that we move beyond a reductive neurological model of depression towards a more trauma informed and socially conscious one. I've included an open access paper giving an in-depth paper discussing St. John's Wort's drug interactions; this being one of the few herbs to merit such a thorough review. Given this complexity it wouldn't be appropriate to attempt to advise here, rather signpost those on pharmaceutical medicine to a professional herbalist who can advise appropriately to your individual circumstances. The most common interactions are listed at the end of this section.

Systemic trauma, childhood adversity and depression

• Hankerson SH, Moise N, Wilson D, Waller BY, Arnold KT, Duarte C, et al. The Intergenerational Impact of Structural Racism and Cumulative Trauma on Depression. Am J Psychiatry. 2022 Jun;179(6):434–40.

• Abbott M, Slack KS. Exploring the relationship between childhood adversity and adult depression: A risk versus strengths-oriented approach. Child Abuse Negl. 2021 Oct;120:105207.

A small selection of clinical trials

• Wölfle U, Seelinger G, Schempp CM. Topical application of St. John's wort (Hypericum perforatum). Planta Med. 2014 Feb;80(2–3):109–20.

• Nobakht SZ, Akaberi M, Mohammadpour AH, Tafazoli Moghadam A, Emami SA. Hypericum perforatum: Traditional uses, clinical trials, and drug interactions. Iran J Basic Med Sci. 2022 Sep;25(9):1045–58.

• Linde K, Ramirez G, Mulrow CD, Pauls A, Weidenhammer W, Melchart D. St John's wort for depression – an overview and meta-analysis of randomised clinical trials. BMJ. 1996 Aug 3;313(7052):253–8.

• Ng QX, Venkatanarayanan N, Ho CYX. Clinical use of Hypericum perforatum (St John's wort) in depression: A meta-analysis. J Affect Disord. 2017 Mar 1;210:211–21.

• Eatemadnia A, Ansari S, Abedi P, Najar S. The effect of Hypericum perforatum on postmenopausal symptoms and depression: A randomized controlled trial. Complement Ther Med. 2019 Aug;45:109–13.

Mechanisms of action and drug interactions

• Nathan PJ. Hypericum perforatum (St John's Wort): a non-selective reuptake inhibitor? A review of the recent advances in its pharmacology. J Psychopharmacol. 2001 Mar;15(1):47–54.

• Linde K, Berner MM, Kriston L. St John's wort for major depression. Cochrane Database Syst Rev. 2008 Oct 8;2008(4):CD000448.

• Kholghi G, Arjmandi-Rad S, Zarrindast MR, Vaseghi S. St. John's wort (Hypericum perforatum) and depression: what happens to the neurotransmitter systems? Naunyn Schmiedebergs Arch Pharmacol. 2022 Jun;395(6):629–42.

• Nicolussi S, Drewe J, Butterweck V, Meyer Zu Schwabedissen HE. Clinical relevance of St. John's Wort drug interactions revisited. Br J Pharmacol. 2020 Mar;177(6):1212–26.

Most common drug interactions: Oral contraceptive pill, immunosuppressants such as cyclosporine and tacrolimus, the heart drug digoxin, anti-retroviral drug indinavir, blood thinners such as warfarin, benzodiazepines such as alprazolam and the anti-cholestorol drugs such as simvastatin. St. John's Wort may also interact with various antidepressants (SSRIs), antiepileptics, chemotherapy agents, opioids, antifungal drugs, calcium channel blockers, and antipsychotics.

Silver Birch Silver Birch is an incredible pioneer tree; I've included some interesting papers below about this as well as the risks involved in tapping Birch for the sap. There's is a growing body of research about betulinic acid's value in cancer, a compound found in Birch. Betulinic acid is also found in Chaga, a mushroom with a rich tradition of anticancer use, which grows on Silver Birch.

Birch ecology and tapping

• Oksanen E. Birch as a Model Species for the Acclimation and Adaptation of Northern Forest Ecosystem to Changing Environment. Front For Glob Change [Internet]. 2021 May 10 [cited 2024 Mar 19];4.

• Franiel I, Kompała-Bąba A. Reproduction strategies of the silver birch (Betula pendula Roth) at post-industrial sites. Sci Rep. 2021 Jun 7;11(1):11969.

• Trummer L, Malone T. Some impacts to paper birch trees tapped for sap harvesting in Alaska. 2009 May [cited 2024 Jun 28]; Available from: https://scholarworks.alaska.edu/handle/11122/3198

Anticancer research related to Birch

• Mu H, Sun Y, Yuan B, Wang Y. Betulinic acid in the treatment of breast cancer: Application and mechanism progress. Fitoterapia. 2023 Sep;169:105617.

• Li X, Jiang W, Li W, Dong S, Du Y, Zhang H, et al. Betulinic acid-mediating miRNA-365 inhibited the progression of pancreatic cancer. Oncol Res. 2023;31(4):505–14.

• Kim SY, Hwangbo H, Kim MY, Ji SY, Kim DH, Lee H, et al. Betulinic Acid Restricts Human Bladder Cancer Cell Proliferation In Vitro by Inducing Caspase-Dependent Cell Death and Cell Cycle Arrest, and Decreasing Metastatic Potential. Molecules. 2021 Mar 4;26(5):1381.

• Jiang W, Li X, Dong S, Zhou W. Betulinic acid in the treatment of tumour diseases: Application and research progress. Biomed Pharmacother. 2021 Oct;142:111990.

Valerian Although impossible to prove, I strongly suspect that the drug Valium, released in 1963, was named with an awareness of the herb Valerian's well-established reputation. While chemically unrelated, their mechanisms of action do overlap, though the effects of Valerian are more complex and multilayered. Both enhance the action of the neurotransmitter GABA, leading to relaxation and sedation. However, Valerian also acts on adenosine receptors (opposite to the effect of caffeine), melatonin receptors, and serotonin through various pharmacological pathways. The effects of this plant are intricate, which may explain the wide variability in individual responses.

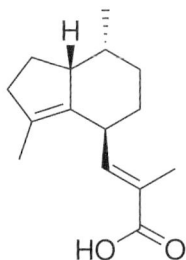

Valerenic acid, a potent sesquiterpenoid sedative found in Valerian and Cramp Bark (*Viburnum opulus*). It is thought to act as a $GABA_A$ modulator and $5HT_{5A}$ agonist, a serotonin receptor involved in sleep-wake cycles. Valerenic acid is only one of many neurologically active molecules found in Valerian.

• Shinjyo N, Waddell G, Green J. Valerian Root in Treating Sleep Problems and Associated Disorders – A Systematic Review and Meta-Analysis. J Evid Based Integr Med. 2020;25:2515690X20967323.

• Miyasaka LS, Atallah AN, Soares BGO. Valerian for anxiety disorders. Cochrane Database Syst Rev. 2006 Oct 18;(4):CD004515.

• Leach MJ, Page AT. Herbal medicine for insomnia: A systematic review and meta-analysis. Sleep Med Rev. 2015 Dec;24:1–12.

• Dietz BM, Mahady GB, Pauli GF, Farnsworth NR. Valerian extract and valerenic acid are partial agonists of the 5-HT5a receptor in vitro. Brain Res Mol Brain Res. 2005 Aug 18;138(2):191–7.

• Bruni O, Ferini-Strambi L, Giacomoni E, Pellegrino P. Herbal Remedies and Their Possible Effect on the GABAergic System and Sleep. Nutrients. 2021 Feb 6;13(2):530.

• Abourashed EA, Koetter U, Brattström A. In vitro binding experiments with a Valerian, hops and their fixed combination extract (Ze91019) to selected central nervous system receptors. Phytomedicine. 2004 Nov;11(7–8):633–8.

Vervain In the chapter on Vervain, I explore how this plant can support individuals through some of the darkest and most profound emotional challenges. Although there is no research regarding this, one study suggests a neuroprotective quality of Vervain. I've also included reviews on the effects of long-term grief and its relationship to loss and trauma to underscore the significant impact these factors can have on health. For myself and many herbalists, Vervain remains one of the most valued allies in providing support during such times.

• Lai SW, Yu MS, Yuen WH, Chang RCC. Novel neuroprotective effects of the aqueous extracts from Verbena officinalis Linn. Neuropharmacology. 2006 May;50(6):641–50.

• Liu WM, Forbat L, Anderson K. Death of a close friend: Short and long-term impacts on physical, psychological and social well-being. PLoS One. 2019;14(4):e0214838.

• Nakajima S. Complicated grief: recent developments in diagnostic criteria and treatment. Philos Trans R Soc Lond B Biol Sci. 2018 Sep 5;373(1754):20170273.

• Kokou-Kpolou CK, Moukouta CS, Masson J, Bernoussi A, Cénat JM, Bacqué MF. Correlates of grief-related disorders and mental health outcomes among adult refugees exposed to trauma and bereavement: A systematic review and future research directions. J Affect Disord. 2020 Apr 15;267:171–84.

Wild Garlic While there is limited medical research specifically on Wild Garlic not involving animal experiments, Wild Garlic contains many compounds similar to those found in other alliums, particularly allicin, which has been extensively researched. Below is a brief overview of some key research papers including some that highlight inter-species similarities among alliums.

• Burton GP, Prescott TAK, Fang R, Lee MA. Regional variation in the antibacterial activity of a wild plant, wild garlic (Allium ursinum L.). Plant Physiol Biochem. 2023 Sep;202:107959.

• Satyal P, Craft JD, Dosoky NS, Setzer WN. The Chemical Compositions of the Volatile Oils of Garlic (Allium sativum) and Wild Garlic (Allium vineale). Foods. 2017 Aug 5;6(8):63.

• Sendl A, Schliack M, Löser R, Stanislaus F, Wagner H. Inhibition of cholesterol synthesis in vitro by extracts and isolated compounds prepared from garlic and wild garlic. Atherosclerosis. 1992 May;94(1):79–85.

• Wang Y, Huang P, Wu Y, Liu D, Ji M, Li H, et al. Association and mechanism of garlic consumption with gastrointestinal cancer risk: A systematic review and meta-analysis. Oncol Lett. 2022 Apr;23(4):125.

• De Greef D, Barton EM, Sandberg EN, Croley CR, Pumarol J, Wong TL, et al. Anticancer potential of garlic and its bioactive constituents: A systematic and comprehensive review. Semin Cancer Biol. 2021 Aug;73:219–64.

• Schwingshackl L, Missbach B, Hoffmann G. An umbrella review of garlic intake and risk of cardiovascular disease. Phytomedicine. 2016 Oct 15;23(11):1127–33.

• El-Saber Batiha G, Magdy Beshbishy A, G Wasef L, Elewa YHA, A Al-Sagan A, Abd El-Hack ME, et al. Chemical Constituents and Pharmacological Activities of Garlic (Allium sativum L.): A Review. Nutrients. 2020 Mar 24;12(3):872.

• Deng Y, Ho CT, Lan Y, Xiao J, Lu M. Bioavailability, Health Benefits, and Delivery Systems of Allicin: A Review. J Agric Food Chem. 2023 Dec 13;71(49):19207–20.

Wormwood Wormwood (*Artemisia absinthium*) has a rich history of use in Europe, supported by extensive research into its digestive, hepatoprotective, and neuroprotective properties. A small clinical trial in patients with Crohn's disease demonstrated significant benefits, improving not only gut symptoms but also mood and quality of life. Emerging research also highlights their potential anti-cancer effects and confirms the traditional use as an antiparasitic and anthelmintic (anti-worm) agent, properties that contributed to their name.

• Szopa A, Pajor J, Klin P, Rzepiela A, Elansary HO, Al-Mana FA, et al. Artemisia absinthium – Importance in the History of Medicine, the Latest Advances in Phytochemistry and Therapeutical, Cosmetological and Culinary Uses. Plants (Basel). 2020 Aug 19;9(9):1063.

• Sohail J, Zubair M, Hussain K, Faisal M, Ismail M, Haider I, et al. Pharmacological activities of Artemisia absinthium and control of hepatic cancer by expression regulation of TGFβ1 and MYC genes. PLoS One. 2023;18(4):e0284244.

• Rashidi R, Ghorbani A, Rakhshandeh H, Mousavi SH. Protective effect of Artemisia absinthium on 6-hydroxydopamine-induced toxicity in SH-SY5Y cell line. Avicenna J Phytomed. 2021;11(3):238–46.

• Omer B, Krebs S, Omer H, Noor TO. Steroid-sparing effect of wormwood (Artemisia absinthium) in Crohn's disease: a double-blind placebo-controlled study. Phytomedicine. 2007 Feb;14(2–3):87–95.

• Lee JY, Park H, Lim W, Song G. α,β-Thujone suppresses human placental choriocarcinoma cells via metabolic disruption. Reproduction. 2020 Jun;159(6):745–56.

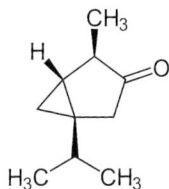

Thujone is a monoterpene that is toxic in relatively small quantities, with a lower estimate of 1.5 mg/kg. Aside from the essential oil, Wormwood contains relatively low levels of thujone, though caution is advised with regular, daily use. Recent research indicates that a liter of traditionally prepared Absinthe contains around 25 mg of thujone, while modern Absinthe is limited to 10 mg per liter. Wormwood essential oil is very high in thujone and should never be taken internally.

• Krebs S, Omer TN, Omer B. Wormwood (Artemisia absinthium) suppresses tumour necrosis factor alpha and accelerates healing in patients with Crohn's disease - A controlled clinical trial. Phytomedicine. 2010 Apr;17(5):305–9.

• He M, Yasin K, Yu S, Li J, Xia L. Total Flavonoids in Artemisia absinthium L. and Evaluation of Its Anticancer Activity. Int J Mol Sci. 2023 Nov 15;24(22):16348.

• de Almeida LMS, de Carvalho LSA, Gazolla MC, Silva Pinto PL, da Silva MPN, de Moraes J, et al. Flavonoids and Sesquiterpene Lactones from Artemisia absinthium and Tanacetum parthenium against Schistosoma mansoni Worms. Evid Based Complement Alternat Med. 2016;2016:9521349.

• Batiha GES, Olatunde A, El-Mleeh A, Hetta HF, Al-Rejaie S, Alghamdi S, et al. Bioactive Compounds, Pharmacological Actions, and Pharmacokinetics of Wormwood (Artemisia absinthium). Antibiotics (Basel). 2020 Jun 23;9(6):353.

• Sotiropoulou N. S. D, Kokkini M. K, Megremi S. F. P, Daferera D. J, Skotti E. P, Kimbaris A. C, Polissiou M. G, Tarantilis P. A. Determination of A- and B-Thujone in Wormwood and Sage Infusions of Greek Flora and Estimation of their Average Toxicity. Curr Res Nutr Food Sci 2016; October 2016).

Recommended Reading

These are all books that have profoundly touched and educated me. I've broadly organised them in four categories: (1) Sensory awakening; (2) Plant wisdom; (3) Undercurrents - systemic themes affecting health; (4) Understanding trauma.

Sensory awakening and perceiving beyond illusions of mind

Abram, David. *The Spell of the Sensuous: Perception and Language in a More-than-Human World.* Pantheon, 1996.

Achterberg, Jeanne. *Imagery in Healing: Shamanism and Modern Medicine.* Shambhala, 2002.

Bates, Brian. *The Real Middle Earth: Magic and Mystery in the Dark Ages.* Pan Books, 2003.

Bates, Brian. *The Way of Wyrd.* Hay House, 2004.

Bortoft, Henri. *The Wholeness of Nature: Goethe's Way toward a Science of Conscious Participation in Nature.* Lindisfarne Press, 1996.

Brennan, Barbara Ann. *Hands of Light: A Guide to Healing through the Human Energy Field.* Bantam Books, 1988.

Buhner, Stephen Harrod. *The Lost Language of Plants: The Ecological Importance of Plant Medicines to Life on Earth.* Chelsea Green Publishing, 2002.

Boothroyd, R. *Warrior, Magician, Lover, King: Archetypes of the Mature Masculine.* Sovereign Books, 2021.

Buhner, Stephen Harrod. *Sacred Plant Medicine: Explorations in the Practice of Indigenous Herbalism.* Roberts Rinehart, 1999.

Buhner, Stephen Harrod. *Plant Intelligence and the Imaginal Realm: Beyond the Doors of Perception into the Dreaming Earth.* Bear and Company, 2014.

Cameron, Julia. *The Artist's Way: A Course in Discovering and Recovering Your Creative Self.* Pan, 1995.

Cowan, Eliot. *Plant Spirit Medicine: The Healing Power of Plants.* Granite Publishing, 1999.

Chödrön, P. *The Wisdom of No Escape and the Path of Loving-Kindness.* Shambhala Publications. 2001

Franz, Marie-Louise von, and Fraser Boa. *The Way of the Dream: Conversations on Jungian Dream Interpretation.* Shambhala Publications, 1994.

Griffiths, Bill. *Aspects of Anglo-Saxon Magic.* Anglo-Saxon Books, 2001.

Harris, Mara Freeman. *Awen: The Quest of the Celtic Mysteries.* Skylight Press, 2018.

RECOMMENDED READING

Hartley, Linda. *Servants of the Sacred Dream: Rebirthing the Deep Feminine.* Elmdon Books, 2020.

Holdrege, Craig. *Thinking like a Plant: A Living Science for Life.* Lindisfarne Books, 2020.

Jung, Carl. *Memories, Dreams, Reflections.* Pantheon Books, 1963.

Kornfield, Jack. *After the Ecstasy, the Laundry: How the Heart Grows Wise on the Spiritual Path.* Rider, 2000.

Lipton, Bruce H. *The Biology of Belief: Unleashing the Power of Consciousness, Matter & Miracles.* Hay House, 2005.

Lyall, Watson. *Jacobson's Organ: And the Remarkable Nature of Smell.* W.W. Norton & Company, 1980.

Mascetti, Manuela Dunn. *Rumi: The Path of Love.* Element Books, 1999.

Merleau-Ponty, Maurice. *Phenomenology of Perception.* Routledge, 2009.

Montgomery, Pam. *Plant Spirit Healing: A Guide to Working with Plant Consciousness.* Bear, 2008.

Myers, David G. *Intuition: Its Powers and Perils.* Yale University Press, 2004.

Nicholson, Shirley J. *Shamanism: An Expanded View of Reality.* Theosophical Publishing House, 1987.

Pelikan, Werner. *Healing Plants: Insights through Spiritual Science.* Mercury Press, 2008.

Price, D. *Unmasking Autism: Discovering the New Faces of Neurodiversity.* Octopus publishing group, 2022.

Rinpoche, Khenchen Thrangu. *Medicine Buddha Teachings.* Snow Lion Publications, 2004.

Seamon, David. *Goethe's Way of Science.* State University of New York Press, 1998.

Sills, Franklyn. *Being and Becoming: Psychodynamics, Buddhism, and the Origins of Selfhood.* North Atlantic Books, 2008.

Stein, Diane. *Essential Reiki: A Complete Guide to an Ancient Healing Art.* The Crossing Press, 1995.

Strand, S. *The Flowering Wand: Rewilding the Sacred Masculine.* Inner Traditions, 2023.

Stewart, R.J. *The Underworld Initiation: A Journey toward Psychic Transformation.* Mercury Publishing, 1998.

Tedeschi, Marc. *Essential Anatomy for Healing & Martial Arts.* Weatherhill, 2008.

Wehr, Gerhard. *Jung & Steiner: The Birth of a New Psychology.* Anthroposophic Press, 2002.

Recommended Reading

Plant wisdom

Allegro, John M. *The Sacred Mushroom and the Cross: A Study of the Nature and Origins of Christianity within the Fertility Cults of the Ancient Near East.* Hodder and Stoughton, 1970.

Bruton-Seal, M and J. *Hedgerow Medicine: Harvest and Make your own Herbal Remedies*, Merlin Unwin Books, 2008.

Chishti, Hakim G.M. *The Traditional Healer's Handbook: A Classic Guide to the Medicine of Avicenna.* Healing Arts Press, 2008.

Culpeper, Nicholas. *Culpeper's Complete Herbal.* Wordsworth Editions, 1995.

Darrell, N. *Conversations with Plants: Volume 1.* Veriditas Press, 2021.

Fischer-Rizzi, Susanne. *Medicine of the Earth: Herbal Remedies for Personal and Planetary Health.* Rudra Press, 1999.

Frawley, David, and Vasant Lad. *The Yoga of Herbs.* Motilal Banarsidass Publishers, 2000.

Freethy, R. *From Agar to Zenry: A book of plant uses, names and folklore*, Crowood Press, 1920.

Graves, Gillian. *The Language of Plants: A Guide to the Doctrine of Signatures.* Lindisfarne Books, 2012.

Grieve, Maud. *A Modern Herbal.* Tiger Books, 1998.

Griggs, Barbara. *Green Pharmacy: The History and Evolution of Western Herbal Medicine.* Healing Arts Press, 1997.

Gurudas. *The Spiritual Properties of Herbs.* Cassandra Press, 1998.

Hughes, N, Owen, F. *Weeds in the Heart.* Quintessence Press, 2018.

Inglis, L. *Milk of Paradise: A History of Opium*, Picador, 2019.

Jones, L. *A Working Herbal Dispensary: Respecting Herbs As Individuals*, Aeon, 2023.

Kimmerer, R. W. *Braiding Sweetgrass: Indigenous Wisdom, Scientific Knowledge, and the Teachings of Plants.* Milkweed Editions, 2013.

Kindred G. *Earth Wisdom: A Heartwarming Mixture of the Spiritual, the Practical and the Proactive*, Hay House, 2004.

Mabey, Richard. *Weeds: How Vagabond Plants Gatecrashed Civilisation and Changed the Way We Think about Nature.* Profile Books, 2010.

Masha, B. *Microdosing with Amanita muscaria: Creativity, Healing, and Recovery with the Sacred Mushroom.* Park Street Press, 2022.

Parvati, J *Hygeieia: A Woman's Herbal*, Freestone, 1978.

Pendell, D. *Pharmako/Poeia: Plant Powers, Poisons, and Herbcraft*, North Atlantic Books, 2010.

Podlech, Dieter. *Herbs and Healing Plants of Britain and Europe.* Collins Nature Guides, 1999.

Pollington, Stephen. *Leechcraft: Early English Charms, Plantlore and Healing.* Anglo-Saxon Books, 2003.

Sistas, Seed. *Poison Prescriptions: Power Plant Medicine, Magic & Ritual,* Watkins, 2022

Wood, Matthew. *The Book of Herbal Wisdom: Using Plants as Medicine.* North Atlantic Books, 1997.

Undercurrents - systemic challenges

Goldacre, Ben. *Bad Pharma: How Drug Companies Mislead Doctors and Harm Patients.* Faber, 2013.

Gøtzsche, Peter C. *Deadly Medicines and Organised Crime: How Big Pharma has Corrupted Healthcare.* CRC Press, 2013.

Kendi, I. X. *How to Be an Antiracist.* Vintage, 2019.

Maté, G. *The Myth of Normal: Trauma, Illness, and Healing in a Toxic Culture,* Vermilion, 2024

Qawas, L. (ed.) *Wort, A Journal of radical, rooted, relational herbalism,* 2023.

Rose, N. *Herbalism and State Violence.* Active distribution, 2021.

Understanding trauma and the healing journey

Dana, D. A. *Polyvagal Exercises for Safety and Connection: 50 Client-Centered practices.* W.W. Norton & Company, 2020.

Kolk, B. *The Body Keeps the Score: Brain, Mind, and Body in the Healing of Trauma,* Penguin, 2015.

Levine, P. *Waking the Tiger: Healing Trauma,* North Atlantic Book, 1997.

Menakem, R. *My Grandmother's Hands: Racialized Trauma and the Pathway to Mending Our Hearts and Bodies,* Penguin, 2021.

Walker, P. *Complex PTSD: From Surviving to Thriving.* Azure Coyote Publishing, 2013.

Schwartz R. *No Bad Parts: Healing Trauma & Restoring Wholeness with the Internal Family Systems Model,* Vermilion, 2023.

Thierry, B. *The Simple Guide to Complex Trauma and Dissociation: What It Is and How to Help (Simple Guides),* Jessica Kingsley Publishers, 2020.

Wolynn, M *It Didn't Start with You: How Inherited Family Trauma Shapes Who We Are and How to End the Cycle,* Penguin 2017.

Yalom, I. D. *The Gift of Therapy: An open letter to a new generation of therapists and their patients.* HarperCollins, 2002.

Index

Index

Index

Index

Index

Index

About Nathaniel and Fiona

Fiona Owen was born and grew up in Wales and has lived, painted and grown plants in the Stroud valleys for 42 years. Her life-long fascination with Nature has always been the inspiration for her work. Her gilded panels of oil on gesso endeavour to capture the Genius Loci, the wild spirit of place, plant and animal. Fiona is a practising Ovate and follows the solitary path of the Awenyddion (the ancient Welsh Druidic caste who gained insight and inspiration through deep dreaming with plants). Her illuminations are an evolution of this; a process she calls 'Drawing Out the Dreaming'. The Moon is a constant presence, whose power and influence affect all Nature.

Magical symbolism is woven through each painting in the form of sacred geometry, ancient Celtic symbols, totemic animals and Welsh myths, creating living invocations of the ancient green Magic of our land, inviting the viewer to transcend everyday reality and enter through a visual portal to connect with the alternative reality of Dream Time.

Nathaniel Hughes trained as a medical herbalist and chemist before exploring the wider realms of spiritual healing and bodywork. He founded the School of Intuitive Herbalism which trains herbalists with a highly somatic, entirely plant-centred approach, in four- to seven-year trainings. In practice, he works in the realms of somatic experience, guiding people into listening to their own body, so that they can discover their own path of healing. In teaching, his passion is in helping guide people into receiving the plants' teachings directly, through a combination of ritual, dream work, somatic awareness and practical herbalism. He has a passion for rekindling the scattered wisdom of these lands through the plants and the deep remembering that we can all access through our bodies and dreams.

WILD EnchAntments

ONLINE RESOURCES

WildEnchantments.org.uk

There's so much more we would love to share with you. To be honest this was meant to be a short book but it kept wanting to grow.

Thanks to the web, we have extended this book for you even more, and hope to keep on extending it.

See online for:

+ Celtic Wheel of the Year showing best times to find each plant

+ Extended chapter from our previous book *Weeds in the Heart*

+ Video and audio links to some of the plants

+ Selected chapter readings

+ Buy prints of the plant cards

For all beings living

at the margins

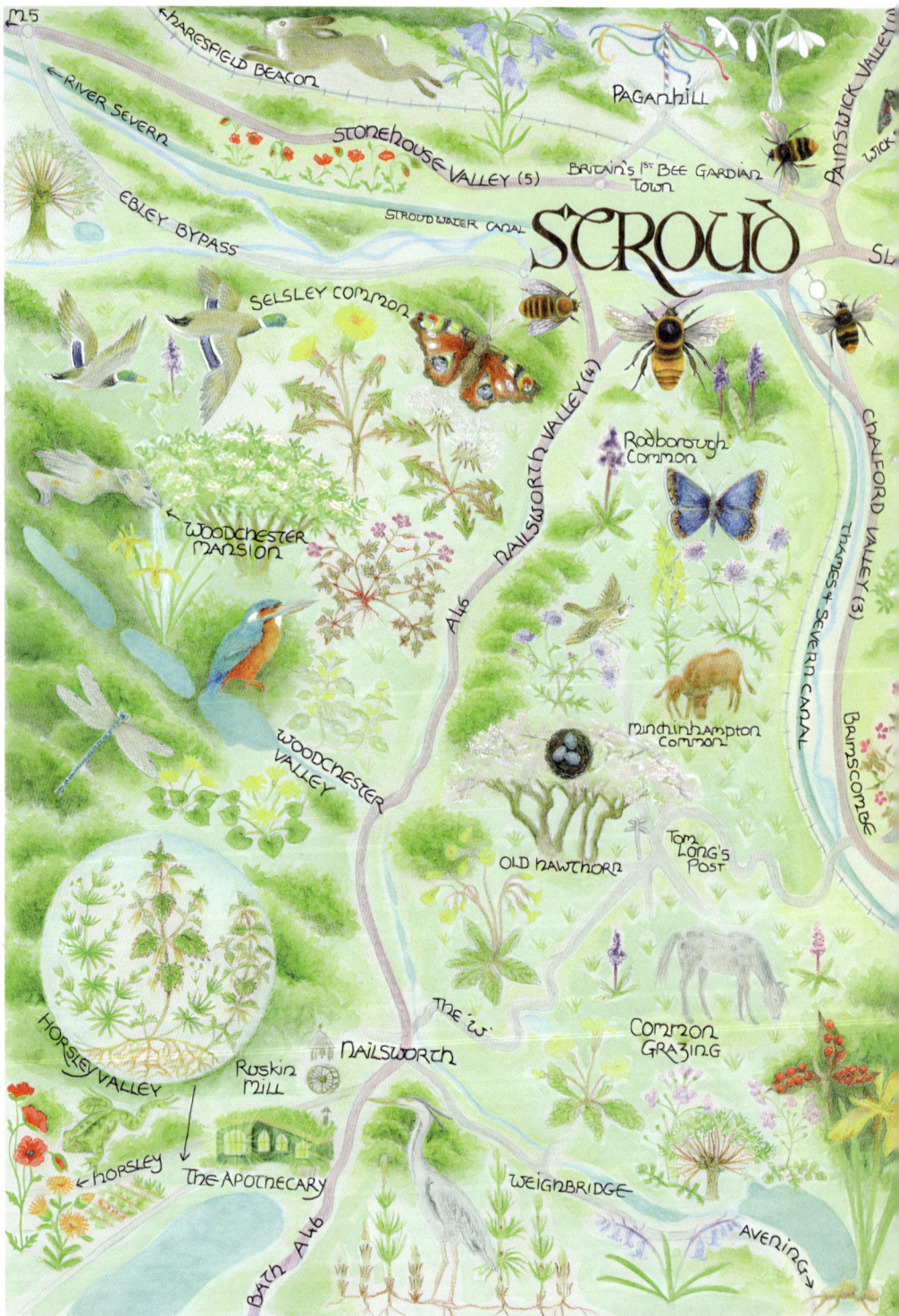

M5

CHARESFIELD BEACON

← RIVER SEVERN

PAGANHILL

STONEHOUSE VALLEY (5)

BRITAIN'S 1ST BEE GARDIAN TOWN

PAINSWICK VALLEY

WICK

EBLEY BYPASS

STROUDWATER CANAL

SCROUD

SLA

SELSLEY COMMON

NAILSWORTH VALLEY (4)

RODBOROUGH COMMON

CHALFORD VALLEY (3)

A46

WOODCHESTER MANSION

THAMES & SEVERN CANAL

MINCHINHAMPTON COMMON

BAUMSCOMBE

WOODCHESTER VALLEY

OLD HAWTHORN

TOM LONG'S POST

THE 'W'

COMMON GRAZING

HORSLEY VALLEY

RUSKIN MILL

NAILSWORTH

← HORSLEY

THE APOTHECARY

WEIGHBRIDGE

AVENING →

BATH A46